JOHN DOUGLAS'S GUIDE TO LANDING A CAREER IN LAW ENFORCEMENT

JOHN DOUGLAS'S
GUIDE TO LANDING A
CAREER IN
LAW ENFORCEMENT

JOHN DOUGLAS

New Lenox
Public Library District
120 Veterans Parkway
New Lenox, Illinois 60451

McGraw-Hill

New York   Chicago   San Francisco   Lisbon   London   Madrid
Mexico City   Milan   New Delhi   San Juan   Seoul
Singapore   Sydney   Toronto

ISBN 0-07-141717-6

This publication is designed to provide accurate and authoritative information in regard to the subject matter covered. It is sold with the understanding that neither the author nor the publisher is engaged in rendering legal, accounting, futures/securities trading, or other professional service. If legal advice or other expert assistance is required, the services of a competent professional person should be sought.
> —*From a Declaration of Principles jointly adopted by a Committee of the American Bar Association and a Committee of Publishers*

McGraw-Hill books are available at special quantity discounts to use as premiums and sales promotions, or for use in corporate training programs. For more information, please write to the Director of Special Sales, McGraw-Hill Professional, Two Penn Plaza, New York, NY 10121-2298. Or contact your local bookstore.

 This book is printed on recycled, acid-free paper containing a minimum of 50% recycled, de-inked fiber.

Library of Congress Cataloging-in-Publication Data

Douglas, John E.
　　[Guide to landing a career in law enforcement]
　　John Douglas's guide to landing a career in law enforcement / John Douglas.
　　　　p.　　cm.
　　Includes index.
　　ISBN 0-07-141717-6 (alk. paper)
　　1. Law enforcement—Vocational guidance—United States. 2. Police—Vocational guidance—United States. 3. United States. Federal Bureau of Investigation—Vocational guidance. I. Title.
　　HV8143.D675　2004
　　363.2'023'73—dc22　　　　　　　　　　　　　　　　　　2004018143

This book is dedicated to the memory of all law enforcement officers who have lost their lives in the line of duty, and in honor of those who will. In this country, about every 57 hours an officer is killed. My hope is that those who succeed these fallen officers will be good and worthy candidates, mindful of the sacrifice made by their predecessors on our streets, highways, waters, and public lands, and in our neighborhoods, downtowns, highways, ports, and everywhere else Americans live safe and free—thanks to the service and protection of our law enforcement officers.

CONTENTS

★

ACKNOWLEDGMENTS

★

The author wishes to thank the following individuals for their generous assistance in the research and writing of this book: Sgt. Marcelino Gonzales of the Austin, Texas Police Department; Sgt. Lee Krebsbach of the Albuquerque, New Mexico Police Department; Capt. Jack McCoy of the Columbus, Georgia Police Department; Deputy Chief Marty Kent of the Bozeman, Montana Police Department; Officer Nadine Taylor-Miller of the Boston Police Department; John E. Chalk; M. Crowell; and the Davies Brothers. In addition, deserved thanks to Jay Acton, my agent; to Tom Dunne, who helped determine the scope and shape of the project; and to editors Barry Neville and Donya Dickerson, who shepherded the book into publication. Finally, thank you to my family.

AMERICA NEEDS YOUR HELP

★

I was in New York City on September 11, 2001. What most of you saw on television, I saw from the center of Manhattan. I am no victim, but I have a visceral sense of the horror of the attacks, as must those of you who were in New York City, Washington, DC, or Shanksville, Pennsylvania that Tuesday morning.

That morning, it quickly became almost impossible to get a working phone line from within New York City. Public transportation was halted, bridges and tunnels were closed (except to those escaping downtown on foot over bridges), and fighter jets were circling. It was a war zone. Your eyes flitted between the black smoke billowing from the Twin Towers—and soon, the collapse of both monumental structures—and close-ups of the same, with updates, on TV. You wished those in the towers would make it, even as you watched some of them leap out of windows to their sure deaths. Once the World Trade Center collapsed, and ash was everywhere, you knew it would take a miracle to bring anyone out of the rubble. And until many hours later, you couldn't feel certain the attacks were over.

My point in recounting that is to remember how shocked, sad, vulnerable, and afraid we all felt on and after September 11th. Millions of people wondered what they could do. Many of you gave money, time, and material donations to help families and friends of victims and the heroic police officers, firefighters, and others who were working to save those they could and to clear away the ruins.

In addition to wanting to help in the short term, many of you were compelled to do more. Law enforcement agencies, particularly on the federal level, experienced a spike in applications after September 11th. So many people realized America needed their help.

One of the reasons I decided to write this book was to help bring qualified candidates into law enforcement. So if you're reading this book and you are the sort of person who could make a real contribution to law enforcement, as an officer in any of the more than 18,000 agencies in this country, I can tell you this much is still true: *America Needs Your Help.*

INTRODUCTION

★

The duties which a police officer owes to the state are of a most exacting nature. No one is compelled to choose the profession of a police officer, but having chosen it, everyone is obliged to live up to the standard of its requirements. To join in that high enterprise means the surrender of much individual freedom.

—President Calvin Coolidge, 1920
(then-governor of Massachusetts)

That quote says it all. I do not think it would be possible to overstate how difficult and important a career in law enforcement can be. During my 25 years with the FBI, I had the privilege of getting to know countless dedicated, hardworking men and women who gave much more than 100 percent to protecting the citizens of this country and enforcing the law. Since I retired from the Bureau in 1995, I've stayed involved with the law enforcement community through consulting work on active investigations, with pardon and parole boards, and through speaking engagements. The work is incredibly rewarding. I always gain as much as I give, and learn as much as I teach. I could never anticipate most of the questions I get, which are interesting, informed, and intelligent. And the answers to my own questions help continue my education in criminal justice and inspire me to continue doing the work that I do.

There are always trends in any workforce, but over the past few decades I have witnessed a change in the aspirations of young people toward more lucrative business and entrepreneurial careers and away from what I consider to be more noble enterprises, like teaching, nursing, and law enforcement. As I've mentioned, since September 11, 2001, that trend has changed to a certain extent, which I find encouraging. But I felt I could do something more than just observe the trend. Creating a guide to careers in law enforcement has been a great way for me to do two things I consider very important: to shed some light on departments and organizations that deserve positive attention and to help bring good, interested candidates to those departments and organizations so they can continue to grow and stay strong.

In today's world, the need to keep those agencies strong is greater than ever. From the local to the federal level, and in every agency, there is a real need for good people to fill thousands of diverse positions. The old world of the separate and distinct local, state, and federal agencies is much more complex now, with greater communication and cooperation among agencies, as evidenced by programs like the Amber Alert system. Likewise, the old image of the law enforcement agent as a middle-aged white man with a gun and a crew cut—that's an antique. While most law enforcement positions require handgun proficiency and require carrying the same, today's officer does much more. More important, today's officer could be male or female, and from virtually any ethnic, racial, or religious background. Agencies are actively pursuing minority candidates, by mandate and by their own initiatives, in an effort to build forces that look like and culturally reflect the public they protect. Whether or not that can ever be achieved across the board, I'm not sure. For instance, according to the Department of Justice Bureau of Justice Statistics, minority representation among local police officers was about 22.7 percent in 2000, and among sheriff's departments was about 17 percent. But I do believe it to be a worthwhile goal, for many reasons, none of them cosmetic or in the interest of political correctness. My reasons boil down to the simple fact that you can better police and protect a citizenry if you can identify with that citizenry, and if the people can identify with you.

My point is, if you're considering a career in law enforcement, and I'm guessing you are if you're reading this, you should take one giant first step right now—forget that middle-aged white man with a gun and a crew cut. I can't say there's a place in law enforcement for everyone. There isn't. But if your personality, psychology, skills, interests, judgment, education, and abilities are right for the job you're interested in, then no matter what your race or gender, there is a place for you. But that job's not going to come knocking at your door. It's up to you to find it. I hope the information in this book will help you do that.

Do I have any advice right from the start? Sure. *Take a look at yourself.* I'll go into this in more detail later, but the upshot is this: Why do you want to be in law enforcement? Do you want to emulate the cops on television, swaggering into bars or crushing suspects against brick walls? Or do you simply want to make neighborhoods safer? Do you make snap judgments about people, or are you considered and careful in your thinking? Do you panic in a crisis, or do you see things clearly? You see where I'm going with this. Personality and psychology are intangibles, but they are more important than anything on your résumé. Your disposition, biases, patience (or lack of it), aggressiveness, curiosity, persistence, judgment, mental clarity—all these and other factors will make you more or less well suited to a career in law enforcement. Be honest with yourself when looking inward. You will not be doing anyone a favor by pursuing this kind of career if you are not suited for it. I can't place enough emphasis on this point. We need thousands more good investigators, patrol officers, corrections officers, and so on. But we do not need even one bad cop, and there are a lot of people who would be good at other things but bad at policework. Size yourself up.

What else? *Prepare yourself.* Education and training are significant factors in determining where you might take your first step on the ladder of a law enforcement career. Absolutely finish high school or get your equivalency diploma. No matter what your aspirations are, this is a basic requirement for most any job. And while there are local law enforcement jobs that do not require a college degree, the trend among all agencies is to increase their educational requirements to include some college, if not a four-year degree. My advice, which applies to much more than the issue of education, is this: Don't go for the minimum. You will never hurt your chances by getting more education or training, whether it's at a four-year college, a community college, in special skills seminars or training classes, or in agency-run cadet or intern programs. Any skill that would make you a better law enforcement officer will make you a better candidate. So consider increasing your skills by getting handgun training or taking a defensive driving class or by learning a second language such as Spanish. These are just examples, but I hope they get you thinking.

But a few words of caution:

- These jobs are not the best-paying jobs in the world. Nobody ever got rich being an (honest) cop or agent. If money is, above all else, what you're after, you should look to the private sector and give this book to your local library.

- These jobs are often dangerous. Like President Coolidge said, no one is going to force you to don a uniform and police our streets, to guard our borders, to bring down drug dealers, or hunt down federal fugitives. If this is where you end up, it has to be because you have chosen it with full knowledge of the risks to your personal safety, and even, at times, to the safety of those you love. There is great honor in risking your life to help others, but the risk is not diminished by that honor. Take steps toward this kind of life with a genuine appreciation for the risks you will be taking.

- Most of these are not strictly 9-to-5, 40-hour-a-week jobs. There will probably be long hours, night duty, weekend work, and potentially extensive travel required. You will, of course, be compensated financially, but it may not come close to outweighing the strain the hours can put on your mental health, physical health, and family life. Be sure to consider that from the beginning. If what you want or need is a guarantee of evenings and weekends at home, and if you hate to travel, many of these jobs won't be for you. There is no shame in that. You just have to be honest with yourself about what you want your life to be like.

- Speaking of travel, many positions in law enforcement will transfer you from city to city or state to state or country to country, particularly those in agencies with larger jurisdictions. You may have to wait a while to put down any real roots, and this can be particularly hard on spouses and children. Consider this now, especially if you are married with children or plan to be.

- The work will sometimes be thankless. If you want or need a reward for every good day you put in, you should look elsewhere. We aren't in it for the praise. While there are innumerable intangible rewards to working in law enforcement—like knowing in your heart you are making the world a better, safer place—there aren't always plaques and bonuses for each case solved, bad guy put away, or bullet dodged. Your accomplishments won't always be in the newspaper. Not every citizen will express gratitude for your help. There will be thanks, often tearful and heartfelt, but it won't come all the time.

- In fact, you may encounter as much derision and scorn as you do praise and thanks. There are people who do not like cops, who resent federal agents, who are afraid of investigators. You can't change that, but you have to be able to deal with it and effectively do your job despite the gestures (verbal and physical) you might get from people. You must be able to treat everyone fairly, regardless of their attitude toward law enforcement.

- Further, as an officer of the law, your work and even aspects of your private life may be subject to public scrutiny, particularly if you become involved in high-profile cases. I can tell you from experience this is a difficult pill to swallow, getting what seems to be unwarranted or at least irrelevant criticism from the very people you're trying to help. But if you can't take that kind of scrutiny, beg off now.

- Finally, these are not jobs you leave at the office. Most of us go home with the details of open cases spinning around in our heads. We dream about them. We take them with us on vacation. We know more about the dark side of life than other people, so we fear more for our children, our spouses, our community. It can be a heavy load, on us and on the ones we love.

What does all that mean? Does it seem like I am trying to discourage you? That's not it. If you went through that list and have new doubts about whether to explore these careers further, that's my point. It's a serious decision and should not be made lightly. Keep reading. More information can only inform your decisions and help you make the right ones.

If you went through the list and are completely undeterred, you either did not take me seriously or you are the Buddha.

Either way, read on. You just might be the man or woman our law enforcement community needs. If not, perhaps this information will help you figure out where you do belong, if only by some part of a long process of elimination. But if so, and if I can help you find the right job in one of these careers—which means I've helped that agency find you—I will consider that a worthwhile accomplishment, one that could stand among the very highlights of my career.

Good luck.

—John Douglas

JOHN DOUGLAS'S GUIDE TO LANDING A CAREER IN LAW ENFORCEMENT

Part One

GETTING STARTED

★

Chapter 1
PERSONAL ASSESSMENT

★

Before you make the decision to go into law enforcement, it is not only useful but necessary to carefully evaluate yourself. On a larger scale, I think we should all undergo a personal assessment so we can make the right decisions for ourselves. Better, we should "update" our assessment as we age and the circumstances in our lives change.

You have probably never done a personal assessment. Don't feel bad. Most people haven't. We go through life making decisions that get us through the hour, the day, the week, and so on. We don't have much time to stop and size things up, especially once we're out of college, on our own, paying taxes, cutting the grass, getting the car fixed, raising kids, saving for their college—when the cycle starts all over.

But as you consider embarking on a new career, you have the perfect opportunity to size yourself up, and a real imperative as well. While I do not believe in fate or destiny, I do know that no one wants to make a dead-wrong decision for him- or herself. Taking a frank, thorough look at yourself will give you a big head start toward the right decision. In the coming pages, I'll supply you with some information about various agencies, from their missions to their recruiting requirements. When you investigate the specific agencies you find yourself interested in, they will provide you with a lot more information about who they are and what they want from you. The personal assessment is your half of the equation: It tells you who you are and what you want from them.

The Truth

The truth is not just a good starting point—it's the *only* starting point. Your personal assessment will be worthless otherwise. The truth should be the starting point for a law enforcement career, and your guide throughout such a career. Telling the truth in your personal assessment will give you the right answers, not just the answers you want or those you think will enable you to please or impress others.

I know it's hard to be honest. There are two main reasons for that, which correlate with the two categories that answers to the questions we should ask ourselves fall into: the complimentary and the critical.

When it comes to acknowledging the good things about ourselves, from our strengths to our talents, most of us are limited by the rules of modesty and good manners. We are taught not to brag, not to boast, not to compete with or compare ourselves to others whom we know aren't as good as we are. For example, take that girl in high school who was able to pull people together to cheer for the football team or turn in a great group science project. Everyone who knew her in high school would say she was a natural leader, but she would probably have a hard time admitting that to herself or saying it aloud to others because those would be immodest things to do. As a natural leader, she might be a great candidate for law enforcement. But she would have to recognize that quality in herself to see it as something that would recommend her for the job. If she were unable to see any of the qualities she had that would make her a good candidate, she might never apply, even though it might be a dream of hers.

It's interesting to note that people who brag the loudest tend to be wrong about themselves. It's one of those strange facts of life. If someone talks a lot about what a great shot he is, he probably can't hit the side of a barn with a shotgun.

Conversely, when it comes to acknowledging the negative things about ourselves, from our weaknesses to our vulnerabilities, most of us do not want to admit the truth about ourselves. It isn't necessarily that we think our muscles are enormous; we just don't want to admit that they're puny. By that I mean we aren't typically lying to ourselves—we are just not admitting the truth. I'll give you an example. I have a friend who really struggles behind the wheel. Whenever he has to merge into traffic, he curses and brakes and slows to a near stop before there is finally what he believes to be enough room for him to get into the lane. Meanwhile, cars are lined up behind him waiting for their chance. Forget parallel parking. But he would never admit he's a bad driver. The problem is always the other drivers: They're overly aggressive, or they've parked too close together to allow room for his car. In this case, my friend might not be the best candidate for law enforcement, particularly local or state law enforcement, since patrol duty requires that you drive a patrol car and drive it well. But if he couldn't admit that he was a bad driver, he might not recognize that jobs that involve patrol duty might not be right for him.

So these are the two reasons we have a hard time being honest with ourselves. But they do not rule out the possibility. They just mean we have to make a point of telling ourselves the truth. You have to put forth the effort to make it a habit, because, as you move toward a potential career in law enforcement, you will be called upon to ask and answer difficult questions. If you get far enough in the hiring process for any given department or agency, you'll find yourself answering written or oral "personal integrity" and situational questions. These questions will cover your past, including any history you might have with drugs, alcohol, legal problems, fights, domestic disputes, and so on. They also include ethical questions, which prompt you to make a choice as to what is the right thing to do in a given situation. These questions are hypotheticals based on real-life situations faced by officers having to decide when to pursue a suspect, when to brandish a firearm, when to report a fellow officer, and so on. These questions speak to good judgment, but also to honesty. Telling the truth is a constant through any law enforcement career.

Strengths and Weaknesses

The first thing you need to ask yourself is this: *What are my strengths and weaknesses?*

What are you good at? What are your talents? There are undoubtedly certain activities or types of activities that come naturally to you. Think hard. We would all consider our physical strength if law enforcement were an area we were interested in. But some aptitudes might not seem as relevant. Don't be so quick to judge. Do you almost always have a sense of what someone is about to say before he or she says it? Are you very organized? Do you have a photographic memory? Are you insanely good at recognizing the celebrity voice-overs in television commercials? Can you do math in your head? Can you identify makes and models of cars on sight and remember details like color, finish, and accessories? Are you a whiz at the computer? All these abilities would be useful in law enforcement. Take a step back when looking at your strengths and include even those that seem inconsequential. You might be surprised.

On the other side of the coin, what are you *not* good at? What do you find yourself struggling with? Maybe you're terrible at math, even with a calculator. Are you a bad driver, like my friend in the previous example? Are you a poor judge of character? Do you have poor communication skills? Do you have a hard time following rules; do you resent authority figures? Again, be honest. None of these things makes you a bad person. They just may not make you the best candidate for law enforcement. Perhaps if you are a poor judge of character, you should try to find work in an area where you aren't called upon to make such judgments. Perhaps if you resent authority figures and have a hard time following rules, you would be better suited to working for yourself.

That said, to the extent that you can improve yourself and make yourself stronger in areas where you are weak, you should do so. Not only will this make you a better candidate for the career you aspire to, but it will make you a better, more well-rounded person. Some things, of course, are easier to change than others. Communication skills can be improved by expanding your vocabulary, by paying attention to those who seem to communicate well and learning by example, and by enrolling in courses in reading, writing, and communication. But others are, obviously, more difficult. For instance, certain prejudices tend to run pretty deep. It takes a lot of soul-searching and work to overcome those. But racial and gender prejudices will take you right out of the running for a job as an officer or agent.

Looking at your strengths and weaknesses should go beyond things you are good at or have no aptitude for. This should address those things that make you nervous or anxious, or situations that make you uncomfortable. Anxieties are common these days. And we all have fears. Try to isolate the situations that put you on edge or, worse, make you incapacitated with fear. For example, does bad traffic make your chest tighten up? Or do you see it as a chance to relax? Do crowds make you hyperventilate? Or do you enjoy observing people? Are you good in emergency situations, keeping a cool head, or do you panic and "let go of the wheel"? Are you uncomfortable asserting yourself?

If the answer to that last question is a meek but certain "yes," you might want to reconsider your career goals—unless you're willing to put a lot of work into rebuilding yourself. Confidence is a must-have trait for officers of the law. In the section that follows on personality, I'll go into that in greater detail. But it's a good example of a weakness that can be improved upon if you're willing to work at it. And I believe it's a key difference between people who can (and should) and people who can't (and shouldn't) be law enforcement officers.

Keep in mind that there is a balance to all of this. One strong point doesn't mean you'll be Supercop, just as one weakness doesn't mean you can't be one at all. Also bear in mind that the training you will undergo if you become an officer or agent will help you become stronger in the ways that will matter most on the job.

Personality

When you think of your personality, you probably think of what other people say about you, such as that you are kind, generous, funny, outgoing, thoughtful, and so on. That's a good starting point.

But as with your strengths and weaknesses, you have to look deeper. Are you patient or hotheaded? Are you fair-minded? Do you like to be the center of attention, or are you a "shrinking violet," someone who would give anything to never have to speak to more than one person at a time? Are you confident and outgoing, someone who likes a rush of adrenaline? Or do you prefer to stick to an established routine, knowing well the boundaries of all your activities?

And going back to the more common traits people are described as having, do you have a good sense of humor? Are you generous? Kind? Ambitious? Clever? Sensitive? Curious? Easily bored? Feisty? Calm, cool, and collected?

Are you wondering what the "right" answers are?

Just a few sentences ago, with regard to strengths and weaknesses, I mentioned that there is a balance to all this. That holds perhaps truest of all when it comes to personality traits. For all of the above, it is best if you have a good balance in the makeup of your personality. Every attitude must be in moderation, and every approach must be consistent with a well-developed sense of proportion.

What does that mean? Here's a good example. For patrol officers on the graveyard shift, as a recruiting officer in an urban area struggling with drug-related crimes emphasized to me, nearly every encounter will be a negative encounter. There is the dealing and use of crack, methamphetamine, and other drugs, there are the domestic and property crimes that go with those enterprises and addictions, and then, of course, there is the gang violence and other activities that inevitably become a huge part of the big picture. Officers on patrol during the day will have some positive encounters. But the graveyard shift is different.

Maybe you're really sensitive. You have too many pets because you can't stop taking in strays. You're definitely a good, compassionate person. Now imagine yourself in a patrol car, driving through a neighborhood just next to the downtown area, where poverty and crime are as apparent as the names on the street signs. If you're too sensitive, you'll be overwhelmed by the conditions some of the citizens you're serving live in—to the point where you lose your objectivity. You won't be able to see the criminals for what they are and protect the innocent from them.

The same works in reverse. If you're too clinical, too analytical, you'll be unable to empathize with those same citizens. If you can't empathize with the people whose safety you're charged with protecting, you will never gain their trust. You will never understand what is important to them or how to communicate with them.

Another good example is a sense of humor. You've got to have one to make it—especially in the FBI, I can tell you from much experience—but you've got to know when it's appropriate to make jokes and when it is absolutely not.

One of the best examples is dedication. You have to be dedicated to your work, but you have to have a life, too. Otherwise you'll burn out, which helps no one.

There has to be a balance. If a supervisor sends an officer out who does not have that balance, which can't help but be manifested in his or her attitudes, there will be a problem. Maybe it's a problem for the public, the criminals, the officer and his or her partner, or maybe it's a problem for them all, which culminates in a really dangerous situation. Knowing that potential exists, departments and agencies try to weed out imbalanced candidates, looking for balance in personality and attitude in all recruits, and trying to select only those who demonstrate a good "happy medium."

Goals

When you imagine yourself in 5 years, 10 years, 15 years, where do you see yourself? Are you in an office, on a rolling leather chair, looking at spreadsheets and making conference calls? (If you're reading this book, probably not.) Are you living on the edge of a national park, enjoying and protecting the wilderness and its creatures? Are you chewing antacids at a desk in a big-city precinct, looking excitedly over cold-case files?

Maybe your goals aren't this specific. Let's start smaller. Do you really see yourself in law enforcement? If so, what about the job appeals to you? *Why* do you want to be an officer or an agent?

Wanting to be in law enforcement is not enough. Believe me. Those of you who've read my other books will remember that there are plenty of criminals who once wanted to be police officers or even

federal agents, among them some of the worst, most violent criminals in our history. Take serial killer Ed Kemper, for example. Before
killing eight women, Kemper aspired to a job as a California Highway Patrol officer. In fact, his mother—who would be one of Kemper's victims—tried to get his juvenile convictions for the murder of
his grandparents expunged so he would have a shot at that goal.

In my investigations and interviews, I found it is very common for
offenders to have been unsuccessful law enforcement candidates. Even
more commonly, serial offenders will be crime or police buffs, scan-
ning the police band for information, following cases (theirs or those
of others) in the media, calling the police to offer clues or ask for
more information, and spending time at cop bars and at diners where
investigators work out the day's kinks over coffee.

Law enforcement recruiting and testing is not an easy process for
anyone. But part of the design of the psychological tests, background
checks, and oral interviews is to weed out people who are in it because
they fantasize about ultimate power and control—the same kinds of
sick fantasies that compel them to rape, torture, and murder.

One of the first questions you'll get from an interview board is
Why do you want to be in law enforcement? If you know the answer
to that question now, and the answer addresses the positive aspects
of police work and investigation, you're on the right track. By those
positive aspects, I mean things like these:

- Keeping people safe
- Making sure the law is equally applied and equally obeyed
- Improving the quality of life for people
- Protecting our borders and natural resources
- Making sure criminals are taken off the streets
- Making sure convicted criminals remain in humane custody
- Ensuring the authorities are fair in their treatment of the
  public

Now, do not go convincing yourself that these, or any other good
reasons to go into law enforcement, are really your reasons for wanting
to do so. Look at your own motivations. If what you look forward

to is more along the following lines, you're not alone, but you may not be the best candidate for the job:

- Carrying a gun and badge and wearing a uniform
- Belonging to a tough, historic, do-or-die brotherhood
- Becoming a hero
- Telling people what to do
- Removing undesirable people from the neighborhood—or the country
- Stopping drug dealers by any means necessary
- Giving a speeding ticket to anyone in a car that cost more than $50,000

Look at yourself. Picture yourself on the job. Imagine how you'd deal with various situations. Do you have good reasons for wanting to be an officer or agent? Are your motives good? Be sure of your answers. If you make it to the oral interview stage of the recruiting process, the men and women asking the questions will be a lot harder on you than I'm being—for your own good, and for the good of the public.

Intangibles: What Are They Looking For?

There are tangible skills departments and agencies seek in recruits. But in this section, we're looking inward, at your strengths, weaknesses, personality, goals, and, finally, at *the intangibles*. We all look for certain intangible traits in those we surround ourselves with, from our friends to the person we share our life with. You should take an inventory of your intangible traits, (of course) telling yourself the truth about what they are and aren't.

Let me give you a head start with some of the intangible traits that make good recruits. In doing the research for this book, I've spoken with many recruiting officers, getting their input as to what they look for in candidates. When it comes to intangibles, everything they said echoed what I experienced in my own career, from interacting with other FBI agents to working with officers from local, state, and other federal agencies. There are certain traits that candidates must possess to become good law enforcement officers.

Here's an overview.

Life Experience and Maturity

You can't discount the importance of life experience. If you have led a relatively sheltered existence, moving from high school to college, living with you parents, then hoping to get a job in law enforcement, you might not be ready for it yet. Those of you who have been in the military, who have real-job experience, or who have worked for private security companies have much more exposure to the realities that an agent or officer will encounter in a day's work. You also have a better sense of the fact that different people are just *different*. Not better, not worse. Having a sense of the variety of ethnicities, religions, values, and other factors that make up our diverse culture is very important to serving and protecting that culture.

Know that if you're of the more sheltered variety, even if your test scores are exemplary, you might not be selected for the department or agency of your choice. They should be honest with you and tell you, for instance, to come back in a few years, after you have gotten some real life under your belt. They want what's best for their force, but they also do not want to jeopardize your life by putting you into a situation you aren't mature enough to handle. If this sounds like you, consider giving it some time and returning to the recruitment process when you're a little more experienced. Or, if the department or agency you're interested in offers a cadet or internship program, consider applying for that. It's a great way for young candidates to get real exposure and experience and to move themselves to the head of the line when it comes time for hiring.

Empathy

I covered this briefly in the section on personality. *Webster's Dictionary* defines empathy as the "ability to share in another's emotions, thoughts, or feelings." No matter what sort of law enforcement career you envision for yourself, you will need to be able to relate to the people you're working for and with and, especially, those you're protecting and serving.

One U.S. Marshal I spoke with, who had spent 20 years as a police officer before joining the Marshals Service, told me that of all the characteristics that make a "good cop," empathy was the most important. He said that while other traits were important, this one was a true dividing line. The ability to move from one social or economic group to another and genuinely communicate with people meant those people would trust you and you could trust them.

Communication Skills

Good communication is vital to safe, efficient, and proper enforcement of the law. There are three pieces to this puzzle: talking, listening, and writing.

Being able to talk to and listen to people, whether in the process of getting information, issuing citations, or making arrests, is very important. As an officer or agent, you may have to instruct people in emergency situations, explain the law, make arrests, ask logical questions in your search for information on a case, even give directions. (Ask an NYPD patrol officer in Times Square how often he or she gives directions to tourists and commuters—the answer will be somewhere between *quite often* and *every minute of every day*.)

Talking is one thing, but listening is another. You may be the most eloquent person on the face of the earth, but if you are unable to listen, you're not a good communicator; you're a speechmaker. You should run for office. You have to actively listen to and hear what people are telling you. Otherwise, instructions may be misunderstood, accounts may be misinterpreted, and worse.

Finally, there is the ability to write clearly. Reports are required at every level of law enforcement. I have written more reports than I care to recall. But they're obviously necessary, because the prosecution of a crime depends upon good, clear written reports and records. It's important that all the facts be entered into a report accurately and thoroughly, and that all the information is presented in a clear and logical manner. An officer or agent may not be around to interpret what he or she meant by something in a report. If you're not a good writer, try to improve your skills. Enroll in a writing class. Try reading more, as it will only improve your ability to write.

Mental Clarity

As an investigator, I had to keep a clear head. You have to look at a crime scene, piece together what might have happened, and do so logically, carefully, and analytically. You can't be some hurry-up person ready to jump to convenient conclusions. A lack of mental clarity might cause an investigator to miss important clues in eyewitness accounts. It might cause a patrol officer to continue a dangerous pursuit of a suspect, while cooler heads would be more concerned about public safety and let the helicopter take over—or even let the suspect get away.

It's easy to keep a clear head in by-the-book situations, in your day-to-day activities. The test comes when the adrenaline gets going, whether it's because of physical danger or emotional stress or both. If you let your anger get the best of you, you'll get tunnel vision. As one recruiting officer told me, that is a fatal error. If an officer loses sight of the big picture, he or she not only risks personal safety but the safety of the public as well.

For example, an officer and his partner answer a call to a dance club where someone has pulled a gun on another patron. The officers are both African-American, but the club is largely populated by Caucasians. Upon entering, two big guys with baggy jackets and tattoos curse at the officers and throw out some racial slurs. One of the officers becomes angry and stops to insist on an apology and pat down the two name-callers. Meanwhile, the suspect who pulled the gun has heard the commotion and noticed the officers—so he has slipped out the back door. The officer made a point but lost the suspect. And this is a *very* mild example.

Mental clarity means keeping a cool head, but it also means thinking on your feet. If you have trouble dealing with multiple tasks or details at once, you will have trouble with police work and may not get that far in the recruiting process. But if you're the kind of person who can multitask, who can see the forest *and* the trees, you might be a good asset to law enforcement. Nothing in law enforcement comes at you in a neat little row. Most of the work is nonlinear, and often unbelievably fast and chaotic. Being able to sort through rapid, sometimes frightening sensory input is key to being a good law enforcement officer.

Good Judgment

Good judgment is a corollary to mental clarity. You cannot have good judgment without it. Input determines output. Imagine that your brain is a calculator. If you want to find out what 36 divided by 7 is, you cannot get to the answer by entering 200 times 2. I know that's an extremely simplified example, but it gets to the heart of the matter. If you are mentally clear, weeding out unnecessary information and organizing necessary input as it comes, you are in a position to make the right judgments with that information. But if you can't work through the information, you won't have the right input. With the right input, you can get the right output.

But it does not mean you will. Some people have good judgment; others do not. And I wish I could say there was a way to improve judgment, other than learning from the consequences of bad decisions and snap judgments. Part of it goes back to that balance in personality and attitude I covered earlier. If you have a good balance of logic and emotion, of confidence and restraint, of patience and resolve, you are probably someone who can make good judgment calls.

Of all the intangibles, this is probably the most difficult to define. But it is one of the most important, because agents and officers do not have the benefit of a supervisor at their side to okay every action they take. They have to be able to make quick, difficult decisions and act on those decisions without supervision. For this reason, you can be sure that some of the questions you will be asked by the recruiting officers during the process are designed to determine whether you have good judgment or not. I'm sure you have a sense of your abilities in this regard.

Integrity

Integrity is defined by the *American Heritage Dictionary* as "steadfast adherence to a strict moral or ethical code." Integrity is what sets apart fictional protagonists like Atticus Finch in *To Kill a Mockingbird* and real-life heroes like Mother Teresa. Having integrity means never taking shortcuts, never making a profit, never gaining acclaim, never making things easier for yourself *if doing so comes at the cost of what you believe is morally or ethically right.* Good judgment depends upon integrity as much as it depends upon mental clarity (you must be beginning to see how these intangibles interrelate). All of us have weaknesses; all of us want to take the easy way out sometimes. But if we cheat on a test or on our taxes, or skip out on a restaurant bill, or cut down a tree across our property line, we're not acting with integrity.

For example, a state trooper pulls over a motorist going 23 miles per hour over the speed limit—in the rain. The motorist expresses regret and is cooperative, but the extent to which he exceeded the speed limit means he should receive a citation. He pleads with the trooper, saying he's just in a hurry to get home for his child's birthday party because his last meeting at work ran late. He doesn't want a ticket because he's had too many recently and it will increase his insurance rates. The trooper sympathizes, knowing how bad insurance premiums can be. But she is resolute about giving the man a ticket, until the man presents the trooper with a $100 bill. The man explains that he knows trooper pay is not great and says he sees it as an even exchange. The trooper is resolute. She likes the guy and feels sorry for him, and a little extra cash would be useful. She's sure the guy will take it slow the rest of the way. But her integrity rules the day. She tells the man in no uncertain terms to put the money away and writes him the ticket.

Not everyone would be able to do the right thing there. And that example doesn't get anywhere near the kind of decisions officers and agents have to make all the time—and quickly.

As part of the recruitment process, you will probably be asked to complete a personal integrity questionnaire. As I've mentioned, this questionnaire will look at your past as well as give you hypothetical situations for which you have to choose how best to respond or take action. Integrity cannot be faked. How you answer these questions, how you respond to oral interview questions along the same lines, and what your history reveals about your integrity will greatly influence your chances of getting into law enforcement.

Flexibility

You've heard the phrase "be flexible" plenty of times. We have to be flexible when it comes to dealing with our kids, learning to work with new technologies, even figuring out how to get to and from work when weather and construction projects get in the way. Being flexible is very important in law enforcement, because the tasks officers and agents perform are rarely linear, step-by-step kinds of tasks. The typical workday is not a typical workday. Things will differ from hour to hour, and you cannot be married to a routine or incapable of adapting to a new routine.

Flexibility in working conditions is important. If you can only work with a certain partner, you may find yourself in a bind. If you cannot stand the suburbs, or hate desk work, or have other restrictive preferences, you may likewise find yourself in a bind. While supervisors like to stick with what works, officers and agents are reassigned, promoted, and otherwise moved within a jurisdiction for a variety of reasons. Depending upon the jurisdiction, that movement could be across town, across the state, across the country, or around the world.

Not only will supervisors dictate changes, circumstances will, and even more commonly. As a patrol officer, you may follow a certain general patrol route, but what you encounter on patrol as well as the calls you receive will determine where you go next and what you do there. If you cannot "roll with it," you will be unable to respond well to these sorts of unpredictable conditions. As an investigator, the facts of the cases will determine where you go, whom you interview, what you analyze, and so on.

Take it from me. It is a rare day in law enforcement when an officer or agent can wake up and say, with any accuracy, *these are the things I will do today.* It's just not that kind of work. That suits me perfectly. I like the challenge. But not everyone does.

Respect for Authority

Law enforcement is not the military, but it's awfully close sometimes. In fact, some of the best officers or agents are former military. I was in the Air Force before joining the FBI, and I know it helped me adjust to the rules and regulations of the Bureau. And that was in the Hoover days.

I just addressed the issue of flexibility, so it may seem strange to turn directly to respect for authority. Being "spit-and-polish" and "by the book" may seem like the direct opposites of "rolling with it." But here again, there is the issue of balance. You have to be flexible, but you must be flexible within the system. There can be no rogues, rene-gades, or vigilantes in law enforcement.

First, officers and agents must respect the ultimate authority of the law. Learn it, pay attention to and learn changes in it, obey it, and enforce it. Second, officers and agents must respect the authority of the rules and regulations of their department or agency. They have to work within the system and, if there is a genuine problem with it, pursue changes within the system. Third, they must respect the authority of their superior officers. This goes for supervisors within the department or agency as well as officers with superior jurisdiction in a particular sit-uation, as when a federal agency assumes jurisdiction over a local case.

Law enforcement can only work within certain set boundaries. There cannot be anarchy, even very localized anarchy. This is not for the sake of power trips or humiliation. This is not for the sake of micromanage-ment. At every level, respect for authority ensures that the process con-tinues efficiently and at its best. Some people have trouble taking orders, because they resent those in power and feel superior to them. Some peo-ple love to bend or break rules, believing they are above them. People who have issues with authority should not go into law enforcement.

Confidence

Finally, we come to confidence. You know whether you're confident or not. If you want to be an officer or agent, you'll need to have confidence in yourself. You'll need to believe in your physical abilities, in your intelligence, and in the decisions you make. Criminals can spot a lack of confidence just like animals can smell fear. One sergeant I spoke with told me that convicted cop-killers will tell you, if you ask them, that they knew they could "take" the officers they killed.

In a face-to-face situation with a suspect, in hostage negotiations, in a natural disaster, or in other emergency situations, an officer or agent must have and convey confidence in what he or she is doing. Think of all the times on television and in movies you've seen an officer pull a gun on a fleeing suspect and told the suspect to freeze and drop his weapon. There is always that dramatic tension, those few moments when the cop and suspect size each other up. Will the suspect do as he is told and surrender? Will he run? Will he fire on the officer? The dramatic tension echoes the real-life sizing-up that goes on when officers come face-to-face with suspects. You can bet the suspects are taking in all kinds of nonverbal clues. A lack of confidence comes across like a loud suit.

In interviews with convicted serial killers and rapists, I had to come across as confident. I had done my homework and knew I would be in no danger, since I was coming face-to-face with these guys in a well-guarded prison scenario. Confidence is naturally enhanced by preparation and a sense of security. But these were men who would make anyone nervous. It was just important not to show it.

Remember, predators are experts at spotting weakness. It's how they choose their victims. If I had not been noticeably confident, the violent criminals I interviewed would have tagged me as weak. They would never have seen me as an equal. I had to approach them as an equal, on their levels, to act like what they did was not repugnant or frightening to me. Sometimes, I had to seem sympathetic or even congratulatory. This was necessary to get information out of them. But it would not have been possible if I had not seemed confident.

Confidence is not just an issue when officers deal with criminals. A lack of confidence can also put the safety of the public at risk. For instance, if an officer is directing the public out of a structure in an emergency situation, like a natural disaster or bomb threat, she must convey confidence or the people she's trying to help will not follow her instructions and will be more likely to panic. Their safety depends on how much she believes in what she's telling them. Likewise, if an individual speaking for his department or agency is interviewed on television or the radio about a suspect who is at large or about another dangerous situation, he must convey confidence. A good example of this was Montgomery County, Maryland Police Chief Charles Moose, who, during the October 2002 sniper attacks in the Washington, DC area, conducted interviews in a calm, confident, professional manner. His attitude helped people live through a time when no one knew who was randomly shooting people or why, or where the next attack would occur.

Of course, much of his confidence no doubt came with time and experience. Chief Moose started his career as a patrol officer, a job in which an officer's confidence is often tested, sometimes shaken, and inevitably built. A candidate is unlikely to reach patrol duty, or any other law enforcement role, if he or she has a pronounced lack of confidence.

Equal Opportunity

If you think you have what it takes to be in law enforcement but are afraid that you might not get hired because of prejudice or closed-mindedness (that is, the hiring body's, not your own), be encouraged. As long as you are able to perform the functions of the position and meet all requirements, you will not be discriminated against. Hiring for all federal, state, and local government positions is subject to regulation and enforcement of antidiscrimination laws by the U.S. Equal Employment Opportunity Commission (EEOC). According to the EEOC, the laws forbidding discrimination against candidates include the following:

- Title VII of the Civil Rights Act of 1964, which prohibits employment discrimination based on race, color, religion, sex, or national origin
- The Equal Pay Act of 1963 (EPA), which protects men and women who perform substantially equal work in the same establishment from sex-based wage discrimination

- The Age Discrimination in Employment Act of 1967 (ADEA), which protects individuals who are 40 years of age or older
- Title I and Title V of the Americans with Disabilities Act of 1990 (ADA), which prohibit employment discrimination against qualified individuals with disabilities in the private sector, and in state and local governments
- Sections 501 and 505 of the Rehabilitation Act of 1973, which prohibit discrimination against qualified individuals with disabilities who work in the federal government
- The Civil Rights Act of 1991, which, among other things, provides monetary damages in cases of intentional employment discrimination

Chapter 2

CIVIL RIGHTS: THE BILL OF RIGHTS AND MIRANDA

★

The police must obey the law while enforcing the law.

—U.S. Supreme Court Chief Justice
Earl Warren, 1959

If you have read this far and are still interested in law enforcement, you should know a few things that are essential to the job no matter which agency on which level you hope to work for. In the United States, all laws are held up to the standards of the Constitution. If a law is passed locally, by a state, or federally, and someone believes it to be unconstitutional, it can be challenged in court and potentially struck down. Debates over the interpretation of the Constitution are as old as the debated provisions of the document itself. Particularly subject to debate is what we refer to as the Bill of Rights, the Amendments to the Constitution that, among other things, outline and guarantee our civil liberties.

If an officer violates someone's civil liberties during the investigation of a crime or the arrest and detainment of that individual, the information and evidence gathered during the investigation, including a confession, as well as the arrest itself, may be thrown out. As an officer of the law, it will be part of your sworn duty to uphold the Constitution. Further, in order to make good arrests and gather evidence that can be used to convict criminals, you should know and understand what these civil rights are. Any academy will cover this in great detail, but I believe it warrants a few pages in this book. If you do not think you can equally and fairly enforce the law while respecting and protecting the civil rights of those in your jurisdiction (including the criminals), you will not make a good officer of the law.

Bill of Rights—The First 10 Ammendments to the Constitution

Officers of the law must be familiar not only with federal, state, and local laws and ordinances but also with the Constitution, especially the Bill of Rights. There are situations in which officers have little time to make decisions and must act in the face of personal danger and risk to the public. It is very difficult to balance this against the backdrop of civil rights, but it is critical, both for the protection of the public and for making good arrests.

Bill of Rights

The Conventions of a number of the States having, at the time of adopting the Constitution, expressed a desire, in order to prevent misconstruction or abuse of its powers, that further declaratory and restrictive clauses should be added, and as extending the ground of public confidence in the Government will best insure the beneficent ends of its institution;

Resolved, by the Senate and House of Representatives of the United States of America, in Congress assembled, two-thirds of both Houses concurring, that the following articles be proposed to the Legislatures of the several States, as amendments to the Constitution of the United States; all or any of which articles, when ratified by three-fourths of the said Legislatures, to be valid to all intents and purposes as part of the said Constitution, namely:

- **Amendment I:** Congress shall make no law respecting an establishment of religion, or prohibiting the free exercise thereof; or abridging the freedom of speech, or of the press; or the right of the people peaceably to assemble, and to petition the government for a redress of grievances.
- **Amendment II:** A well regulated militia, being necessary to the security of a free state, the right of the people to keep and bear arms, shall not be infringed.
- **Amendment III:** No soldier shall, in time of peace be quartered in any house, without the consent of the owner, nor in time of war, but in a manner to be prescribed by law.
- **Amendment IV:** The right of the people to be secure in their persons, houses, papers, and effects, against unreasonable searches and seizures, shall not be violated, and no warrants shall issue, but upon probable cause, supported by oath or affirmation, and particularly describing the place to be searched, and the persons or things to be seized.
- **Amendment V:** No person shall be held to answer for a capital, or otherwise infamous crime, unless on a presentment or indictment of a grand jury, except in cases arising in the land or naval forces, or in the militia, when in actual service in time of war or public danger; nor shall any person be subject for the same offense to be twice put in jeopardy of life or limb; nor shall be compelled in any criminal case to be a witness against himself, nor be deprived of life, liberty, or property, without due process of law; nor shall private property be taken for public use, without just compensation.
- **Amendment VI:** In all criminal prosecutions, the accused shall enjoy the right to a speedy and public trial, by an impartial jury of the state and district wherein the crime shall have been

committed, which district shall have been previously ascertained by law, and to be informed of the nature and cause of the accusation; to be confronted with the witnesses against him; to have compulsory process for obtaining witnesses in his favor, and to have the assistance of counsel for his defense.

- **Amendment VII:** In suits at common law, where the value in controversy shall exceed twenty dollars, the right of trial by jury shall be preserved, and no fact tried by a jury, shall be otherwise reexamined in any court of the United States, than according to the rules of the common law.

- **Amendment VIII:** Excessive bail shall not be required, nor excessive fines imposed, nor cruel and unusual punishments inflicted.

- **Amendment IX:** The enumeration in the Constitution, of certain rights, shall not be construed to deny or disparage others retained by the people.

- **Amendment X:** The powers not delegated to the United States by the Constitution, nor prohibited by it to the states, are reserved to the states respectively, or to the people.

Miranda

You've watched enough television, no doubt, to have memorized the Miranda warning:

You have the right to remain silent.

Anything you say can and will be used against you in a court of law.

You have the right to have an attorney present before any questioning.

If you cannot afford an attorney, one will be appointed to represent you before any questioning.

Do you understand these rights?

But do you know how it came about, why it's required, or who Miranda was?

The case was *Miranda v. Arizona*. In 1963, Ernesto Miranda was accused of kidnapping and raping an 18-year-old woman. During questioning, Miranda confessed in writing to the crime. He was tried and convicted by a jury, and sentenced to two concurrent 20- to 30-year sentences. Miranda appealed the verdict on the basis that he had not been informed—before confessing—of his right to representation (as guaranteed by the Sixth Amendment) or of his right not to incriminate himself (as guaranteed by the Fifth Amendment). The case went all the way to the U.S. Supreme Court.

The Supreme Court ruled that his confession must be thrown out because Miranda was not advised of his rights, including his right to remain silent. Therefore, the conviction was overturned. In the Supreme Court's majority opinion to reverse the Supreme Court of Arizona's decision to uphold Miranda's conviction, Chief Justice Earl Warren wrote the following:

> The principles announced today deal with the protection which must be given to the privilege against self-incrimination when the individual is first subjected to police interrogation while in custody at the station or otherwise deprived of his freedom of action in any significant way. It is at this point that our adversary system of criminal proceedings commences, distinguishing itself at the outset from the inquisitorial system recognized in some countries. Under the system of warnings we delineate today or under any other system which may be devised and found effective, the safeguards to be erected about the privilege must come into play at this point . . .
>
> We reverse. From the testimony of the officers and by the admission of respondent, it is clear that Miranda was not in any way apprised of his right to consult with an attorney and to have one present during the interrogation, nor was his right not to be compelled to incriminate himself effectively protected in any other manner. Without these warnings the statements were inadmissible. The mere fact that he signed a statement which contained a typed-in clause stating that he had "full knowledge" of his "legal rights" does not approach the knowing and intelligent waiver required to relinquish constitutional rights.

Miranda did not go free, however. He was eventually convicted without the confession.

Since this Supreme Court ruling, before any pertinent questioning of a suspect, the police have been required to advise the suspect of his or her rights by reciting the Miranda warning. Once a suspect has been thusly informed, he or she has been "Mirandized."

If a suspect is questioned without first being Mirandized, anything the suspect says, up to and including a confession, may be disallowed at trial. Further, if evidence is gathered as a result of information given to the police by a non-Mirandized suspect in response to police questions, that evidence may be disallowed.

Imagine your chagrin as an officer if by a simple omission—not reading a suspect his Miranda rights—you set events in motion that make it impossible for prosecutors to convict someone who is guilty of a terrible crime. This is a quandary you do not want to find yourself in, so begin now taking the Miranda warning seriously. By the time you're an officer of the law, it'll be second nature.

Chapter 3
PREPARE YOURSELF

★

O bviously, just declaring a desire to be a law enforcement officer won't get you a badge. Regardless of the agency or jurisdiction, there are certain steps in recruitment, testing, and hiring that you will have to undergo before realizing your dream. While, particularly on the federal level, there is a huge difference from agency to agency regarding what is specifically required of officers, it's a good idea to familiarize yourself with some common steps in the process.

Oral Interviews

The oral interview is your best chance to impress the people who will decide whether or not you are a good candidate for their department. Just like any other job interview, the number one rule is that old cliché: *You never get a second chance to make a first impression.* They will be judging you on a number of factors, and only one of them is the substance of the answers you give to their questions. Fairly or not, they will be judging you on the following:

- Appearance, including your dress, grooming, body language, and posture
- Eye contact
- Tone of voice and apparent sincerity

- Knowledge of the position you are applying for and the department as a whole
- Whether your answers indicate that you understood the questions
- Whether your answers indicate that you would make a good officer

How to Prepare

First, go back to what you know about the position. Investigate the particulars and consider whether you really want the job, or you just want *a* job. If you are not certain that the position is for you, there's no need to prepare—you'll be wasting the interviewers' time by going in. However, if the job sounds like it's what you want, there are many things you can do to prepare yourself.

Remember as you go through the process of preparing that nobody enjoys a job interview. Everyone gets nervous; you're not alone, and nervousness does not mean you are an inferior candidate. Take the time to prepare and you can reduce the amount by which your nerves may negatively impact your performance in the interview.

Try to find out as much as you can about the position and the department from unofficial sources, not just from the department's official materials. Speak with current or former officers. Read articles in the newspaper about issues and/or changes in the department, especially concerning leadership and personnel. Consider participating in a ride-along, or taking a tour of the correctional facilities and precincts. Once you're armed with knowledge about the places you might work, the people for and with whom you might work, and the types of situations they face, you will be able to give informed answers to questions about how well you understand the risks and rewards of the job, and about your goals within the department.

If you are uncomfortable in an interview setting, as most people are, try practicing with friends or family. They can ask you questions like the following, and you can practice answering them. This is not to suggest you go into the interview armed with a bunch of speeches you've committed to memory—you want to be sincere and responsive, not a robot. But practicing will help you gather your thoughts into cohesive answers to questions you're liable to be asked, including:

- When did you first become interested in law enforcement?
- Why do you want to be a law enforcement officer?
- What in your background has prepared you for such a career choice?
- Do you understand the duties and responsibilities of the position?
- Do you understand the powers assigned to officers, and the limits to those powers?

As for the first three items on my list of things the interviewers will be watching for, you should do your best to look clean, well-rested, professional, and relaxed. Here are my tips for the interview:

- Wear a suit or a nice matching professional outfit.
- Adhere to departmental grooming standards. If beards are not allowed among officers, go in with a clean face. If short hair is required, get a haircut. If women must keep their hair pulled back, wear your hair pulled back to the interview.
- Sit with your back straight and do not fidget during the interview.
- Make good eye contact.
- Try not to look away or touch your face (rub your nose, scratch your chin) when you're answering the questions—these behaviors may suggest you are lying, though they may just be part of your nervous repertoire.
- Do not rush to answer their questions. If you need to think for a few seconds, do so. They do not want rash candidates, and they will appreciate your considered responses.
- Avoid "um" and "like" and "you know" in your answers.
- Refer to them by rank and name, and use "sir" and "ma'am" when addressing them, as in, "Yes sir, Captain Jones, I believe I would make a good police officer."
- Try to incorporate their questions in your answers, which should be phrased in complete sentences. For example, if

you're asked, "Why do you want to be a police officer?" you might begin your answer with, "I would like to be a police officer because . . ."

- When it's over, smile and thank them for the interview, regardless of how well or poorly you believe it went.
- **Above all else, be honest.** This is in bold for a reason. Be candid, even and especially when discussing mistakes you have made that you are afraid might disqualify you. Any misinformation you give them may be revealed as such, and you will be disqualified for lying.

If you get this far, remember that you are being interviewed by a law enforcement agency. Of all the times you might get away with a lie, big or small, this is not among them. Remember that they will be conducting a background check on you, which may include your record in every place you have ever lived and information gathered from schools, friends, and family, as well as information gathered from government sources like your various current and former local Departments of Motor Vehicles and your former employers. What you tell them in the interview had better match what they find in their investigation. If you fail to tell the truth, you will be summarily dismissed from the process. They may be able to work with a black mark in your personal or professional history—if you're honest about it. But they will not be able to work with you if you are dishonest.

Written Tests

While written tests are different depending upon the department's needs and requirements, there are some basic guidelines for preparing for and taking the tests. It is a great idea to prepare, no matter how confident you are in your desirability as a candidate or your abilities to take tests, because testing situations create a lot of nervous tension. A method psychologists recommend basically suggests that if you're studying for a test to be taken in a cool, brightly lit, quiet classroom, you should study in cool, brightly lit, quiet room. Subconsciously you will register the similarities and, it is believed, you will test better. If this works for you, great. It works for many people. But if you can only study by lamplight with the music cranked, then do what you need to in order to prepare.

One piece of advice that applies to every aspect of the application process is to *get enough sleep*. Do not drag in on half your usual amount and expect to be sharp. Though you may find yourself pulling some late nights and early mornings if you end up in law enforcement, you're out to make a first impression here and shouldn't risk being at less than your best.

Reading Comprehension

The first thing any written test will indicate to examiners is your ability to comprehend what you have read. Take your time reading the questions, and make sure you have understood everything before rushing to answer. If you have trouble reading, you will have difficulty getting into law enforcement.

How to Prepare   If you have trouble reading, get a tutor or enroll in a class oriented toward adult reading skills. No matter your reading skills, it will be of benefit to you to practice by reading a paragraph or two at a time from your local newspaper or national magazine—anything with real content—then put it away and try to summarize what it said. You can do this alone by writing a summary and then comparing it to the paragraph, or you can have a study partner who can "grade" you on how well you summarized what you just read.

Grammar/Spelling/Writing Skills

Beat cops spend a great deal of their time writing police reports, and the prosecution of the crimes, minor or major, depends largely upon the breadth and clarity of these reports. For this reason alone, though there are others, if you cannot communicate clearly in writing, you will not be able to get into law enforcement. Written tests will often include multiple-choice sections to test your grammar and spelling skills. (Note that in an oral interview, your ability to communicate orally will be evaluated as much as the content of your responses.)

How to Prepare   If you take my advice under Reading Comprehension and practice summarizing text from periodicals, you will be preparing for this aspect already. But instead of just evaluating whether you summarized the paragraph correctly, look at how well you wrote your summary. Watch for grammar, spelling, and punctuation errors. If these are areas in which you are weak, get a tutor or enroll in a class oriented toward adults.

Retention

Examiners will want to know how well you remember details about what you have seen or read. In some cases, written tests will include photographs of crime scenes, which you'll be given a limited amount of time to look at before being asked specific questions about them. For instance, after viewing a photograph of a hotel room strewn with clothes and bedding, you might be asked whether the shirt on the floor by the bathroom door was a T-shirt, a button-down shirt, a tank top, or a sweater.

How to Prepare   There's no doubt some people have better memories than others. But you can sharpen your memory in many ways. Try doing memory exercises (don't discount the old children's card game "Memory"). Look at a photograph in a magazine for one minute. Time yourself. Then close the magazine and write down all the details you remember about the photograph. When you're done, check your work against the picture. You'll find you will improve quickly, both in your ability to observe and to remember what you have observed.

Analytical Ability

It's one thing to be able to read and understand something, but to analyze it and make judgments about it is another. Apply this to the field: If on patrol you come upon a crime in progress, you will need to take in all the details about what's happening quickly and correctly in order to decide what to do next.

How to Prepare   This is one area where I believe maturity, education, and work experience have a lot of bearing. Size yourself up. Do you think you make good decisions? Have other people commented on your decision making? Do you find yourself making a lot of snap judgments about people or situations that later prove to be way off the mark? If so, you may not be ready for a career in law enforcement. If not, you can prepare for this aspect of testing by making sure that your head is clear going in and that you check any hastiness and prejudice at the door. Take the test seriously and take your time, and if you have good analytical ability, you will do fine.

★ ★ ★ ★ ★ ★

All my advice can't equal a real-world example. Please review Appendix A, which is the study guide prepared by the Albuquerque, New Mexico Police Department to help candidates prepare for that department's written test. Their test is a great example of the types of questions these tests may contain, and their study guide is a great preparation tool.

Physical Fitness or Physical Abilities Test/Medical Examination

Like it or not, law enforcement is a physical job. Again, there are similarities to the armed services here. Most departments and agencies require candidates to undergo a physical fitness test, in addition to a medical examination. The physical fitness test may involve any of a number of activities, most of which are timed, and these are usually graded on a curve according to age and gender. In other words, a 20-year-old man will have slightly more strict requirements than a 35-year-old woman.

Many departments and agencies follow the testing methods and requirements of the Cooper Institute in Dallas, Texas. Founded in 1970 on the premise that preventing disease is as important as treating disease, the institute developed a set of criteria for measuring healthy levels of physical fitness, among many other endeavors and accomplishments. The Cooper Institute for Aerobics Research has worked with law enforcement fitness programs for nearly 30 years. Their norms are the basis for most of the tests given in the recruitment process, as well as in physical fitness reviews given annually, or more often, to current law enforcement officers. The Cooper standards involve the following:

- Vertical Jump
- 1-Minute Sit-Up
- 300-Meter Run
- Maximum Push-Up or Bench Press
- 1.5-Mile Run

Real-life results from law enforcement are ranked by the institute. Most departments and agencies have a pass/fail cutoff at the 70-percent mark.

In addition to the standards of the Cooper Institute, departments and agencies will have other tests that you must pass. These tests may test your ability to handle firearms, drive a police vehicle, run an obstacle course, and perform other activities.

The best advice I can give for preparing for a physical fitness test is to find out what will be on the test and practice doing it. Before you jump-start your fitness, however, please check with your doctor if you have any doubts or questions about what you should or should not try to do, and how rapidly you should or should not try to do it. It may make sense to hire a personal trainer, or take a running class that is structured for healthy improvement over a reasonable amount of time.

That said, if you know the department will require that you do 40 sit-ups in under one minute, start doing sit-ups every day until you can do more than 40 in one minute. If you know you will be required to run a mile in less than 10 minutes, run at least four days a week until you can run a mile in less than 9 minutes.

Do you see my point? Practice for the specific tests, but don't shoot for the minimum, as you may not perform at your peak on the day of the test.

To get a really good idea of what a physical fitness test may include, please review Appendix B, which is the Physical Ability Test overview given in the Austin Police Department's Applicant Information Packet. Departments and agencies like the Austin Police Department do you the service of telling you exactly what they require on their physical fitness test. Do yourself the service of reviewing their requirements, practicing the specific activities, and showing up prepared.

A medical examination is trickier. You can try to keep yourself in good shape, but there are some tests with outcomes you cannot influence. For instance, you can lower your cholesterol, but you cannot improve your vision or hearing. There are certain minimum standards for vision and hearing that you must meet to become a law enforcement officer. Find out what the requirements are. If you use corrective lenses or have had laser eye surgery, these factors will influence whether you meet the vision requirements. If either of those are true in your case, then you should know whether you have uncorrected vision of 20/40 or 20/200. If you do not meet the minimum, you will know from the outset that you will not qualify. Hearing is tougher, as most of us do not get our hearing tested. If the department or agency you aspire to join has a hearing requirement and you know you have hearing problems or hearing loss, find out what it is and consider getting your hearing tested before you apply. It may save you some trouble and even disappointment.

As for the rest of the medical examination, if you are in good cardiovascular health, that's a good start. If you have no chronic or untreated conditions, and if you have no conditions or diseases that could be considered a risk to other officers, you should be able to pass. If you're concerned about whether you're healthy enough, see your own doctor and get a complete physical. Take him or her the criteria used by the department or agency you're applying for, and ask the doctor to conduct the appropriate tests to determine whether or not you meet the criteria. It may cost you some money, but you'll know where you stand in terms of getting the job you want, and you'll benefit by having a good idea about your general health.

One important note: For nearly all law enforcement jobs, *true color blindness is a disqualifier*. If you are color-blind or have anything more serious than minor hue impairment, you have little chance of becoming a law enforcement officer. There are other jobs in criminal justice for which hue impairment is not an issue.

Psychological Test

I won't lie to you. I included this because it is an area that candidates are tested in, but I don't believe you can prepare for it. Psychological tests are usually written, though there may be oral interviews as well.

They are designed to find out whether you are psychologically fit to perform the duties of the department or agency you're applying for.

Don't let me scare you. If you are intelligent and have a good mental health history, you should not have any trouble with the psychological test. As with other subjective testing, be honest. You will do no one any good by trying to seem like someone you are not.

Background Check

Like the previous area, here is another one for which you cannot really prepare yourself. As I'll mention later, you can conduct yourself leading up to your application in such a way that will leave a clean and impressive background for the investigators to check. But your background is what it is. Based on information in your application, on your résumé, and in answers you supply to questions about your personal history, investigators will look at any or all of the following:

- Criminal record in every jurisdiction in which you have ever lived
- School record at every school you have attended
- Financial records
- Medical records
- Military records
- Employment history

In addition, investigators will seek out and interview any or all of the following:

- Former employers
- Personal and professional references
- Friends and former friends
- Spouse and ex-spouse(s)
- Other family members

The process is long and involved, and it is usually conducted during other steps in the recruitment process. No decision will be made as to whether you will or will not be hired until the background check is complete and has been evaluated. For the FBI, the background investigation can take up to four months, and the FBI conducts background checks for other federal agencies, so take this as the norm for federal law enforcement.

Appendix C is the Columbus, Georgia Police Department's Background Investigation Booklet, which applicants must complete and turn in for use in the department's background investigation and screening process. Look over the information this department requires from applicants. It's very thorough, and it's indicative of what other departments and agencies require.

Polygraph Examination

Licensed polygraphers ask questions of a candidate to determine whether there are things in the candidate's past that he or she is not revealing or being candid about. These days, information supplied by the candidate, as cross-referenced and supplemented by a background check, is used in the questioning. Almost everyone gets nervous about a polygraph test. There are some criminals who are so far inside their own actions and motivations that they are unafraid, and their lies are often undetectable by even the best polygraphers. But most law-abiding citizens become nervous when faced with the lie detector test. What if you tell the truth but your heart is racing from nerves? Will your true statement look like a lie? Those are a couple of the questions people have going in.

Also, for many people there's something about the process that implies extraordinary perception on the part of the examiner. It has the air about it of mind reading, so people are sometimes overly anxious that not only their relevant actions, especially with regard to criminal activity and drug use, will be under scrutiny, but that their thoughts, inclinations, and so on may be as well. They might also be concerned about mistakes they have made that have nothing to do with their viability as candidates but that they do not want to reveal.

If you're required to take a polygraph test and are nervous for any of these reasons, try to relax. The test is not magic, and it's not ESP. If you're required to take one, take your time, try to breathe, and be honest.

Criminal Records

You might think it odd for me to include this in a chapter called "Prepare Yourself." No amount of studying or preparation is going to change what the hiring officer or human resources person sees when he or she pulls up your criminal record. The preparation starts earlier than that. If you have the dimmest hope of going into law enforcement, you have to keep your record clean.

Of course, you should obey the laws simply because they're the laws, not just because disobeying them could keep you from reaching your goals. But we were all young once, even me. I had my share of close calls with the law when I was in college—mind you, it was for underage drinking and not any "hard crime." But if I had known then that I was going to end up applying for a job with the FBI, I would've been more careful. I would've made better choices. If one close call had gone the wrong way for me, I wouldn't have been a Special Agent, I wouldn't have developed the profiling techniques that I built my career on and that are now used worldwide in investigations—and I certainly wouldn't be writing this book. Everything would be different. I hate to think what a little too much beer and some dumb, youthful decisions might've done to my life—past, present, and future.

I have a friend, a local law enforcement officer who shall remain nameless, who pulled a common stunt in college. He streaked down a stretch of interstate highway. Some of you youngsters may not remember the streaking craze. In the 1970s, you could almost count on some fool in nothing but socks or a necktie running across the corner of the end zone in a televised football game, or jumping into the outfield during a baseball game. College graduations, groundbreaking ceremonies—almost any public event was a forum for streaking. So naturally college kids took to it and made new games of it. This guy took it all off as a fraternity stunt and ran down the median, about 100 yards, according to his account. Now, it was probably more like 100 feet, but I imagine he was nervous and every step felt like three. Anyway, had he gotten caught (which he didn't, luckily), and had he been convicted of indecently exposing himself, he would not have been able to become an officer in the department for which he is now in charge of recruiting. Why? His department won't hire someone who has a misdemeanor conviction if that conviction involves acts of "moral turpitude." Among such acts is indecent exposure.

So take my advice and start acting like an agent now. I don't mean you should make citizen's arrests or start calling in anonymous tips on your friends for accidentally driving without their licenses. But do try to live like you have already taken an oath. Obey the law. Do not bend the rules and expect to get away with it, even if your intentions are innocent, good-natured, and "all in good fun." Learn one of life's biggest lessons as early as possible: Once it's done, you can't take it back.

Disqualifying Convictions

As you might expect, convicted felons cannot be law enforcement officers. They cannot possess a firearm, so they cannot be law enforcement officers. For non-felony drug convictions, there are some mitigating factors within departments that allow for exceptions. Armed robbery, murder, and rape are all felonies. But depending on where you live, passing a bad check for more than $500 is too. So keep an eye on your checking account balance.

For law enforcement jobs, a misdemeanor conviction for domestic abuse is also a disqualifier. Just as with a felony conviction, you won't be able to carry a firearm if you've been convicted of misdemeanor domestic abuse. In accordance with the Lautenberg Amendment, effective as of 1996, to the Gun Control Act of 1968, it is a felony for any person convicted of a misdemeanor crime of domestic violence to possess, ship, transport, or otherwise dispose of firearms or ammunition.

Beyond that, if you have a history of domestic disputes, if the police have been called to your house repeatedly, even if you have never been convicted, you may be disqualified. If you have a domestic abuse conviction on your record, most agencies will not hire you.

In addition to the preceding disqualifications, most agencies and departments also refuse to hire individuals convicted of misdemeanors involving "moral turpitude"—crimes involving a sexual component, like indecent exposure or public urination. Some departments and agencies have a recent time limit on misdemeanor convictions of any sort; for example, if you have been convicted of a misdemeanor within the last three years, you would be disqualified.

You will not be surprised to hear that having a DUI or DWI (Driving Under the Influence or Driving While Intoxicated) on your recent record will likely be a disqualifier. Having a DUI or DWI shows poor judgment and a reckless disregard for public safety that does not recommend you for law enforcement duty. For some jobs, the recent time limit may be three years, for others much longer. For some, such a conviction anywhere on your record will keep you from getting hired.

You might be surprised to find that even having a large number of traffic citations, particularly if they are unpaid or were paid late, can bar you from getting hired by some departments. This is for two reasons. First, police officers and sheriff's deputies start out on patrol, so they will be charged with safely handling a department vehicle in conditions ranging from rush-hour traffic to the pursuit of a speeding vehicle. If you can't handle your own car safely and without incident, odds are you won't be the best candidate for driving a patrol car. Second, officers of the law should have a healthy respect for the law. If you have repeatedly or substantially exceeded the speed limit, or parked in a red zone, or passed on a double yellow line, you have shown a disregard for the law. Everyone makes mistakes and we've all gotten tickets, but if you have gotten a lot and/or have failed to own up to the ones you have received, you may have a hard time getting hired.

Other Disqualifiers

Any history you might have with illegal drugs will be especially important to the chiefs, captains, and commanders looking to fill their ranks. This is for obvious reasons: First, you have to be sober to enforce the law; second, you have to be healthy to enforce the law (i.e., not crippled by an addiction, even if your use is restricted to off-duty hours); third, you have to follow the law to enforce the law.

Since drug use is an acknowledged common fact in our society, there is usually a recent time limit on drug use, and drug use is usually classed by type of drug. Typically, if you have used a drug for which a conviction would be a misdemeanor, like marijuana, the time limit is shorter. But if you have used a felony drug, the time limit is longer. For instance, if you used marijuana within the last three years, you would be disqualified, while use of cocaine within the last 10 years would disqualify you. This depends entirely upon the hiring rules of the department or agency. Be sure to find out what those rules are. If your own drug use, however minor or experimental, does not fall outside of their time limits, you need to wait to apply.

Notwithstanding the preceding, if you have ever demonstrated a pattern of drug use, regardless of the drug, you will probably be disqualified, at the discretion of the department or agency.

Another disqualifying factor may not seem fair; however, your financial history may come to bear on your chances of getting into law enforcement. You don't have to be a Rockefeller, and everyone has lived paycheck-to-paycheck, but if you have a history of chronic financial problems, it can be an indicator of irresponsibility or instability. If you have had repeated financial problems and you have a good explanation, offer it candidly and show that you are resolved to keep your finances straight going forward. Regardless of what your financial record is like up to now, this is another example of something you can start working on at any point before applying for a law enforcement job. Keep your checkbook straight and your debts under control, and this won't be an issue for you.

This all goes back to my original point: *Live like you're already an agent.* If you do that, you'll not only protect your chances of getting a job in law enforcement; you'll find yourself being a good citizen. That's not a bad by-product. I know that is a corny, 1950s kind of thing to say. But to my mind, if we all did a better job of living according to and with respect for the law, we'd be safer and happier as a nation.

Chapter 4

ASSOCIATED CAREERS IN CRIMINAL JUSTICE

★

There are many careers in law enforcement. As you may have guessed, for the scope of this book, I have chosen to concentrate on law enforcement jobs as defined by the Department of Justice Bureau of Justice Statistics: those with arrest and firearm authority. This is for several reasons.

First, these jobs are available to the greatest number of people. Generally speaking, aside from minimum requirements for educational levels, such as a high school diploma or four-year college degree, these jobs to not require special degrees or advanced training. If you have the advanced training and post-graduate education in an area of specialization, you are probably aware of the specific opportunities that would take advantage of your training and education.

Second, in terms of specialized assignments, I have covered those within agency profiles. But if you wish to become a cold-case investigator, you will have to start out on patrol like everyone else and work your way toward that specialization, if it suits you by that point and you are deemed suitable for it.

Third, while my focus is on jobs with arrest and firearm authority, this entire chapter is devoted to other careers in criminal justice, within the context of which law enforcement careers fall. I enthusiastically recommend, to anyone qualified and interested, these other sorts of jobs in law enforcement—from laboratory positions to crime scene photography to medical examination. A large percentage of cases would never be solved without the work of sketch artists, forensic analysts, and even profilers.

It used to be more difficult to enter such areas without first becoming an officer or agent. Take the FBI. In my day, you couldn't work in the lab without first being a Special Agent. That meant, in my opinion, that some highly qualified people were turned away because, for instance, their uncorrected vision wasn't 20/200 or better. The thinking was sound, but flawed. The idea was that the folks in the lab should have an investigative background so that they could see the case from all the right perspectives, something it was thought could only be gained by field experience. But the need for qualified forensic scientists and others outweighed the Bureau's desire to have only seasoned field agents in every aspect of the investigative process.

The change is good, and I hope it reflects a trend. Some of the most important jobs in law enforcement do not have arrest and firearm authority and have different requirements than those that do. Following is an overview of some of these crucially important jobs within law enforcement departments or agencies.

Examiners and Experts:
The Crime Scene to the Laboratory

The men and women who analyze evidence amaze me. From the crime scene to the lab, they provide the stepping stones for investigators that lead to closing a case. Crime scene and laboratory analysts come from a variety of backgrounds and have varying levels of education and specialized training. For instance, a crime scene photographer may start in local law enforcement as an officer with photography experience and an interest in the position, or as a certified crime scene photographer hired outside of the requirements of officers in that department. Evidence analysts may be certified and, depending upon the requirements of the department or agency, may have various undergraduate or graduate degrees in fields like medicine, chemistry, and biology, and experience in laboratory analysis of tissues, hair, fiber, blood and other fluids, as well as just about anything you can put under a microscope.

As for evidence examination experts, there are too many areas of expertise to list. Among them are experts in the analysis of fingerprints, ballistics, footwear, and bloodstain patterning. Experts in these fields are designated as such in a variety of ways, including education, training, experience, and certification. For instance, the International Association for Identification (IAI) requires that fingerprint experts have at least 80 hours of training and pass IAI tests for certification, in addition to having at least two years of fingerprint examination experience and a college degree, or a combination thereof. Bloodstain patterning experts must have at least 40 hours of training for certification, three years of practice within the area, and 240 hours of training in a related field of study, such as documentary photography.

Forensic Scientists

Among the most specialized in criminal justice are the forensic scientists, including the forensic anthropologist, pathologist, and odontologist. These individuals may work for medical facilities or universities and consult with law enforcement, or be employed directly with law enforcement departments or agencies. They are instrumental in determining causes of death and identities of bodies in all sorts of conditions.

Imagine finding a body buried 50 years ago in the tropics. All you're going to have, probably, are bones and teeth, and you may only have partial remains of those. Forensic anthropologists piece together such evidence. They apply anthropological knowledge and techniques to investigations, skillfully recovering and examining skeletal remains for evidence of identity and cause of death. A forensic anthropologist usually has a PhD in biological anthropology.

Forensic pathologists are medical doctors who specialize in disease and, as detailed later in the chapter, perform autopsies. Looking at biological evidence, they determine the presence and extent of disease in the deceased, and how it contributed to death, among other analyses.

You're no doubt familiar with dental records being used to identify bodies. Forensic odontologists are responsible for such identification. They also analyze bite marks and dental records or impressions of those investigators believe might match them. Forensic odontologists are doctors of dentistry who have been certified through a strict process that requires at least two years' experience with a coroner's or medical examiner's office; participation in a number of autopsies; experience with dental and bite mark identifications; and experience conducting lectures, writing articles, and more. Forensic odontologists are certified by The American Board of Forensic Odontology.

Coroner's or Medical Examiner's Office

The office of a coroner or medical examiner is typically responsible for the investigation of sudden, violent, or unusual deaths that occur within the jurisdiction of the office. The coroner, medical examiner, and deputies determine the cause of death, which generally falls into one of the following categories: homicide, suicide, accidental death, death by natural causes, and indeterminate. Cause of death determinations dictate which deaths will be investigated by law enforcement and which will not.

In addition to determining cause of death, the coroner's or medical examiner's office will do their best to identify the deceased if such identity is unknown or uncertain. Coroners and medical examiners use crime scene investigation, analysis of evidence, interviews, medical records, body chemistry and toxicology tests, and autopsy examinations to determine cause of death. They use fingerprints, DNA, dental records, X-rays, and other evidence to determine identity, or to determine elements of identity in the case of badly decomposed or partial remains; for instance, they may be able to determine only the general age, the gender, and the race of the deceased. This information is, of course, very important in an investigation and in attempting to find and notify next of kin, to determine whether the deceased was previously reported missing, or even to determine whether the deceased fits the profile of victims of a certain serial killer. Coroners and medical examiners and their deputies may have to appear in court to testify as to their findings.

In many places, medical examiners are replacing coroners. Whereas coroners are not necessarily medical doctors, medical examiners are, and the latter have forensic specialization. The coroner or medical examiner may be elected or appointed. Within the coroner's or ME's office, the forensic pathologist is an expert in determining cause and manner of death. The forensic pathologist is trained to perform autopsies, incorporating case information into his or her evaluation, and to collect evidence (from secretions to tissue under the fingernails of the deceased). The forensic pathologist looks at how wounds occurred, coming up with logical scenarios for fatal, coincidental, and previous injuries. (Think television's *CSI* with realistic lighting and cases that are not solved in an hour.)

The requirements for deputy and other positions at coroner's and medical examiner's offices vary, but college and specialization in medicine, anthropology, chemistry, toxicology, or another related field may be required or sought. If you are interested in working with your local or state office, contact them for specific information. Many offices offer internship programs to acquaint individuals with the work they do.

Sketch Artists

Sketch artists are also called forensic artists or forensic illustrators. Everyone is familiar with the work of sketch artists, who take eyewitness information and develop plausible composite drawings or sketches of suspects or others whose identities are required in the course of an investigation. To become a forensic artist certified by the International Association for Identification, you must take between 40 and 120 hours of training at approved institutions, with many levels of testing and minimum numbers of actual drawings to be completed. Requirements vary, and nothing recommends a sketch artist as well as that artist's ability to convey in a composite drawing the descriptions of often frightened, shaken witnesses who may have had only a fleeting look at the subject of the composite.

There is much work for competent sketch artists, but much rests on their shoulders. Remember, they aren't drawing from their memory; they're drawing from the memory of others. If the descriptions they are given are inaccurate or of the wrong individual, the resulting composite can be a hindrance to an investigation rather than a tool. And if they are unable to accurately render what they are told, the same may happen. But when suspects are identified on the basis of a composite, that is obviously and rightly gratifying for the artist.

Polygraph Examiners

Polygraph examiners are specially trained and certified, and they may be employed by law enforcement departments or agencies, by private sector companies, or as independent consultants. As I've often said, a polygraph test is only as good as its examiner. The men and women I've worked with have been well-trained, are highly experienced, and are fluent in the nuances of human behavior.

Requirements vary by jurisdiction, but specialized training is required. Certain schools are accredited by the American Polygraph Association, which is made up of examiners from across the country and which sets the examiner's code of ethics, provides information about training and certification, and offers other resources to examiners and the public.

Probation and Parole Officers

Members of law enforcement on the correctional side—probation and parole officers—have a great deal of responsibility. They are law enforcement's overseers of individuals on the fringe, individuals who are moving from incarceration to free citizenship or who have committed a relatively mild or first offense, a repeat of which could land them in prison. As such, they can be lifelines for individuals trying to readjust to life "outside" or working to avoid life behind bars.

For those who are unfamiliar, a couple of definitions will help. *Probation* is ordered by the court in lieu of a prison term. While on probation, an offender is under the supervision and care of a probation officer. The terms of probation often involve certain behavioral restrictions. These may include regular drug screens, a curfew, and travel restrictions. Violating any terms of probation can result in the offender going to prison. *Parole* is a conditional release of an offender after a period of incarceration. During an offender's parole term, the offender is supervised by a parole officer and subject to strict rules governing the terms of that parole. Violation of these rules may result in the offender being returned to prison.

According to the Department of Justice Bureau of Justice Statistics, at the end of 2002 there were 3,995,165 adult men and women on probation in this country, and 753,141 on parole. To those men and women, probation and parole officers can offer a sympathetic ear, while maintaining a hard line of instruction and guidance for those under their supervision. They can spot signs of trouble—social, marital, or emotional or problems of another nature.

The requirements for such jobs vary. Usually a four-year college degree is required, with a major in social work or a related field preferred. Post-graduate education is required for promotions and supervisory positions. If you are interested in working in one of these jobs, investigate the position locally. Know in advance that they are demanding jobs, but they can also be very rewarding.

Other Careers in Criminal Justice

There are other ways to be involved in criminal justice. Social workers who oversee child safety and custody and victims' rights champions who protect and fight for crime victims are part of the process. Obviously, prosecutors and defense attorneys are inextricably important to the criminal justice system. So are jurors, and, of course, the judges who preside over trials, sentence or free those who have been tried, set precedents that change the way laws are interpreted, and sometimes rule certain laws unconstitutional. The men and women in legislatures and other law-making bodies on every level are at the most formative phase of criminal justice.

In fact, criminal justice goes all the way back to each of us. We can affect what laws are passed with our votes, we can choose to abide by or break those laws, and we can choose to report crimes or look away.

Chapter 5

LAW ENFORCEMENT CODE OF CONDUCT

★

The best expression of how police officers should conduct themselves is given in the International Association of Chiefs of Police Code of Conduct. The International Association of Chiefs of Police (IACP) is a great professional organization. In addition to working with the U.S. government on law enforcement policy and performing other important functions, they publish *Police Chief Magazine*. If you're interested in learning about law enforcement, from advances in technology to interagency investigations to new trends in crime, getting this publication would be a good idea. It is pretty inexpensive, and if you would prefer to see it virtually, you can do so online at www.policechiefmagazine.org. They also post job openings. Another great magazine is *The Chief of Police*, which is published by the National Association of Chiefs of Police (NACOP). I am a subscriber, and I can recommend *The Chief of Police* for its compelling content, including profiles of law enforcement leaders. I must also take time here to commend the NACOP for their efforts to recognize and remember injured and fallen officers.

The Law Enforcement Code of Conduct from the IACP follows. You should review this code of conduct now, and if you are chosen, you should read it once you are a member of the law enforcement community, and then reread it often thereafter. There are more than 18,000 law enforcement agencies in the United States, but within every department and agency at every rank, this code of conduct will apply. It clearly states the guidelines adopted by departments and agencies to determine how officers and agents should conduct themselves, on the job and off.

Law Enforcement Code of Conduct

All law enforcement officers must be fully aware of the ethical responsibilities of their position and must strive constantly to live up to the highest possible standards of professional policing.

The International Association of Chiefs of Police believes it important that police officers have clear advice and counsel available to assist them in performing their duties consistent with these standards, and has adopted the following ethical mandates as guidelines to meet these ends.

ICAP's Law Enforcement Code of Conduct
Primary Responsibilities of a Police Officer

A police officer acts as an official representative of government who is required and trusted to work within the law. The officer's powers and duties are conferred by statute. The fundamental duties of a police officer include serving the community, safeguarding lives and property, protecting the innocent, keeping the peace and ensuring the rights of all to liberty, equality and justice.

Performance of the Duties of a Police Officer

A police officer shall perform all duties impartially, without favor or affection or ill will and without regard to status, sex, race, religion, political belief or aspiration. All citizens will be treated equally with courtesy, consideration and dignity.

Officers will never allow personal feelings, animosities or friendships to influence official conduct. Laws will be enforced appropriately and courteously and, in carrying out their responsibilities, officers will strive to obtain maximum cooperation from the public. They will conduct themselves in appearance and deportment in such a manner as to inspire confidence and respect for the position of public trust they hold.

Discretion

A police officer will use responsibly the discretion vested in his position and exercise it within the law. The principle of reasonableness will guide the officer's determinations, and the officer will consider all surrounding circumstances in determining whether any legal action shall be taken.

Consistent and wise use of discretion, based on professional policing competence, will do much to preserve good relationships and retain the confidence of the public. There can be difficulty in choosing between conflicting courses of action. It is important to remember that a timely word of advice rather than arrest—which may be correct in appropriate circumstances—can be a more effective means of achieving a desired end.

Use of Force

A police officer will never employ unnecessary force or violence and will use only such force in the discharge of duty as is reasonable in all circumstances.

The use of force should be used only with the greatest restraint and only after discussion, negotiation and persuasion have been found to be inappropriate or ineffective. While the use of force is occasionally unavoidable, every police officer will refrain from unnecessary infliction of pain or suffering and will never engage in cruel, degrading or inhumane treatment of any person.

Confidentiality

Whatever a police officer sees, hears or learns of that is of a confidential nature will be kept secret unless the performance of duty or legal provision requires otherwise.

Members of the public have a right to security and privacy, and information obtained about them must not be improperly divulged.

Integrity

A police officer will not engage in acts of corruption or bribery, nor will an officer condone such acts by other police officers.

The public demands that the integrity of police officers be above reproach. Police officers must, therefore, avoid any conduct that might compromise integrity and thus undercut the public confidence in a law enforcement agency. Officers will refuse to accept any gifts, presents, subscriptions, favors, gratuities or promises that could be interpreted as seeking to cause the officer to refrain from performing official responsibilities honestly and within the law.

Police officers must not receive private or special advantage from their official status. Respect from the public cannot be bought; it can only be earned and cultivated.

Cooperation with Other Police Officers and Agencies

Police officers will cooperate with all legally authorized agencies and their representatives in the pursuit of justice.

An officer or agency may be one among many organizations that may provide law enforcement services to a jurisdiction. It is imperative that a police officer assist colleagues fully and completely with respect and consideration at all times.

Personal-Professional Capabilities

Police officers will be responsible for their own standard of professional performance and will take every reasonable opportunity to enhance and improve their level of knowledge and competence.

Through study and experience, a police officer can acquire the high level of knowledge and competence that is essential for the efficient and effective performance of duty. The acquisition of knowledge is a never-ending process of personal and professional development that should be pursued constantly.

Private Life

Police officers will behave in a manner that does not bring discredit to their agencies or themselves.

A police officer's character and conduct while off duty must always be exemplary, thus maintaining a position of respect in the community in which he or she lives and serves. The officer's personal behavior must be beyond reproach.

Part Two

OPPORTUNITIES AT THE LOCAL LEVEL

★

Chapter 6
GENERAL INFORMATION

★

I'm so used to pressure I'm afraid if it stopped I'd get the bends.

—Walter Headley, Miami Chief of
Police, 1968

Local law enforcement is not easy. It is certainly not, as some people outside of law enforcement imagine, the lowest level on the totem pole—an elementary school to federal law enforcement's college. As first responders to emergency calls, in homes, businesses, and on roadways, local law enforcement officers are our first hope for assistance when we most need it. In their role as officers patrolling our streets and neighborhoods, they keep us safe from dangers we may not realize are there. They get criminals off the streets, protecting us and our children from harm. And as investigators, they solve crimes, from stolen property cases to assault and worse.

Imagine if they weren't there for us when we need them. And that need is increasing, particularly in large cities. According to the U.S. Department of Justice Bureau of Justice Statistics (BJS), between 1990 and 2000, the number of big-city residents served increased by 10 percent, but the number of officers serving them increased only 7 percent. Across the board, in sworn and non-sworn positions, police departments increased their total employment by about 2 percent from 1996 to 2000; sheriff's departments increased theirs by about 3.5 percent. And even a quick look across the country indicates that, wherever there's the budget for it, departments are hiring.

In addition, the makeup of these departments is coming to increasingly reflect the diversity of our culture. According to the BJS, minority representation among local police officers was about 22.7 percent in 2000, and among sheriff's departments was about 17 percent. This was up from 14.5 percent and 13.4 percent, respectively. That is an encouraging increase, and the trend is continuing, so you should not by any means be discouraged if you are not Caucasian.

If you want to work at the local level, as a police officer or sheriff's deputy or other type of officer, your options are going to vary greatly depending upon the size of the department and need for new recruits where you live or want to work. On the following points, departments around the United States vary greatly.

Minimum/Maximum Age

Unlike federal jobs, for which, as a rule, the minimum age is 21 and the maximum age is 37, local departments vary greatly in their minimum and maximum ages for recruits. Some don't have maximum ages at all. Of course, you have to be at least 18, the age of majority, to become an officer, but many departments require that you be 19 or 21 to join. Bearing on this are the various departments' educational requirements. For example, a department may require a four-year college degree but have a minimum age of 21. Few students can achieve a four-year degree before the age of 22, so that minimum age may mean less than the educational requirement does.

Educational Requirements

According to the BJS, from 1990 to 2000, the percentage of departments requiring new officers to have at least some college rose from 19 percent to 37 percent, and the percentage requiring a two-year or four-year degree grew from 6 percent to 14 percent. In 2000, about 11 percent of sheriff's departments required some college education for new officers. I believe this is a very good trend, and I hope it continues. Policing is a difficult job. The ability to assess and assimilate information quickly and make good decisions is critical to policing, and most people in law enforcement agree that education helps people develop this ability. From such basic skills as reading and writing well to understanding diverse cultures as a result of learning about and encountering them on campus, post-high-school education provides a real maturity.

Categorical Preference

By federal, state, or local decree and/or the discretion of individual departments, certain groups of people are given categorical preference in hiring. This means if there are two equally qualified candidates going for one job and one belongs to such a group, that individual will probably get the job. This may seem unfair if you're not a member of any of these groups, but there are good reasons for such preferential practices. Look at this list of some of these groups and see if you don't agree:

- Children or siblings of fallen officers
- Honorably discharged veterans
- Members of minority segments of the population
- Women

Each department will state such preference, if any, in its recruiting materials and information. In addition to varying from department to department, these preferences change over time as the demographics of employees of the departments change.

Salary and Benefits

There is a vast difference in pay and benefits for officers in small areas to large, rural to metropolitan, low income to affluent. Since many departments require you to have been a resident for at least one year prior to applying, you should seriously consider the pay versus the local cost of living before you make a residency commitment. Look at overtime pay and requirements as well. Typically, law enforcement jobs pay relatively well with regard to the local economy and almost always have superior benefits for full-time employees, sworn and civilian. But you should look into the numbers well in advance of applying.

Chapter 7
JOB DESCRIPTIONS

★

___

J ob descriptions, responsibilities, and specializations will vary from department to department as well. But some general statements can be made about certain roles within any given department.

Patrol Officers

Officers on patrol duty are the ones you will see most often as you go about your daily business. They are the foot soldiers, as it were. They are usually in uniform. They are also the officers with the most direct, continuous contact with and knowledge of their community. So, in addition to their law enforcement responsibilities, they are important ambassadors for their department.

For most departments, all officers begin on patrol and must serve a mandatory amount of time in the field, usually two years. From there, officers may explore specialized units or assignments, or be given promotions within patrol. Patrol officers are assigned to certain geographic areas within the department's jurisdiction and are responsible for the prevention of crimes, protection of citizens, apprehension of suspects, and response to emergency calls within that area or other areas when required.

Officers typically patrol in pairs, sometimes in marked cars and sometimes in unmarked vehicles. Mounted officers in some areas patrol on horseback. Bicycle patrols, particularly in urban areas and cities with good bike lanes, may allow officers quicker access to arising situations than vehicular patrol. Also, officers in many areas patrol on foot in downtown sections and near public events.

Patrol officers respond to calls, suspicious or unusual activity, alarms, and other indications that crimes may be occurring or may have occurred. They also respond to and evaluate indications of risks to public safety, from open fire hydrants to abandoned vehicles to unruly crowds to drunken and disorderly individuals. Patrol officers enforce all applicable local, state, and federal laws; respond to vehicular accidents and emergency calls; answer questions from the public; administer first aid in the absence of emergency medical personnel; conduct preliminary investigations; prepare police reports; and appear in court. They also provide crowd control and security details for certain events and public figures.

Traffic Officers

Traffic officers are also uniformed and drive police vehicles. But traffic duty differs from patrol in that it is focused on the regulation of traffic flow, both vehicular and pedestrian, and the enforcement of traffic laws. Traffic officers often work alone. They direct traffic when it must be rerouted because of an accident or other incident, and in certain school and work zones at key times of day.

Traffic officers issue citations for parking violations, and for excessive speed, running a stop sign, failure to yield, and other moving violations. They make arrests for driving while intoxicated, driving without a license, and other violations of the law. They are responsible for analyzing and documenting traffic accidents in their police reports, and they often testify in court.

Detectives

Detectives investigate crimes, interrogate suspects and question witnesses, analyze evidence, make arrests, and perform other functions related to investigating and solving crimes. An officer must generally serve as a patrol officer for a period of time before being made detective. In larger departments, investigative divisions differentiate between the sorts of crimes being investigated by detectives within those divisions.

For instance, vice detectives investigate crimes like prostitution. Narcotics detectives investigate illegal drug manufacture, use, and distribution. Homicide detectives, obviously, investigate murders. Special victims or sex crimes detectives investigate sexual assault and abuse cases. White-collar detectives investigate corporate and financial crimes. And so on. In some large departments, there may even be cold-case detectives, assigned to cases that have remained unsolved for a long period of time and bear reinvestigation. Detectives may also be in internal affairs, investigating internal and external allegations of impropriety or criminal behavior against their own personnel.

Detectives dress in street clothes and drive marked or unmarked cars. They usually operate in pairs.

Correctional Officers/Detention Officers

Correctional officers or detention officers oversee individuals who are in custody pending trial or who have been convicted and are serving time. They are responsible for security and inmate safety and are assigned to prevent assaults and escapes, among other disturbances. Such officers maintain order, an important role. They do so by observing inmate behavior, conducting inspections, and employing other means of monitoring the tenuous balance that exists among the incarcerated. Most correctional officers are unarmed within prison facilities but are armed in situations such as monitoring prisoner transport or other assignments outside of the prison facility. Local departments often, but not always, have designated correctional or detention officers, depending upon the size of their jurisdiction and the volume of inmates they deal with. In rural areas with no prison facilities but rather just a jail or holding facility, there may be no such designated officers. In those cases, correctional duties fall to police officers or sheriff's deputies within the department.

Specialized Units and Assignments

After gaining experience as an officer, you may be eligible for assignment in a specialized unit. Such assignment will usually require additional training and is considered a promotion. Some specialized units that may be found within local departments, depending upon size and location, are as follows:

- Anti-Gang Unit
- Anti-Terrorism Unit
- Arson Squad
- Bomb Squad
- Canine (K-9) Unit
- Major Crimes Division
- Special Weapons and Tactics (SWAT) Team
- White-Collar Crimes Division

Municipal and County Departments

There are several key differences between municipal departments and county departments. Municipal and county departments are usually led by a police chief who is appointed. County departments are typically led by a sheriff who is elected by popular vote (although in the case of county police departments, there may be an appointed police chief). While there are similarities among their responsibilities, there are also key differences, addressed more thoroughly in the text that follows. For instance, both police and sheriff's departments enforce traffic laws, but only sheriffs serve civil summonses. One thing they share is the responsibility for many functions that we take for granted. For example, police and sheriff's departments may serve as funeral escorts, offer directions to lost pedestrians or motorists, and provide security at big public events like groundbreakings and parades.

Local Police Department Responsibilities

Local police department responsibilities generally include patrolling within city limits, responding to calls (including 911 calls), enforcing traffic laws, investigating crimes, executing warrants, and collecting and analyzing crime scene and forensic evidence. In addition, there may be numerous specialized divisions, including bomb squads, arson units, anti-terrorism units, special security and crowd control details, and even divisions to license and police taxicabs and other vehicles for hire.

Local police are typically first responders to emergency calls. In this regard alone, they do far more than enforce the law. They are also our lifeline in health emergency and disaster situations.

Sheriff's Department Responsibilities

Generally speaking, sheriff's departments respond to calls (including 911 calls), patrol the highways, enforce traffic laws, investigate property crimes, investigate accidents, and investigate narcotics crimes. In unincorporated rural and small-town areas where there is no local police department, sheriff's deputies are the first responders to emergencies. They may also conduct search-and-rescue missions and participate in major crime investigations, often in cooperation with state agencies and other departments. Many sheriff's departments have highly specialized units, including narcotics and K-9 units, and SWAT teams.

It is in their service to the courts that sheriff's departments differ the most from local police departments. Sheriff's departments serve the judicial system by serving criminal and civil court papers upon citizens in their jurisdictions. Such papers may be subpoenas, summonses, or other calls to serve or appear. They also provide bailiffs to aid in court processes and provide security, and they transport prisoners to and from facilities, including courts, holding facilities, and incarceration facilities.

Chapter 8

REPRESENTATIVE
DEPARTMENTS

---★---

In the following you'll find detailed information on municipal and county departments of varying sizes and locations. Obviously, I can't go into detail about every department in the United States, but I hope the specific information about these will inform your decision about pursuing a career in local law enforcement.

Please take the time to fully investigate the department you're interested in joining. You may find that there are advancement opportunities or specialized assignments in one local department that are not available in another, even within the same locality. Or you may find that if you explore opportunities in the next county or in another city, you will be able to work in an environment that appeals to you and is well matched to your interests and experience.

For instance, if you would prefer a lot of interaction with the public, you would probably be better suited to a department with patrol duties in a highly populated area. If you are interested in someday becoming involved with major crimes investigations, you would want to try to join a larger department with a division devoted to the same.

If your interest is in antiterrorism, you might want to focus on the one or more departments in your state that serves as a nucleus for inter-agency antiterrorism initiatives, or pursue a career with a department in a very large metropolitan area. If you are interested in the judicial system and would like to serve papers for the courts, you might want to look into a sheriff's department near you.

Boston, Massachusetts

Boston Police Department

James M. Hussey, Acting Police Commissioner
Boston Police Headquarters
One Schroeder Plaza
Boston, Massachusetts 02120-2014
Telephone: (617) 727-3777 (Massachusetts Human Resources
   Division)
Fax: (617) 343-4481
Web site: www.ci.boston.ma.us/police/default.asp

CAREER QUICK FACTS

Minimum age:	19
Education:	High school diploma or GED
or	
Military equivalent:	Three years with honorable discharge or release
Criminal record:	No felony convictions; no misdemeanor conviction of domestic violence; any prior convictions may prevent acceptance
Base salary:	$40,000 (after three years)
Benefits:	13 paid holidays and full retirement
Tests:	Background check; written, medical, psychological, and physical exams
Academy:	Six months
Categorical preference:	Preference is given to children and siblings of fallen officers and to veterans of the armed services

Mission Statement and Introduction

> We dedicate ourselves to work in partnership with the community to fight crime, reduce fear and improve the quality of life in our neighborhoods. Our Mission is Neighborhood Policing.

The Boston Police Department (BPD) prides itself on being the oldest police department in the United States, but it is by no means old-fashioned. Boston proper, as of 2002, is a city of about 600,000 people, with that number increasing to over 2 million during the day. Boston has grown into a world-class business, finance, and technology center. Since its inception nearly 165 years ago, the BPD has adapted to the changing times, introducing initiatives that address advancements in technology while staying in touch with the individuals it serves and protects.

The updated Crime Lab, for example, houses the only public forensic DNA laboratory in Massachusetts and is one of only 18 in the country. On a neighborhood level, the "Same Cop/Same Neighborhood" program ensures that a beat officer spends 60 percent of his or her time in the same neighborhood, allowing the residents to get to know the officer, and vice versa. Since trust is an enormous factor in police/community relations, and since informed observation is one of the basics of good police work, I think this is a fantastic idea.

A Brief History of the BPD

The Boston Police Department has quite a history. The first night watch was established in 1635—more than 350 years ago. A formal department was initiated in 1838, when a bill was passed that enabled the city to appoint officers. Then in 1854, the force was formalized and named the Boston Police Department. Modeled after the London Police, the BPD was the first professional, paid department in the United States.

At first, the mission and jurisdiction of the BPD were somewhat general. Under supervision of the city marshal, the department was officially given "care of the streets, the care of the common sewers, and the care of the vaults, and whatever else affects the health, security, and comfort of the city."

In those days, a force of under 300 officers carried long blue and white poles as their sole weapons. To call for backup, they used police "rattles." There weren't telephones until 1878; until then, the police communicated with headquarters by telegraph. Granted, the population, both criminal and civilian, was tiny compared to today. In 1903, the BPD began its first motor patrol. Fast-forward to 1972, when the 911 emergency system was established as part of a vastly improved radio communication system. From then until now, change has been swift.

Obviously, the department has grown and adapted with the times and with changing technology. Through crises like the Great Fire of 1872 and the St. Valentine's Blizzard of 1940, and infamous cases like the Boston Strangler, the BPD has responded to the needs of the citizens. Today it is a well-respected force, with about 2,130 sworn officers and just over 800 civilian support staff. According to its own annual report, that's one police officer to every 276 residents. Working to police its neighborhoods with equal emphasis on staying rooted in knowing its citizens well enough to protect them, while striving to incorporate new technologies to help prevent and to solve crimes, the BPD is moving its proud tradition forward.

Overview

The BPD is divided into six bureaus and one office.

Office of Police Commissioner   One big compliment to the BPD is the recent appointment of Commissioner Paul F. Evans to London's Metropolitan Police, where he heads up Scotland Yard's Police Standards Unit. Acting Commissioner James M. Hussey and his staff are, obviously, part of the Office of Police Commissioner (OPC), which also includes a variety of support staff who research and develop policy, direct community and employee relations, and interact with the media. They also cooperate with state and federal law enforcement agencies; for example, the Office of Research and Evaluation briefed the Anti-Terrorism Task Force on the department's systems for evaluating potential terrorist threats.

Bureau of Administrative Services   The Bureau of Administrative Services (BAS) provides the essential administrative and support functions to the BPD, including human resources, licensing, property and evidence maintenance, and fleet maintenance. One interesting function of the BAS is supplying donated bicycles to the "Bikes Not Bombs" program, which invites young teens to earn the donated bikes by repairing them under the instruction of older teens.

Bureau of Professional Development   The Bureau of Professional Development includes the Police Academy (Training and Education Division) and focuses its attentions on training and retraining, both in practical police practice and in ethics and integrity.

Bureau of Investigative Services   Within the Bureau of Investigative Services (BIS) are the investigative divisions of the sort you're used to seeing on television dramas: Homicide Unit, Major Case Unit, Sexual Assault Unit, and Forensic Technology Division, among others. In 2002, two types of crime that were on the rise and represented challenges for the BIS were bank robberies and techno-frauds (like identity theft). By the end of the year, as a result of the BIS's efforts, suspects were identified for 95 percent of bank robberies committed as well as a major techno-fraud scheme involving ATMs.

One major initiative of the BIS originated from the Sexual Assault Unit, which initiated the Boston Area Sex Investigators Network (BASIN). Incorporating local, state, and university police departments, the network was formed to share intelligence, planning, and collective resources to better investigate sexual assaults in and around Boston. In addition, the BASIN provides education and information for high-risk youths. Programs like this should be more common.

Bureau of Internal Investigations   This bureau polices the police, as it were, primarily through its Internal Affairs (IA) Division and Anti-Corruption Division. IA is often represented negatively on television and in movies, but it is a vital part of any department. Nobody, especially not the police, wants the men and women who risk their lives every day in extremely stressful situations to exercise their armed authority without checks and balances.

Bureau of Field Services   Bureau of Field Services (BFS) is the largest section of the BPD, including about two-thirds of the department's sworn staff. Working from 11 police stations are the men and women Bostonians encounter every day—the men and women in blue. Also included in the BFS are the Court Unit, Special Police Unit, Neighborhood Crime Watch Unit, and Juvenile Detention Facility. In addition to patrolling the streets 24 hours a day, all year long, the BFS has taken part in a couple of programs that deserve highlighting. One is its initiative with Boston University Medical School to train officers in recognizing and assisting seniors suffering from Alzheimer's disease. Another is Operation Crosswalk, which has resulted in more than 13,000 citations issued since 2001 at busy intersections; pedestrian and vehicle accidents declined by more than 350 incidents in 2002.

Bureau of Special Operations   Several specialized and highly trained units, including the Mobile Operations Division and Environmental Safety Division, make up the Bureau of Special Operations. These men and women are called upon to carry out some of the department's most dangerous missions—missions like dealing with bombs and hazardous materials, and executing warrants in extremely high-risk situations.

Recruiting

To become a police officer in Boston, you must first get into the Boston Police Academy. There are several requirements. As is common throughout the United States, applicants must pass a civil service exam given by the state (or in this case, the commonwealth). The civil service exam in Massachusetts is given every two years. For information about the next exam date, contact the Massachusetts Human Resources Division at (617) 727-3777.

As mentioned in our *Career Quick Facts*, the minimum age for applicants is 19. You must be a U.S. citizen, reside in Boston, and have a Massachusetts driver's license; you must have lived there for at least one year before you can take the civil service exam. You need either a high school diploma, a GED certificate, or three years of service in the U.S. military with an honorable discharge or release. Preference is given to children or brothers/sisters of fallen officers. I think this is a great tribute to officers who have died in the line of duty. Some may question whether kids or siblings of fallen offices might be (even subconsciously) motivated by guilt or a desire for vengeance, but there are two reasons this doesn't concern me. First, if someone goes into law enforcement for the wrong reasons, they usually don't make it to their first day of work. Second, psychological tests and good controls make it difficult for anyone coming in with emotional problems to slip through.

Tests

There are four tests administered by the Commonwealth of Massachusetts to applicants to the academy:

- Background investigation
- Written civil service police examination
- Psychological testing
- Physical agility test

The Academy

Training at the Boston Police Academy lasts for six months. It is a difficult six months—mentally and physically—and it should be. You'll learn constitutional and criminal law; you'll get in the best physical shape of your life; you'll learn how to safely and effectively handle a firearm, how to deal with crisis situations, and how to handle that police cruiser in harrowing situations without endangering others; and you'll learn how to do things procedurally according to department rules and traditions. That's an overview—the point is, after six months you will be thinking and acting less like a civilian and more like a police officer, which will go a long way toward getting you through your rookie year.

Getting Started Early

The BPD is a very selective department. According to Human Resources, if you're 19 years old and have no military experience, your chances of becoming a police officer are very slim. However, if you first become a cadet, your chances are much better. Preference is given to academy applicants who are or were cadets, and about 80 percent of cadets become BPD officers. To become a cadet, you must be between 19 and 25, submit an application, and take a written exam. For more information, contact Human Resources at (617) 727-3777.

Columbus, Georgia

Columbus Police Department

Willie L. Dozier, Chief of Police
Personnel Unit
Box 1866
Columbus, Georgia 31902-1866
Telephone: (706) 653-3154
Web site: www.columbusga.org/police/

CAREER QUICK FACTS

Minimum age:	21
Education:	Approx. two years of college
Criminal record:	No felony convictions; no misdemeanors involving moral turpitude (i.e., public indecency, lewdness); no misdemeanor conviction of domestic violence
Base salary:	Approx. $25,000 (varies with education)
Benefits:	11 paid holidays plus sick leave; city and state retirement
Tests:	Background check; written, psychological, physical, and polygraph exams
Academy:	Eleven weeks at the state academy plus six weeks of local training; all training is paid

Columbus, Georgia, is a medium-sized city with a population nearing 200,000. The city and county governments are consolidated, making for an interesting jurisdictional overlap between the police and sheriff's departments. Adding to this mix is Fort Benning, the adjacent U.S. Army base, which of course has its own police force.

My unit at the FBI worked with the CPD in 1978. A serial killer was strangling elderly white women in their homes with the victims' own nylon stockings. Six victims had been attributed to the "Stocking Strangler" by the time my unit became involved. We were brought in at the request of police officer Jud Ray. If his name sounds familiar to you, it's because he eventually became a member of my unit, and one of the best at that. In addition, he became one of my closest friends. But at the time, he was a shift commander who enlisted our help through the Georgia Bureau of Investigation because the case of the Stocking Strangler had been compounded by letters from someone claiming to speak for a hate/vigilante group threatening to kill a black woman if the Stocking Strangler—widely and publicly thought to be a black man—was not caught. The CPD, working with officers from Fort Benning, incorporated our profile and acted swiftly to catch the author of the letters, who confessed to murdering three women. The Stocking Strangler was ultimately apprehended as well.

The Columbus Police Department: Then and Now

Back in 1831, citizens were required to serve on patrol duty as part of the police department. There were no sworn officers until 1840. In the ensuing 170 years, the force has grown to employ nearly 500 individuals, about 80 percent of them as sworn officers and the rest as civilian support.

The makeup of the department is currently about 12 percent female, which compares pretty well to the national average of about 14 percent. In terms of minority makeup, the department calculates its makeup to be about 32 percent black and 4 percent "other" non-Caucasians.

One of the things the Columbus Police Department is proudest of is its accreditation. The CPD works hard to maintain state, national, and international accreditation, an accomplishment only 2 percent of such agencies in the United States can claim as their own.

Perhaps the biggest source of pride for the department, according to Personnel Officer Captain Jack McCoy, is its close relationship to the community. The department gets a lot of support and feedback from the citizens of the city and county, and it offers proactive programs like Juvenile Diversion and Conditional Discharge. These programs offer first-time drug or alcohol offenders the chance to lessen or eliminate the charges against them by paying a fee and undergoing court-mandated counseling, classes, and random drug and alcohol testing.

The CPD can also boast of a well-trained SWAT team and bomb and terrorism squad, which works in Georgia as well as across the state line in Alabama. The department is fortunate to have a very new multiuse facility, which includes a fitness center (a very good idea, of course) and offices for associated agencies, like the coroner's office and the fire department, as well as space for resident agents of several federal agencies.

The department is divided into four bureaus: Patrol Services, Investigative Services, Administrative Services, and Professional Standards. This is a typical structure, and the duties of each bureau are well defined and differentiated.

Patrol Services   Patrol Services is the largest of the bureaus, as you might expect. This is where most of the police officers you'd encounter would be, and where all recruits spend their first four years. These are your uniformed officers—beat officers—assigned to respond to emergency calls and to patrol the community to prevent crimes. In addition to vehicular patrol, there are bicycle patrols in certain areas, like parks and the historic riverfront, where citizens engage in leisure activities.

Investigative Services   This bureau investigates major crimes and comprises several specialized units, including the Gang Task Force, Juvenile Diversion Unit (JDU), and Gang Resistance Education and Training (GREAT) program. I'm impressed with the Juvenile Diversion Unit, which offers a great outreach program. Working with local schools, the JDU offers mentoring and observation of kids who have committed crimes; this helps those kids who have made mistakes but aren't hardened criminals and can be deterred from a life of committing crimes, and it helps the kids around them by offering protective supervision of offenders whose actions might put other kids at risk.

Support Services   Support Services includes the 911 Emergency Center, Motor Transport, Property and Evidence, Central Record Unit, and the Quartermaster supply center. Working in these units may not seem as glamorous, as made-for-TV, as the others, but there are some very important duties you would be responsible for as part of Support Services, like being a lifeline for emergency callers or maintaining evidence that would convict a violent criminal or prevent an innocent person from being wrongly convicted of a crime.

Administrative Services This would be the first bureau you would encounter as a candidate, as they oversee recruitment and training. They are also responsible for community relations and public safety programs. Special training in many specialized areas is coordinated by this bureau, as are the CPD's firing ranges. Columbus's community antidrug program operates out of Administrative Services, as does the aforementioned progressive program of Conditional Discharge.

Professional Standards This is the internal affairs office. Now those of you who watch cop shows may have a tendency to categorize internal affairs officers as "rats," but that's just a stereotype; we need checks and balances at every level of government, and internal affairs protects civilians and the police equally by investigating complaints against officers.

Recruiting

As mentioned in the *Career Quick Facts*, you must be a U.S. citizen and at least 21 years old to apply to the CPD. If you have a felony on your record, or a misdemeanor with moral turpitude, you need not apply. In addition, if you have a great number of traffic citations on your record, this may count against you as a candidate. Showing a prior disdain for the law, even when the law is something as ordinary as the speed limit, demonstrates that you may not be the best person to enforce the law.

Educationally speaking, the CPD requires about as many college hours as would be needed for an associate's degree, approximately two years' worth at an accredited school. There is no military equivalent accepted; the requirement for two years of college education is one of the basic requirements of the department.

Testing

There are four tests given to applicants:

- Background investigation
- Polygraph test
- Psychological exam
- Physical fitness test

If you meet the educational requirement, the department finger-prints and photographs you, then administers the physical fitness test, which includes push-ups, sit-ups, an obstacle course, and a 1-mile run. The next step is the written entrance exam for the state academy. It is a pass-or-fail exam that largely covers basic skills, including reading comprehension and writing, and most people who make it this far pass.

Simultaneous with your being tested, the department will begin its investigation into your background, checking your criminal history, personal references, and professional references. This is often the most important test of all. The CPD's Applicant Background Booklet, which applicants must complete, is included as Appendix C. It is a great example of the sorts of in-depth information most departments and agencies will ask you to provide, and upon which they will base some of their investigation into your background. For better or worse, parts of your history that don't appear on your record or in the information you provide will be revealed during the thorough background check.

Next come the polygraph and psychological tests, which are usually given on the same day. There's a set bank of questions for the polygraph test, the purpose of which is to a large extent to find out whether you've got a history with theft or drugs. This isn't to say that no mistake will be overlooked; the department recognizes that people, especially when they're young, make bad judgment calls. The best approach is to tell the truth in response to every question, no matter how nega-tively you think your answer might impact your chances, because the polygrapher will know if you're lying and that always looks much worse. This is true for any polygraph situation.

The psychological test is very basic. It's written and sent via fax to experts who review your responses and grade them for the department.

If all goes well, you're on to a preliminary interview with the personnel officer, then to an interview with the chief of police, assistant chief, and two bureau majors. The chief of police makes the final decision on all hires.

Training

Once you pass the preceding tests and are selected for the department, you're hired. At that point, you're sent to the Georgia Public Safety Training Center's West Georgia Police Academy in Columbus for 11 weeks of training with pay. Finally, you'll have about five weeks of local training, which includes exposure to the different bureaus, class-room instruction, and ride-along exercises with field training officers.

Around 95 percent of candidates who are sent to the state academy make it through all the training. The department is very selective in its hiring, so it does not experience much washout in the training phases.

The Future

The biggest challenge to the CPD these days isn't getting good officers—it's keeping them. Like many departments of its size, the CPD loses experienced officers to larger cities like Atlanta, or to suburbs of Atlanta like Stone Mountain and Decatur. The pay can be 20 percent higher or more in such areas, which may actually be safer and have a smaller population and/or a lower crime rate.

Albuquerque, New Mexico

Albuquerque Police Department

Gilbert G. Gallegos, Chief of Police
Recruiting and Selection Unit
5412 2nd Street Northwest
Albuquerque, New Mexico 87107
Telephone: (505) 343-5020 or (800) 7POLICE
Web site: www.apdonline.com

CAREER QUICK FACTS

Minimum age:	21
Education:	High school diploma or GED
Criminal record:	No misdemeanors within last three years; no DWI within last 10 years; no felony convictions; no misdemeanor conviction of domestic violence
Base salary:	$28,412.80 per year for cadets
Benefits:	Health and dental insurance; 12.5 vacation days per year; city retirement
Tests:	Physical fitness; written and oral tests; personal integrity questionnaire; background check; polygraph, psychological, and medical exams; drug screen
Academy:	23 weeks

The metropolitan area that includes Albuquerque, New Mexico, is populated by more than a million people. Among the challenges facing this Southwestern city are drug dealing and drug use, and related property crimes. Its proximity to the West Coast and the Mexican border, as well as its positioning on two major interstate highways, make it a crossroads for drug trafficking.

On a more positive note, the Albuquerque PD has some great incentive programs in place for its officers. Among them are increased pay for officers who are bilingual. Another exciting feature of the Albuquerque PD is its high proportion of female officers, who account for nearly 17 percent of the force. Albuquerque is also at the forefront of technology implementation, with programs that implement mobile computers in patrol cars, electronic police reports, and other advancements to increase efficiency and reduce errors. Given that, according to the Department of Justice Bureau of Justice Statistics, about 75 to 80 percent of local law enforcement agencies rely primarily on paper reports, the Albuquerque PD is on the cutting edge of moving toward a more streamlined, computerized approach.

Overview

There are just over 900 sworn officers of the Albuquerque PD. In addition to specialized assignments, which are covered in the text that follows, officers in the APD serve in the following divisions:

- Metro Division is the Albuquerque PD's traffic unit.
- Field Services Bureau is their patrol unit.
- Criminal Investigation Division is their detective unit.

Requirements

To be considered as a candidate for a position as an Albuquerque police officer, you must be at least 21 years old as of the day you would graduate from the academy. You must be a U.S. citizen and have a high school diploma or equivalent (i.e., a GED). If you have ever been convicted of a felony crime, you will not be considered. If you have committed a misdemeanor crime within the previous three years or have received a DWI within the previous 10 years, you will not be considered.

There are many other disqualifiers. If you have a history that includes a pattern of traffic citations, arrests, or convictions within the previous three years, you may be disqualified. Disqualifying pattern violations include running red lights, speeding, or reckless driving. A recent history with illegal drugs may disqualify you as well. If you have used any drug within the past three years, the use of which would amount to a misdemeanor crime, you will be disqualified. Such drugs include marijuana, hashish, hallucinogenic mushrooms, steroids, LSD or "acid," and inhalants. If you have used a drug within the past five years, the use of which would amount to a felony crime, you will be disqualified. Such drugs include cocaine, crack, heroin, methamphetamines, or amphetamines. In addition, any pattern of use or abuse, no matter how recent or how far in your past, may disqualify you.

Applicants must demonstrate a history of satisfactory employment. Applicants who have served in the armed forces must not have been dishonorably discharged. In addition, applicants must have a healthy financial history. If you have a chronic pattern of financial problems, you may not be considered.

Any dishonesty in the recruitment process results in disqualification. In addition, if an applicant has committed an act in his or her past that indicates a lack of morality or personal integrity, that candidate may not be considered.

Recruitment

If you are interested in becoming an Albuquerque police officer, you must first fill out the Interest Card, or Initial Application. On it you will include the usual personal information necessary for a job application, from your name to your social security number, and you will answer some questions that will determine your eligibility. Then, the testing begins.

Testing

You must undergo a series of tests in the recruitment process, and they are nearly all administered in one inclusive testing weekend. The tests are as follows.

Physical Fitness Test The first step is the physical fitness test. The physical fitness test is composed of a 1.5-mile run, a 300-meter run, a flexibility test, one repetition of a bench press, and a one-minute sit-up test. A minimum score of 40 percent for each test is required, based upon the Cooper Institute's rankings as addressed earlier in this book.

One very generous thing the Albuquerque PD's Recruiting and Selection Unit does is offer pretesting assessments for interested candidates. Candidates are tested in all five categories of the physical fitness test administered to actual recruits and are advised of their results. If their results do not meet the minimum requirements of the job, they are given advice on ways to improve their performance and achieve those minimum levels. This kind of "practice test" would be a great idea for anyone unsure of how well he or she would perform on the real test, especially as it would simulate the stress and conditions of the test, a simulation that is difficult to do at the track or in a home gym.

You will be interested to know that, according to recruitment officer Sergeant Lee Krebsbach of the Albuquerque PD, more applicants fail the physical fitness test than are disqualified by any other test result. The Albuquerque PD places a premium on physical fitness, both for recruits and for established officers. Officers are tested annually, with incentives for high scores that include free days off. I think this is a great way to encourage physical fitness and to reward discipline.

Written Tests   The first written test given by the Albuquerque PD is the Nelson-Denny Reading and Comprehension Test. It includes 116 multiple-choice questions on vocabulary and reading comprehension. Included as Appendix A is the Albuquerque PD's test preparation kit. It is a great way to learn the types of questions administered not only by the Albuquerque PD but by many departments and agencies nationwide.

The second written test is the City Police Entrance Exam. This written test is composed of 100 multiple-choice questions divided into the following five sections: observation and recall, cognitive abilities, personal maturity and integrity, technical skills, and written and oral communication.

Personal Integrity Questionnaire   This questionnaire is composed of 132 questions designed to gain insight into your personal history and personal integrity. It is reviewed by a recruiting or background detective with you upon completion.

Behavioral Personnel Assessment Device (Oral Exam) This test consists of eight verbal questions built around hypothetical or actual police scenarios. Your responses will indicate your ability to communicate and respond to certain situations.

Personal History Statement This is not exactly a test, but it does test one important characteristic: your honesty. The Personal History Statement requires you to provide information including personal references, your employment and residential history, and your military background. Applicants who omit information or are dishonest in their responses are disqualified.

Background Investigation The background investigation includes research into your criminal and arrest history, driving record, educational history, and personal references, among other things, and is based in part on your Personal History Statement. The background investigation can take from a month to a month and a half. Any discrepancies between the Personal History Statement and the results of the background investigation can result in disqualification.

Polygraph Examination A licensed polygrapher will test candidates to verify that all the information they have provided to the Albuquerque PD about themselves and their history is correct.

Chief's Selection (Oral Interview) Applicants may be interviewed by the Chief's Selection Committee after the committee has gotten input from the Background Detective about the applicant. The Chief's Selection Committee will then make an offer of conditional employment to selected applicants, with the understanding that their hire is dependent upon passing the remaining tests.

Psychological Written Tests and Psychological Interview You will complete a number of written psychological tests and undergo a psychological interview, based in part on the results of the written tests.

Medical Examination and Drug Screening Test Hearing, vision, medical, and physical evaluations are required at this stage of the recruitment process. If you meet the minimum requirements, a test for illegal drugs is performed on a sample of your urine.

Training

If you pass all the tests and interviews and are hired, you will be sent to a preorientation session at the police academy, then on to an orientation session. Trainees take the physical fitness test again at this point in the process, then proceed to academy training.

Training at the police academy in Albuquerque is paid at the cadet's current base rate of pay of $28,412.80 per year. Academy training lasts for 23 weeks and includes hundreds of hours of training on all topics of professional law enforcement. Academy training is followed by three months of on-the-job training with rotating training officers, then by a year of probation. During probation, a cadet may be dismissed for any reason and without recourse.

Career Opportunities

All officers must spend two years on patrol duty before applying for specialized duty. Specialized assignments include the Police Academy, Armed Robbery Division, Auto Theft, Bicycle Patrol, Criminal Intelligence, Crisis Negotiation Team, Gang Unit, Homicide, Horse Mounted Patrol, Narcotics, Property Crimes, Repeat Offender Project, Special Weapons and Tactics (SWAT), Traffic Investigation, Vice Squad, and White Collar Crime.

Bozeman, Montana

Bozeman Police Department

Mark Tymrak, Chief of Police
615 S. 16th
Bozeman, Montana 59715
Telephone: (406) 582-2000
Web site: www.bozeman.net/safety.html

CAREER QUICK FACTS

Minimum age:	18
Education:	High school or equivalent (GED)
Criminal record:	No felony convictions; some misdemeanors will disqualify depending on nature and length of time since; no misdemeanor conviction of domestic violence
Base salary:	$34,620 during the first (probationary) year
Benefits:	Medical and life insurance and city retirement
Tests:	Physical fitness; medical (release); background check
Academy:	Twelve weeks (basic course)

Mission Statement and Introduction

The Bozeman Police Department, in partnership with the citizens of Bozeman, is committed to improving the quality of life by identifying and resolving public safety concerns.

Bozeman, Montana, is a beautiful Western town, and one with which I am quite familiar. As you may know, I attended undergraduate school for two years of underachievement at Montana State University. I can't say the town was left with a good impression of me, as I was a worse-than-typical college student in those days—my extracurricular activities led me to two encounters with the Bozeman PD from the other side of the law. As I've said before, if there is any truth to the expression "the cops are never around when you need them," Bozeman, in 1965 and now, is definitely an exception.

The Bozeman PD is a great example of a small-town department with as many challenges from the environment as from criminal activity.

The Department

There are about 50 employees of the Bozeman PD, about 80 percent sworn and the rest civilian. There are three divisions: Administrative, Patrol, and Investigation. Within these divisions are the drug task force, the community antidrug program, a canine unit, and a bicycle patrol unit.

As you often find with small police departments like Bozeman's, responsibilities handled in larger areas by other agencies fall under their jurisdiction. For instance, among the duties assigned to the Bozeman PD is animal control—which, in Bozeman, Montana, can mean much more than stray dogs.

Requirements

To be considered for the Bozeman Police Department, you must be at least 18 years old and have a high school diploma or equivalent (GED). If you have any felony convictions, you will not be considered. If you have certain or very recent misdemeanor convictions, you may be disqualified. The department takes these types of convictions case by case.

Testing

To be eligible for hire and training, candidates must take a physical fitness pretest and undergo a background check. In addition, a medical release must be submitted.

Career Opportunities

Successful applicants are hired for a one-year probationary period. Upon completion of this first year, officers may be confirmed and receive a commensurate pay raise.

The Academy

Montana has a state academy for police candidates. Located in Helena, Montana, the Montana Law Enforcement Academy provides criminal justice officers with basic and specialized law enforcement training. More than 2,000 officers and other individuals in criminal justice attend the academy each year. Basic programs are given to entry-level law enforcement officers, corrections and detention officers, and others. In addition to training new police officers for departments like Bozeman's, the Montana Law Enforcement Academy offers specialized and advanced training.

Los Angeles, California

Los Angeles County Sheriff's Department

Leroy D. Baca, Sheriff
LASD Recruitment Unit
Star Center
11515 S. Colima Road Bldg. F-115
Whittier, California 90604
Telephone: (800) A-DEPUTY or (800) 233-7889

North County Recruitment Office
LASD Recruiting
45100 60th St. West
Lancaster, California 93536
Telephone: 661-949-3877
or: (800) A-DEPUTY or (800) 233-7889
Web site: la-sheriff.org/

CAREER QUICK FACTS

Minimum age:	20 years (at time of appointment as deputy sheriff trainee)
Education:	U.S. high school or equivalent or two- or four-year U.S. college degree
Criminal record:	No felony convictions or certain serious or numerous misdemeanor/traffic violations; no misdemeanor conviction of domestic violence
Base salary:	Deputy sheriff—about $42,000 depending on education
Benefits:	Varied bonuses available plus 10 paid holidays, 10 vacation days, and 12 sick days per year; retirement
Tests:	Written exam; background check; fingerprint search; medical, psychological, and polygraph exams
Academy:	Up to 22 weeks

Mission Statement

Lead the fight to prevent crime and injustice.
Enforce the law fairly and defend the rights of all.
Partner with the people we serve to secure and promote safety in our communities.

Core Values

As a leader in the Los Angeles County Sheriff's Department, I commit myself to honorably perform my duties with respect for the dignity of all people, integrity to do right and fight wrongs, wisdom to apply common sense and fairness in all I do and courage to stand against racism, sexism, anti-Semitism, homophobia and bigotry in all its forms.

Brief History

Formed in 1850, the department's first sheriff was George T. Burrill; he had a total of two deputies. As the Los Angeles Sheriff's Department (LASD) proudly lays claim to the title of the largest sheriff's department in the world, things have changed a lot in 150 years.

The LASD has always been on the vanguard. In 1912, Mrs. Margaret I. Adams became the first female deputy in U.S. history when she was sworn in as an LASD deputy. In 1928, communications were modernized by a countywide Teletype system. That same year, officers began wearing uniforms instead of the civilian clothes they had historically worn. This made them immediately recognizable.

In 1972, communications leapt forward again when a high-speed computerized dispatch system was implemented. Four years later, the crime lab was brought up to speed with the latest techniques.

As of 2003, there are more than 10 million people living in Los Angeles County, making it the largest county in the nation. To put this in perspective, the county's official information states there are only eight *states* with greater populations than L.A. *County*. Approximately 28 percent of the population of California live in L.A. County. Serving this population with nearly 9,000 sworn officers, the LASD is not only the largest sheriff's department in the world; it is the third-largest metropolitan law enforcement agency in the United States.

Though it is quite large, the LASD thinks locally, offering many community programs. They have a very positive program called the Sheriff's Youth Foundation, which offers L.A. County youths safe and supportive places to come after school and interact with positive role models, including members of law enforcement. Kids receive tutoring and participate in various activities at youth activity centers.

Overview

There are 9 divisions within the LASD.

Sheriff's Headquarters Bureau   Sheriff's Headquarters Bureau (SHB) is the contact bureau for members of the media and the public who are seeking information. SHB maintains and disseminates information on the LASD's operations.

Administrative Services Division   As with every department, there are a great many administrative issues, from budgetary items to personnel to the supply and maintenance of computer hardware and software.

Correctional Services Division   You'd expect the Correctional Services Division, or COSD, to administer the necessities of the Los Angeles County inmate population, from medical and mental health screening to food and medicine. But the COSD also provides special programs for the incarcerated, including religious and volunteer programs, educational opportunities, and commissary services. COSD helps inmates upon their release with their transition into society with continuous support services. With repeat offenses—unfortunately the rule rather than the exception—this is an especially worthwhile endeavor.

Court Services Division   In Los Angeles County, protection and security of all superior and municipal courts, of which there are more than 50, falls to the Court Services Division of the LASD. This division provides court security personnel, including bailiffs; is responsible for inmate transportation; and maintains order in and around court proceedings. Given the great number of courts, it's no surprise this is the second-largest division in the LASD, with about 2,000 individuals in the workforce, about 75 percent of them sworn.

Custody Operations Division   Along with the Correctional Services Division, Custody Operations runs L.A. County jails and holding facilities within the LASD. This includes the care and custody of individuals before and during trial and, if convicted, after sentencing.

Detective Division   The Detective Division is made up of experienced investigators who work in the following bureaus, which are charged with the investigation of certain types of crimes:

- **Homicide Bureau** is responsible for the investigation of all homicides, questionable deaths, and possible suicides, as well as missing persons cases. A grim fact of life for homicide detectives in L.A. County: 42 percent of all L.A. County homicides are gang-related.
- **Major Crimes Bureau** (MCB) investigates crimes that fall into a category referred to as "criminal enterprise crimes." Formed by the merger of several bureaus, including Vice, MCB cases include organized crime, terrorist groups, serial robberies, kidnapping for ransom, and contracts for murder.
- **Commercial Crimes Bureau** is responsible for investigating white-collar crimes, including forgery, fraud, real-estate, elder abuse, and computer crimes. I doubt that L.A. County is proud to be the site of forgery and fraud cases that accounted for 10 percent of the financial losses *nationwide* in 1997. Clearly, Commercial Crimes has its hands full.
- **Family Crimes Bureau** investigates child abuse cases. An incredibly difficult type of crime to investigate with any impartiality, child abuse is also one type of crime whose victims cannot defend themselves. Because of the sensitive nature of the crimes, detectives in this bureau have highly specialized training.

- **Narcotics Bureau** is charged with investigating controlled substances crimes, including possession, manufacture, sale, and transport of narcotics. Given its proximity to the United States' border with Mexico, L.A. County continues to be a hub for the transportation of drugs. In addition to issues of drug traffic across the border, the Narcotics Bureau faces rising challenges in its fight against local drug production and use, including the rise in popularity of methamphetamine.

Field Operations Division and Sheriff Stations   The patrol operations of the LASD are conducted by the Field Operations Division. There are three patrol divisions, each assigned to a region, within which are headquarters and sheriff stations in unincorporated areas, community colleges, and contract cities, like Carson, which the LASD serves.

Office of Homeland Security   The Office of Homeland Security was inaugurated on October 27, 2002, as a center for first responders in the LASD to coordinate preparedness and response strategies in the face of terrorist activities and attacks. Many departments across the country have taken similar steps since September 11th.

Technical Services Division   Technical Services Division's responsibilities include maintaining and overseeing the LASD's vehicle fleet, records, data, statistics, and crime analysis.

Recruiting

Interested candidates should respond to advertised open positions. Between applying and becoming a deputy sheriff, you will have to pass an oral interview, a background check, a written examination, a polygraph test, a medical examination, and a psychological examination, not to mention nearly six months of academy training.

Career Opportunities

The non-sworn trainee position of deputy sheriff trainee brings candidates into the LASD and provides classroom and field training in areas including criminal and traffic law, evidence and investigation, police and community relations, and jail operations. After 18 weeks of academy training, appointees may receive permanent positions as deputy sheriffs. From there, the first assignments are in Custody/Court Services Division and then on patrol in Field Operations.

The job description of a deputy sheriff includes driving a patrol vehicle and detecting violations of federal, state, and local laws and ordinances, including traffic laws, responding to emergency calls, pursuing suspects, using firearms when necessary, arresting and transporting suspects, interviewing witnesses and suspects, collecting and protecting evidence, writing reports, recovering stolen property, serving civil and criminal process papers, and testifying in court.

Nassau County, New York (Long Island)

Nassau County Police Department

James H. Lawrence, Commissioner of Police
1490 Franklin Ave.
Mineola, New York 11501
Telephone: (516) 573-7000
Web site: www.police.co.nassau.ny.us

CAREER QUICK FACTS

Minimum age:	17 (to take written exam)
Maximum age:	35 (minus up to six years served in the military)
Education:	32 college credits required for appointment
Criminal record:	No felony convictions; no misdemeanor conviction of domestic violence
Base salary:	$30,000 after academy training; $35,000 after one year plus 10 percent differential pay for night duty
Benefits:	Generous paid time off and retirement
Tests:	Written exam; background check
Academy:	Six months

MISSION STATEMENT

To serve the people of Nassau County and to provide safety and improved quality of life in our communities through excellence in policing.

Nassau County

Nassau County is a large county department located on Long Island, New York. I know a lot about Nassau County—my family moved to

Hempstead, Long Island, in Nassau County, when I was eight years old. So while I'm a Brooklyn man by birth, I grew up a few train stops east on Long Island. I was a regular hometown boy, playing baseball and football for Hempstead High. In fact, our football team, with me on the defensive line, was the best high school football team on Long Island. But that's enough nostalgia.

Overview of NCPD

Nassau County was and is safer than my birthplace of Kings County (Brooklyn) and its neighbor, Queens County (Queens). There were only 17 murders in Nassau County in 2002—not a small number, but quite low compared to the 600 reported murders in New York City that year. But Nassau County is still part of that New York metropolitan area, and it is adjacent to New York City.

With about 2,400 sworn officers operating out of eight precincts, the Nassau County Police Department is one of the largest in the United States. Within its organization are the following.

Patrol Division　The officers you'll encounter every day, as you escape the city to Nassau County, are most likely the officers in Patrol. Every new officer must first serve as a patrol officer. There are eight precincts from which officers patrol the county.

Patrol Division includes the following Field Services bureaus:

- **Bureau of Special Operations (BSO)** executes high-risk search warrants and entries. The Precision Firearms Team and Crisis Negotiation Team, as well as the Anti-Gang Strike Force, are coordinated by the BSO.
- **The Emergency Ambulance Bureau** operates the ambulance service and emergency medical personnel for the NCPD and coordinates all other ambulance providers in the county.
- **Highway Patrol Bureau** (HPB) is responsible for enforcing laws and supervising auto and pedestrian traffic. The HPB's coverage area includes one of the New York City metro area's largest commuter and distribution highways—the Long Island

Expressway (LIE). In addition, K-9 patrol is part of the Highway Patrol Bureau's responsibilities.

- **The Patrol Division** also includes the Marine/Aviation Bureau and Mounted Unit, as well as the Community Safety Unit, Traffic Safety Unit, and Auxiliary Police.

Detective Division   The NCPD's Detective Division operates a squad at each of the NCPD's eight precincts, as well as the following squads:

- **Central Detectives Squad** includes the Main Office for the division, as well as several specialized sections. Among them are the Crime Stoppers Section, Fugitive Section, and Polygraph Section. You may encounter detectives from that last section of this squad as part of your preemployment screening if you are a candidate for the NCPD.
- **Electronics Squad** does what it sounds like it would do— coordinates, services, and installs surveillance equipment for the NCPD.
- **The Forensic Evidence Bureau** is made up of several distinct sections, all of which contribute to the analysis of forensic evidence for the NCPD. The Crime Scene Search Section deals with the collection, examination, and preservation of crime scene evidence. The Criminalistics and Documents Section conducts the kinds of tests you see all the time on television forensic shows, like examining hair, fibers, and fluids. The Drug Chemistry Section examines controlled substance and blood alcohol evidence. The Evidence Assessment Section collects, analyzes, and preserves forensic evidence, sending it to the appropriate section for further analysis if the item or specimen warrants examination. The Photography and Rogues Gallery Section keeps the photographic laboratory and the photographic criminal database. In addition to these sections, there are the Firearms Identification Section and Latent Fingerprint Section.
- **Special Investigation Squad** investigates crimes of a special nature, including bias or hate crimes and gang crimes. It also protects local and visiting dignitaries and governmental figures.

- **Narcotics/Vice Squad** investigates controlled substance crimes, including possession or sale of narcotics and other controlled substances. In addition, Narcotics/Vice investigates gambling, prostitution, pornography, and other vice crimes in Nassau County.
- **Arson/Bomb Squad** investigates arson and suspicious fire cases, including deaths and injuries caused by such fires. It is also charged with the serious and dangerous responsibility of inspecting and disarming/rendering harmless explosive devices and other dangerous items and substances, including fireworks.
- **Crimes Against Property Squad** coordinates with precincts to investigate auto theft cases, forgeries, bank fraud cases, counterfeiting, and computer crimes that victimize children. This squad works with detective squads at each precinct on pattern robberies that occur across precincts. Analysis of seized computers and electronic information is undertaken by this squad, as computer crimes are investigated by its detectives.
- **District Attorney Squad** investigates organized crime.
- **Homicide Squad** investigates murders, suspicious and accidental deaths, and possible suicides.
- **Robbery Squad** works with precinct detectives on high-stakes robberies, from banks to armored cars.
- **Special Services Squad** is made up of the Juvenile Aid Section, Missing Persons Section, and Special Victims Section.

Career Opportunities

All new officers begin on patrol. There are opportunities for promotions and special assignments after required time on patrol has been satisfied. The NCPD offers highly competitive salaries and benefits, with salary after academy training at $30,000 per year, rising to nearly $75,000 after seven years—not to mention the pay differential of at least 10 percent for night duty.

The NCPD also offers a generous time-off package. After one year, officers are entitled to the following paid days off: 13 holidays, 15 vacation days, 5 personal days, and 26 sick days.

Requirements

All candidates must be residents of Nassau, Suffolk, or Westchester Counties or New York City for one year prior to taking the written exam. You must be at least 17 years old to take the written test and will need to complete 32 hours of college to become a police officer, though you can take the exam before you've obtained those credits. If you have been convicted of a felony, you will not be considered.

More intangibly, the NCPD values loyalty, integrity, fairness, and the pursuit of excellence.

Arapahoe County, Colorado

Arapahoe County Sheriff's Office

J. Grayson Robinson, Sheriff
13101 East Broncos Parkway
Centennial, Colorado 80112
Telephone: (303) 795-4711
Web site: www.co.arapahoe.co.us

CAREER QUICK FACTS

Minimum age:	21
Education:	High school or equivalent (GED)
Criminal record:	No felony convictions; no domestic violence convictions; certain misdemeanors will disqualify
Base salary:	$38,400 for sheriff's deputy
Benefits:	Medical, vision, dental, life insurance; retirement
Tests:	Written exam; medical, psychological, polygraph exams; background check; drug screen

Mission Statement

Committed to quality service with an emphasis on integrity, professionalism, and community spirit.

Values

We respect the rights and individuality of all people.
We are committed to personal and organizational integrity.
We are committed to providing quality service in partnership with our community.

Overview

Located just south of Denver, Colorado, Arapahoe County is home to a number of small cities and unincorporated areas. The citizens within the jurisdiction of the Arapahoe County Sheriff's Office number about 165,000. A highly professional department, the Arapahoe County Sheriff's Office prides itself on being given the Triple Crown Award by the National Sheriff's Association, in recognition of accreditation by three major accrediting agencies. This is a rare honor.

One positive initiative of the Arapahoe County Sheriff's Office is their Citizen Law Enforcement Academy, a 10-week course for citizens that covers neighborhood watch programs, community-oriented policing, firearms, and other issues of interest to citizens. It takes a lot of work to conduct this kind of dedicated public service and public relations project, and I'm sure those who take the course find it edifying and informative. It is always a good idea to increase communication and contact between the community and law enforcement. This facilitates better, more responsive policing, as well as increased cooperation and support from the public.

There are four bureaus within the Arapahoe County Sheriff's Office, each with distinct duties and personnel.

Administration   This bureau includes the sheriff and undersheriff and their staffs, budget officers, and the Office of Emergency Management, which prepares for and responds to natural and man-made disasters in the area, and cooperates with the Federal Emergency Management Agency (FEMA), the Red Cross, and other disaster preparedness and relief organizations.

Detention/Administrative Services Bureau   This bureau is responsible for county court and prisoner-related duties, from transport and detention of prisoners to the service of court papers and court security. The Civil and Warrants Section of Administrative Services is responsible for the service of court papers, including summonses and eviction notices. This bureau also maintains the Sheriff's Office records within the Administrative Services Sheriff's Records Section. Detention Services Bureau manages the jail, and deputies within the bureau serve in court protection and judicial order enforcement capacities.

Professional Standards Bureau   This bureau is responsible for internal investigations of employee misconduct, staff inspections, and maintenance of the Sheriff's Office's three accreditations. In addition, the Professional Standards Bureau conducts employee hiring and training, as well as the Citizen Law Enforcement Academy mentioned previously.

Public Safety Bureau   This bureau includes patrol officers and investigators. Deputies on patrol cover approximately 850 miles of roads and highways in the jurisdiction of the Arapahoe County Sheriff's Office, enforcing applicable laws, including traffic laws; responding to accidents and stranded motorists; responding to over 50,000 emergency or assistance request calls per year; and evaluating potential threats to public safety.

Unincorporated Arapahoe County has a curfew for individuals under 18 years of age. The curfew is 11 P.M. Sunday through Thursday and midnight Friday, Saturday, and the night before a state holiday. Patrol officers are responsible for enforcement of the curfew, which has been credited with reducing juvenile crime.

Requirements

The Arapahoe County Sheriff's Office stresses intangible qualities as requirements alongside minimum age and education. Among these intangibles are honesty, maturity, self-discipline, and initiative, and an exceptional ability to deal with people and traumatic events is expected of all applicants.

Applicants for the position of deputy sheriff/deputy recruit must be 21 years of age and have a high school diploma or equivalent (GED). Disqualifiers include any felony convictions, any domestic violence convictions or permanent restraining orders resulting from domestic violence, a negative police history or record, a bad driving record, a pattern of aggressive or assaultive behavior, negative prior work history, certain misdemeanor convictions, and current or recent use of illegal drugs. If you have used marijuana within one year of applying or any other illegal drug within five years of applying, you will be disqualified. Other drug use is considered case by case.

Testing

There are several tests required of applicants for positions with the Arapahoe County Sheriff's Office. Applicants must take a written test, undergo an oral interview, and may have to take a skills test pertinent to the position applied for. In addition, candidates receiving a conditional offer of employment will undergo a background examination, a polygraph examination, a psychological evaluation, and a medical examination that includes a drug screen.

Getting Started Early

Young men and women between the ages of 14 and 20 have the opportunity to get acquainted with the Arapahoe County Sheriff's Office and law enforcement in general through the Sheriff's Office Patrol Operations' Explorer Post program. Explorer scouts, also known as cadets, have been around for more than 20 years. The young people who become explorer scouts meet monthly to learn about law enforcement. They wear uniforms, and assist sheriff's deputies with certain tasks, including report writing, communications functions, and security details.

Part Three

OPPORTUNITIES AT THE STATE LEVEL

★

Chapter 9
GENERAL INFORMATION

★

There is, of course, a great variety among state law enforcement agencies, from departments of corrections to highway patrol departments to bureaus of investigation. But, as with local agencies, there are some commonalities.

State law enforcement agencies are often run through a central public safety department. This department will genuinely function to oversee and protect public safety, from its administration of the highway patrol department to its oversight of the state's department of corrections and bureau of investigation. As you'll see in the information to follow about several sample agencies, to join a specialized agency within a state's department of public safety, you may be required to perform a certain amount of duty as a trooper in an area such as highway patrol before being given the opportunity to specialize. It works much like the common requirement that local law enforcement agents start on patrol, satisfy a certain experience requirement, and only then are given the opportunity to specialize through promotions and special assignments.

Some state bureaus of investigation are run by the respective state's department of justice, rather than through a department of public safety. In an instance like this, the bureau of investigation will hire directly rather than be an avenue of specialization and advancement for troopers or other officers hired through a department of public safety.

That is all assuming, of course, that you meet the requirements for a position in law enforcement within the state you're hoping to serve. The requirements vary, as you'll see, on all points, from minimum age to minimum education. But all agencies screen candidates by the following steps and processes:

- Written examination
- Oral interview
- Physical fitness or abilities test(s)
- Background investigation
- Medical examination
- Drug screen
- Psychological examination

Please see the Introduction for information on preparing for these tests and other steps.

Chapter 10
JOB DESCRIPTIONS

★

It would be difficult to list all the jobs within all the state law enforcement agencies. But I will briefly cover the three primary law enforcement positions: trooper, corrections officer, and special agent. Of course, these roles are defined differently from state to state, with overlap in duties and more or less defined distinctions between them. For more information, please contact your state's department of public safety or specific law enforcement agency or bureau.

Highway Patrol Officer or State Trooper

An American icon, thanks to Jackie Gleason's "Smokey," Eric Estrada's "Ponch," and Bruce Springsteen's "State Trooper" and others, the highway patrol officer or state trooper is a true guardian of travelers on our nation's roads, highways, and interstates. I'll admit I don't want to see blue lights coming up behind me when I travel, but I try to obey the speed limit and know I have it coming if I get pulled over. Troopers do much more than pull over speeding motorists. They respond to emergency calls, pursue and apprehend wanted individuals, help stranded motorists, identify risks to public safety, license and rehabilitate drivers, enforce commercial vehicle restrictions, and perform many other functions. As drugs are moved across state lines, state highway patrol officers or troopers are on the front lines of the war against the distribution of illegal drugs, particularly in states on established drug routes.

Correctional Officer

Correctional officers oversee individuals who are in custody pending trial or who have been convicted and are serving time. They are responsible for security and inmate safety and are assigned to prevent assaults and escapes, among other disturbances. Officers maintain order, an important role. They do so by observing inmate behavior, conducting inspections, and using other means of monitoring the tenuous balance that exists among the incarcerated. Most correctional officers are unarmed within prison facilities but are armed in situations such as monitoring prisoner transport or other assignments outside of the prison facility.

Special Agent/ Investigator

Criminal investigations within state agencies may be carried out by special agents or field agents. These agents conduct major crime investigations over which their agency has original jurisdiction, meaning they investigate those crimes independent of or in the absence of requests from the department within the state that has local jurisdiction. They assist local departments, at the request of the department or certain state officials, with investigations, evidence analysis, and high-risk situations such as hostage negotiations. They also work with federal agencies in the investigation of certain crimes, including drug crimes, kidnappings, and homicides.

Agents may specialize in areas such as counterterrorism, arson investigations, white-collar or financial crimes, and forensic evidence analysis. Special training and experience are required for positions in these areas.

Chapter 11

REPRESENTATIVE AGENCIES

★

In this chapter you'll find detailed information on various state agencies. As with local departments, I obviously can't go into detail about every state agency in the United States. But I hope the specific information about these will inform your decision about pursuing a career in state law enforcement.

Please take the time to fully investigate the agency you're interested in joining. These agencies are often looking for good candidates and are more than willing to share information about who they are, what they do, and what they look for in prospective troopers and agents.

Oklahoma Department of Public Safety

Oklahoma Highway Patrol

James H. Lawrence, Commissioner of Police
Oklahoma Department of Public Safety
Robert R. Lester Training Center
Academy Personnel Coordinator
P.O. Box 11415
Oklahoma City, Oklahoma 73136
Telephone: (405) 425-2165
Web site: www.dps.state.ok.us/
E-mail: OHPjobs@dps.state.ok.us

CAREER QUICK FACTS

Minimum age:	21
Maximum age:	37
Education:	Associate's degree or 62 semester hours of college
Criminal record:	No felony convictions; no misdemeanor crimes of domestic violence
Base salary:	$27,000 with health and life insurance and retirement plan
Benefits:	10 paid vacation days and 15 paid sick days, plus holidays
Tests:	Written; physical agility; background check; polygraph, psychological, and medical exams; vision test
Academy:	14 to 18 weeks
Categorical preference:	Preference may be given to veterans

Mission Statement and Introduction

Working to provide a safe and secure environment for the public through courteous, quality and professional services.

According to the Oklahoma Highway Safety Fact Sheet for 2002, there were 636 fatal vehicular crashes involving 1,639 people, 736 of whom died. Based on that alone, it's clear that officers of the Oklahoma Highway Patrol (OHP) have their work cut out for them, and their job makes a big difference. But like many states, Oklahoma has been dealing with an extremely tight budget for several years, and the state has not had the money for an academy class in two years. I hope by the time this book is published they will have better funding. You can't reinforce your patrol staff if you don't recruit, and you can't recruit if you don't have the capacity to train your recruits. These people do important work, and I hope the budget woes that have been holding them (and so many other agencies) back will be relieved soon.

Brief History

Established in 1937, the Oklahoma Department of Public Safety now has more than 1,300 employees, including civilians and sworn officers. About 650 of these are highway patrol officers. The mandate of the Oklahoma Department of Public Safety (DPS) is to protect citizens, to uphold and enforce state and federal laws, and to respond to emergencies. Their jurisdiction includes 111,994 miles of city, county, and state maintained roads and highways in Oklahoma, as well as 4,400 miles of shoreline and nearly 500,000 water acres along and on lakes and rivers throughout the state.

In addition, DPS officers perform security and law enforcement functions for the governor and the governor's family and at the state office buildings in Oklahoma City and Tulsa. You no doubt recall the Oklahoma City bombing of April 19, 1995, when Timothy McVeigh set off a car bomb that destroyed the Alfred P. Murrah Federal Building in Oklahoma City, killing 168 people and wounding more than 500 others. With that tragic event, the dangers that come with guarding public and government buildings became much clearer. I imagine that since that event, officers in Oklahoma City feel it even more acutely.

Enforcement of motor vehicle laws, requirements, and restrictions is another duty of the DPS. Highway safety is promoted through the Oklahoma Highway Safety Office, which dispenses federal funds for highway safety projects in the state. Drivers are licensed through

DPS, and vehicle inspection, maintenance, and hazardous materials regulation falls under their domain. In addition, they maintain all of the state's traffic collision reports.

Overview of Highway Patrol

The Oklahoma Highway Patrol has four divisions. Most of the officers of the OHP are assigned to the 13 Field Troops. These are the officers you'll see coming up in your rear view mirror if you're driving on one of those nearly 112,000 miles of roads they patrol. Don't sneer at the trooper because he or she issues speeding tickets. Keep in mind that in addition to patrolling for violations ranging from exceeding the speed limit to driving without a license plate, field troopers are first responders to emergencies on those roads. If you break down or have an accident, the troopers are there for you. They respond to calls ranging from collisions to disabled vehicles to natural disasters. They are also there to assist lost drivers and officers from other agencies.

In addition to Field Troops, divisions of the OHP include Special Service Troops, Aircraft Division, and Executive Security. Special Service Troops are assigned to specialized tasks. Aircraft Division personnel patrol from the air, providing airborne assistance to ground units in vehicular patrol, refugee and manhunt situations, and search-and-rescue operations. The Executive Security Division protects the executive officers of the state—the governor and lieutenant governor and their families.

In addition to these four divisions of the OHP, the Oklahoma Department of Public Safety oversees the Oklahoma Capitol Patrol and Lake Patrol sections. The Oklahoma Capitol Patrol polices the State Capitol Complex and State Office Building in Tulsa, providing security to employees as well as visitors. The Lake Patrol Section polices 38 state lakes and recreation areas with nearly 4,400 miles of shoreline and 490,215 water acres. Duties of the Lake Patrol troopers include water patrol, search-and-rescue missions, investigation of boating accidents and drownings, and response to natural-disaster situations. Special Operations troopers within Lake Patrol carry out special operations such as marine theft investigations and boating safety training and education programs. Lake Patrol also conducts free inspections of vehicles for citizens concerned about their vehicles' maintenance status and safety.

Requirements

Candidates must be at least 21 years of age and no more than 37, must be U.S. citizens, and must have an associate's degree or at least 62 semester hours of college. Any felony conviction will disqualify you as a candidate, as will a misdemeanor domestic violence conviction, as both preclude the carrying of a firearm. There are many levels of testing along the way to the Oklahoma Highway Patrol Academy, and failing those tests can disqualify you as well.

There is an application available at the OHP Web site (www.dps. state.ok.us/), or you can contact the Academy Personnel Coordinator at the address and phone number given at the beginning of this section. If your application meets their requirements, you will be asked to take a written test and physical agility test, and to undergo an oral interview. The written test focuses on reading, writing, and spelling. Lucky for most of us, there's no math. The physical agility test includes a 1.5-mile run, a 300-meter run, sit-ups, and push-ups, with minimum requirements for each. The oral interview is conducted by Patrol personnel. You are scored not only by your answers but by how you give them—so be honest and be professional.

If you do well enough on the preceding and are offered a position, a thorough background check will be conducted on you. Further, you will undergo polygraph testing, a medical examination, including a vision test, and a psychological evaluation made up of written and oral testing. Finally, you will be interviewed by executives of Public Safety and Highway Patrol.

Training

Training at the Oklahoma Highway Patrol Academy is 14 to 18 weeks. At this point, candidates have cadet status. They live in dormitories during training and receive training pay of about $2,000 per month. Upon successful completion of training, cadets are sworn in as officers of the OHP. After a one-year probationary period, graduates of the academy become full-fledged officers of the Oklahoma Highway Patrol at a starting salary of $27,000 and a current maximum potential salary of about $48,000.

One thing the OHP does that is uncommon is offer a weekend mini-academy to applicants. This weekend mini-academy familiarizes candidates with what the Oklahoma Highway Patrol Academy is like. This is a great opportunity to find out if the OHP is truly for you and if you have what it takes to get through the academy before you've made a 100-percent investment of your time and ambitions toward this goal.

Oregon Department of Public Safety

Oregon Department of Corrections

Max Williams, Director
Recruitment and Career Services
1793 13th Street, SE
Salem, Oregon 97302
Phone: (503) 945-9090
Fax: (503) 378-5449
E-mail: recruitment@doc.state.or.us

CAREER QUICK FACTS

Minimum age:	21
Education:	High school or equivalent (GED)
Criminal record:	No felony convictions; various other convictions are automatic disqualifiers
Base salary:	About $30,000
Tests:	Written tests; medical examination; background check

Mission Statement

The mission of the Oregon Department of Corrections is to promote public safety by holding offenders accountable for their actions and reducing the risk of future criminal behavior.

Overview

The Oregon Department of Corrections operates within the state's Department of Public Safety. The state's approximately 1,700 correctional officers are responsible for overseeing state prisoners at 12 state prisons and other facilities and preventing disturbances within state correctional facilities. They provide continuous supervision of inmates through observation and person-to-person contact. Correctional officers secure state corrections facilities and demonstrate and encourage appropriate behavior among inmates, giving inmates positive reinforcement for good behavior.

Officers work in shifts, and the environment can be harsh. Inmates can be verbally assaultive and offensive, and even threatening. Officers may have to use force, including firearms, when warranted by an emergency situation or disturbance that reasonably dictates force is necessary. They are required to complete reports, restrain violent inmates, conduct walking patrols of cell blocks, and search cells and inmates.

Observation is key to maintaining a safe and orderly prison environment. In their patrols and during the performance of other duties, officers must observe and recognize early signs of trouble, from prisoner health and safety issues to escape attempts.

Requirements

Candidates must be at least 21 years of age and possess a high school diploma or equivalent (GED). If you have been convicted of a felony, you will not be considered. There are many other crimes for which a conviction is an automatic disqualifier, including sexual abuse crimes and assaulting a police officer. If you have lost your license because of a DWI or DUI conviction, you may be disqualified.

Testing

Applicants undergo a physical fitness and medical examination. Hearing and vision requirements must be met. Applicants undergo a background check, including criminal and driving history. There is also a Work-Style Behavior Survey and, if you pass the survey, a Correctional Officer multiple-choice test.

Career Opportunities

Specific duties for correctional officers vary. Officers may be assigned to supervisory and observation duties at towers, in gate control, within housing units, and during recreation, special details, and inmate work details.

Corrections is a "growth industry," and there are plenty of opportunities at every level for qualified correctional officers. Within the Oregon Department of Corrections, officers can achieve promotions to the following security classifications: corporal, sergeant, lieutenant, and captain.

North Carolina Department of Justice

North Carolina State Bureau of Investigation

Robin Pendergraft, Director
North Carolina Department of Justice
Personnel Division
114 W. Edenton Street
P. O. Box 629
Raleigh, North Carolina 27602
Telephone: (919) 716-6494
Fax: (919) 716-6710
Web site: sbi.jus.state.nc.us/sbimain/ncsbi.htm

CAREER QUICK FACTS

Minimum age:	21
Education:	Four-year college degree
Criminal record:	No felony or other serious crime conviction
Base salary:	Salary depends on assignment and experience
Benefits:	Medical insurance; state retirement; 96 hours sick leave; 94 hours paid vacation
Tests:	Polygraph, medical, and psychological exams; drug screen
Academy:	26 weeks

Values

Truth, Integrity, Justice

Overview

The North Carolina State Bureau of Investigation (SBI), headquartered in the state capital of Raleigh, investigates major homicide, burglary, arson, and narcotics crimes. In its role as an assisting agency, the North Carolina SBI helps local law enforcement departments with their investigations through case and evidence analysis, including scientific analysis of evidence in its state-of-the-art forensic laboratory, and investigation. The North Carolina SBI also helps prepare evidence as part of investigations and for use in court.

There are certain crimes over which the North Carolina SBI has original jurisdiction. Among those are drug crimes. For crimes over which the SBI does not have original jurisdiction, local law enforcement can request assistance or state officials, including the governor, can involve the SBI in an assistance role. In drug investigations, the SBI works with federal agencies, including the National Guard, DEA, and FBI, in addition to local departments.

To achieve its goals and be accessible to law enforcement and citizens in all regions of the state, the bureau has eight district offices located throughout North Carolina. In addition to its investigative efforts, the SBI works hard to provide information to and solicit information from the public about wanted persons and potential threats, including those from possible terrorist acts.

Brief History

Originally established as the State Bureau of Identification and Investigation in 1937, the bureau's first director, Frederick C. Handy, a former FBI Special Agent in Charge of the Carolinas, was appointed by Governor Hoey in 1938. North Carolina was only the eighth state to establish a state law enforcement agency. The bureau became the State Bureau of Investigation in 1939 and was moved under the auspices of the state's Department of Justice, where it remains.

Though it started as basically a two-man unit, the North Carolina SBI has come a long way. In 2001, Robin Pendergraft was sworn in as the bureau's first female director.

Requirements

If you are interested in becoming a sworn agent of the North Carolina State Bureau of Investigation (SBI), you must be at least 21 years old and have a four-year degree from an accredited college or university.

If you have been convicted of a felony or other serious crime, you will not be considered. In addition, if you have used marijuana within the past three years, if you have used any other illegal drug, or if you have possessed with intent to sell any illegal drug, you will be disqualified.

Testing

Applicants must undergo a comprehensive background investigation, which includes contact with employers, references, friends, and investigation of your criminal record, driving record, credit history, and other factors. Applicants undergo polygraph, medical, and psychological examinations, and a drug screen.

Training

Agents undergo 26 weeks of training at the Special Agent Academy in Raleigh, followed by three months of formal training in the field.

Career Opportunities

New agents are initially employed for a probationary period of one year, including training at the SBI Special Agent Academy. Agents can be assigned permanently anywhere in the state of North Carolina, and temporarily in other locations. The hours can be irregular, and include nights, weekends, and holidays. Agents may be required to work undercover or travel for extended periods. All agents must be willing to carry a firearm and use deadly force when necessary and warranted.

Special agents may be assigned to any type of investigation, and they have the opportunity to specialize and obtain special certification for certain jobs and types of investigations.

For example, there are 86 certified agents working within field and laboratory services in the SBI's Clandestine Laboratory Program in its drug enforcement efforts. These agents investigate the possible manufacture of illegal drugs in the often dangerous settings of clandestine laboratories. The SBI is the sole state agency in North Carolina conducting such investigations.

The Clandestine Laboratory Team is often backed up by the Special Response Team, another specialized unit of the SBI. Its mission specializes in high-risk situations, such as raids and hostage situations. There are currently 27 agents on this team.

The SBI's Arson Program is a third specialized unit of the SBI. It currently includes 17 agents and four canine teams. Agents in the Arson Program conduct arson and fire investigations throughout the state.

The SBI is organized as follows.

Crime Laboratory Division   As mentioned, the SBI has a very advanced forensic laboratory located in Raleigh, and a regional facility in Asheville. Within the Crime Laboratory Division are specialized sections, including Drug Chemistry and Toxicology, Firearms and Tool Marks, Latent Evidence, Questioned Documents, and Trace Evidence. To work within this division, your required four-year college degree may have to be in a physical science, including chemistry or biochemistry.

Field Division   Within the Field Division, special agents assigned to one of the SBI's eight district offices or special units investigate violations of state law. Field agents interview and interrogate witnesses and suspects, collect evidence, and otherwise conduct case investigations. They may work undercover and run surveillance operations. They investigate major cases in conjunction with other agencies on the federal, state, and local levels.

Financial Crimes Unit   The Financial Crimes Unit has special educational requirements, as its agents must be familiar with the standards, transactions, methods, and terminology of the crimes it investigates. Agent positions in the Financial Crimes Unit require a minimum of 18 semester hours of accounting in college, within or in addition to the four-year college degree required for all agents, and four years of professional financial or accounting experience.

Airwing   Airwing is the SBI pilot unit. Obviously, there are highly specialized requirements for agent positions within Airwing. The unit performs an important function in the SBI's Marijuana Eradication Program, surveilling from the air to locate marijuana plants, which agents are adept at recognizing.

Getting Started Early

The North Carolina SBI offers an internship program for college students interested in a law enforcement career. If you are a student and qualify for the program, it is a great opportunity to become familiar not only with the SBI but with the range of law enforcement careers at the state investigative level, in a real-life setting.

Students can apply after they have completed their sophomore year. Depending upon major and area of interest, among other factors, a student will select certain internship opportunities. These are competitive positions, and worth the competition. Internships are available in, among other areas, crime laboratory, field offices, Financial Crimes Unit, and Diversion & Environmental Crimes Unit.

Texas Department of Public Safety

Texas Troopers

Thomas A. Davis, Jr., Director of Texas Department of Public Safety
Street address:
5805 North Lamar Blvd.
Austin, Texas 78752-4422

Mailing address:
P. O. Box 4087
Austin, Texas 78773-0001
(Applications may be made in any Texas DPS office.)
Telephone: (866) 898-7667
Web site: www.txdps.state.tx.us

CAREER QUICK FACTS

Minimum age:	20
Maximum age:	No maximum age
Education:	90 semester hours
or	
Military equivalent:	Three years
or	
Law enforcement experience equivalent:	Three years (on sliding scale)
Criminal record:	No felony convictions; certain misdemeanors disqualify; no family violence convictions
Base salary:	About $33,000 per year after training
Benefits:	Two weeks' vacation; 12 paid holidays; sick leave; health insurance; retirement
Tests:	Competitive examination; medical examination; background check; drug screen
Academy:	26 weeks

Mission Statement

> The Department of Public Safety of the State of Texas is an agency of the state to enforce the laws protecting the public safety and provide for the prevention and detection of crime.
>
> The department is composed of the Texas Rangers, the Texas Highway Patrol, the administrative division, and other divisions that the commission considers necessary.

The Texas Department of Public Safety (DPS) is a large department in a very large state, and it encompasses a great many functions, responsibilities, and divisions. Texas Troopers are the law enforcement officers of the Texas DPS and have statewide authority as peace officers of the state of Texas. After required years of service, troopers are eligible for promotions in the DPS's Criminal Law Enforcement Division, including the elite Texas Rangers, which are covered in the next section.

Overview

The Texas Department of Public Safety is organized by division as follows.

Director's Staff The division includes the Public Information Office and performs budget and accounting functions within the Accounting and Budget Control Office, Legal Services, and other executive departments. Also within the Director's Staff is the office of Internal Affairs.

Traffic Law Enforcement Division As you might expect, this division enforces highway and traffic laws, from speed limits, inspections, and safety regulations for passenger vehicles to weight limits on commercial trucking vehicles. Within the Traffic Law Enforcement Division is the Highway Patrol Service, where most troopers you'll come face-to-face with are assigned. Also within this division are the Safety Education Service, License & Weight Service, and Breath and Alcohol Test

Program. Drivers under the influence are a deadly problem on our nation's roads and highways, and Texas Troopers have a lot of miles to cover to protect Texans and travelers from that danger.

Criminal Law Enforcement Division   This includes Narcotics Service, Special Crimes, Motor Vehicle Theft Service, and the Texas Rangers. Also included are the crime laboratories, in which some part of most investigations is undertaken for the aforementioned investigative departments within Criminal Law Enforcement. Criminal Law Enforcement Division officers are authorized to enforce Texas law throughout the state. They also assist local law enforcement, as well as other state and federal agencies.

Texas Ranger Division   This division is covered in the next section.

Administration Division   This group includes the Emergency Management Service, which manages emergency calls and crime records. Texas Trooper staff functions are performed by the Administrative Division as well.

Driver License Division   This division oversees licensing of Texas drivers, from issuance and renewal to revocation and reinstatement. It is not an easy job, especially since most Americans have little patience for the necessary paperwork and procedures involved in getting and maintaining their licenses. It can be especially difficult in a border state like Texas with significant immigration.

Requirements

To become a Texas Trooper, you must be at least 20 years old on the date of appointment to the probationary position of trainee. The Texas DPS sets no maximum age limit for applicants. You must have completed at least 90 semester hours of college from an accredited school or have prior law enforcement experience of three years as a complete equivalent to the educational minimum. The equivalence is accepted on a sliding scale. For instance, if you have 45 hours of college completed and two years of law enforcement experience, you will meet their minimum requirements.

The Texas DPS includes some intangible requirements, setting the bar high for applicants. Texas Trooper candidates "must be of good moral character and habits."

Among the disqualifiers for the position are a criminal record that includes any felony convictions or convictions for certain misdemeanors within the past 10 years. In addition, any conviction for a family violence offense will disqualify you. If you have had your driver's license suspended for habitual violations within the past five years, or have received four or more convictions for hazardous violations of traffic laws within the past year or seven within the past two years, you will not be considered. Any conviction, regardless of the time frame, for DWI, indecent exposure, or delivery of marijuana will disqualify you.

Testing

The screening process for applicants to the Texas Trooper position includes an oral interview. A thorough background check is conducted on applicants. In addition, applicants undergo a medical examination and must have 20/200 uncorrected vision. If hired, you will have to pass a drug screen before commencing training.

Upon completion of training (see below), trooper-trainees must pass a written state licensing test administered by the Texas Commission on Law Enforcement Officer Standards and Education.

Training

Once you are hired as a trooper-trainee, you will undergo 26 weeks of basic training at the Texas Law Enforcement Academy in Austin. This includes firearms training, emergency response training, education in driver license and traffic laws, and physical defense tactics.

Career Opportunities

As a trooper-trainee or trooper, you must be willing to relocate within the state. Troopers may be assigned anywhere in Texas, although some consideration is given to preference.

New officers of the Texas DPS are assigned as troopers to either the Highway Patrol Service, License & Weight Service (Traffic Law Enforcement Division), Vehicle Inspection Service (also within the Traffic Law Enforcement Division), or the Driver License Division. Troopers are assigned as follows within the divisions of the Texas Department of Public Safety.

Highway Patrol Troopers   Highway Patrol troopers enforce traffic laws, apprehend and cite violators, investigate rural vehicular accidents, apprehend wanted individuals, and perform other functions, including stolen vehicle and property recovery.

Vehicle Inspection Troopers   This division is responsible for supervising vehicle inspection stations and inspecting mechanics, according to state requirements for each.

License & Weight Troopers   These troopers are responsible for enforcing laws pertaining to commercial traffic, including weight restrictions and registration requirements for long-haul and other commercial vehicles.

Safety Education Troopers   This division performs a public service by providing informational programs on traffic safety, responsible driving, and the prevention of crime.

Capitol Troopers   Capitol troopers provide security at the Texas State Capitol Complex located in Austin, where much of the work of state government is conducted.

Driver License Division Troopers   This group licenses drivers and rehabilitates those who have broken certain laws.

Once troopers have gained experience in one of the preceding capacities, they are eligible for promotions within the uniformed services, Driver License Division, Criminal Law Enforcement Division, and Administrative Division. There are specific eligibility requirements for postings, especially within the latter two divisions.

Texas Department of Public Safety

Texas Rangers

C.J. Havrda, Senior Captain
Chief of the Texas Rangers
Headquarters
P.O. Box 4087
Austin, Texas 78773-0600
Telephone: (512) 424-2160
Web site:
   www.txdps.state.tx.us/director_staff/texas_rangers/index.htm
E-mail: rangers@txdps.state.tx.us

CAREER QUICK FACTS

Experience:	Eight years of major investigations experience in law enforcement; must be at least a Texas State Trooper II
Education:	90 semester hours of college
or	
Military equivalent:	Three years
Criminal record:	No felony convictions; no misdemeanor crimes of domestic violence
Tests:	Written; background check

How could I give an overview of state law enforcement agencies in this country without shining a spotlight on the Texas Rangers? Without a doubt the oldest, most well-known state law enforcement agency in the country, the Texas Rangers are the only agency I know of with a Major League Baseball team named after them. More to the point, the Rangers have a venerable history that includes some of the most recognizable figures in Texas and U.S. history, on both sides of the law, from Sam Houston to Bonnie and Clyde. They are so important an organization that a 1987 Texas statute stipulates they cannot be disbanded:

> *The division relating to the Texas Rangers may not be abolished.*

They even inspired a now-syndicated and still popular drama starring martial arts movie star Chuck Norris. No doubt you'll remember these words:

> *'Cause the eyes of a Ranger are upon you,*
> *Any wrong you do, he's gonna see,*
> *When you're in Texas,*
> *Look behind you,*
> *'Cause that's where the Ranger's gonna be.*
>
> **—Theme song from *Walker, Texas Ranger***

Brief History

The Texas Rangers were formed in 1823 to protect the fewer than 1,000 colonists who had by then settled west in what is now Texas. Organized by Stephen F. Austin, the Rangers were so named because they had to range over a broad expanse of land to protect those colonists. Their duties included fighting off Indians, and they protected the settlements even as Sam Houston faced off against and defeated Santa Ana in 1836's Battle of San Jacinto.

As part of the Confederacy, Texas seceded from and fought against the Union in the Civil War. Upon readmittance and throughout Reconstruction, the Rangers' mandate grew from protecting citizens against Indians to include the enforcement of some unpopular laws. The discovery of oil in Texas and the Prohibition era gave the Rangers more than they could handle. One of the most famous crime sprees in outlaw history and lore, that of Clyde Barrow and Bonnie Parker, came to an end after 102 days of pursuit by Texas Rangers when Bonnie and Clyde were trapped by officers in Louisiana. The outlaws reached for their weapons, and the officers, who had hoped to take the two alive, shot them dead. At the time of their death, the duo were believed to have committed 13 murders, including those of two police officers.

It wasn't until more than a half-century later, in 1935, that the Texas Ranger came to be known as a peace officer rather than a semi-soldier. For many years now the Rangers have been within the Texas Department of Public Safety (DPS) but operate as a unified force with special, separate duties within the DPS.

Overview

Texas Rangers are charged with many duties. Statewide, they investigate crimes, apprehend felons, protect the lives and property of citizens, and assist local law enforcement with the same in their jurisdictions. In 2002, the Rangers conducted more than 5,300 investigations resulting in more than 1,500 indictments and convictions and 12 death sentences. It's hard to imagine, but that's one death sentence per every 10 Rangers.

The Rangers investigate crimes that include murder, robbery, sexual assault, burglary, theft, fraud, threats against public officials, missing persons, questionable deaths, and unidentified bodies. They are responsible for investigating organized crime, serve as officers of the court, and protect public officials, including the governor and other dignitaries. Their forensic capabilities are exceptional, and they conduct thorough, state-of-the-art investigations.

The Texas Rangers are an elite group, with 140 members, including 118 commissioned officers, three crime analysts, a forensic artist, a fiscal analyst and 17 civilian support personnel. The sworn officers are organized into six companies, A through F as follows:

A: Houston
B: Garland
C: Lubbock
D: San Antonio
E: Midland
F: Waco

Other Rangers are stationed throughout the state, with each Ranger being responsible for two or three counties. Rangers operate with great autonomy and must be able to make decisions without direct supervision. They must be mature, careful, and courageous.

In addition, the Rangers have an Unsolved Crimes Investigations Team (UCIT) formed to pursue open murder and serial crimes.

Requirements

To be a Ranger you must first be a Texas State Trooper. The Texas Department of Public Safety's requirements for troopers are as follows. You must be 20 years old with at least 90 semester hours of college, although three or more years of military or law enforcement experience may be counted as equivalent.

The Texas Ranger is by no means an entry-level position. In 2001, the average Ranger was 44 years old and had 117 hours of college education. You cannot join the Rangers without significant prior law enforcement experience—eight years to be exact, and that spent in the investigation of major crimes. You must, of course, be a U.S. citizen, be employed with the Texas Department of Public Safety at least at the level of Trooper II. Candidates should have good moral character and habits that would be reflected in the very thorough background examination the Rangers conduct.

An entrance exam is given to applicants. The highest scorers go on to oral interviews. There are always many more applicants than open positions, with a tiny percentage of applicants reaching their goal of becoming Rangers.

Rangers must attend 40 hours of in-service training every two years and are encouraged to take part in additional, specialized courses as well.

Part Four

OPPORTUNITIES AT THE FEDERAL LEVEL

★

Chapter 12

GENERAL INFORMATION

★

Working for the Federal Government

Federal jobs are appealing for many reasons, including job security, good pay, and good benefits. Pay for most of the positions covered in this book is set according to the government's General Schedule (GS) plan, with special salary rates for law enforcement officers. Note that there is a schedule for Foreign Service (FS), which is utilized by the Bureau of Diplomatic Services and in other instances for which assignments are largely overseas. Also note that executive positions have their own pay scale, but positions on that scale aren't covered in this text.

The General Schedule includes 15 tiers, from GS-1 to GS-15. For 2004, the GS plan for GS-1 through GS-10 is as follows.

GS-1	$15,625
GS-2	$17,568
GS-3	$19,168
GS-4	$21,518
GS-5	$24,075
GS-6	$26,836

GS-7	$29,821
GS-8	$33,026
GS-9	$36,478
GS-10	$40,171

For 2004, the GS plan for law enforcement officers, from GS-3 through GS-10, is as follows.

GS-3	$23,002
GS-4	$25,820
GS-5	$29,696
GS-6	$31,311
GS-7	$33,797
GS-8	$35,228
GS-9	$37,694
GS-10	$41,510

There is an additional geographic adjustment (increase in pay) for most law enforcement jobs that ranges from about 8 percent to about 20 percent. For instance, the following table shows the rates for the general Washington, DC/Baltimore, Maryland area, including a locality payment of 14.63 percent.

GS-3	$26,367
GS-4	$29,597
GS-5	$34,041
GS-6	$35,892
GS-7	$38,742
GS-8	$40,382
GS-9	$43,209
GS-10	$47,583

Other areas, including Atlanta, Boston, Los Angeles, San Francisco, St. Louis, and others, have special locality pay. The San Francisco general area has a 24.21 percent locality pay adjustment. To illustrate the difference that makes, GS-3 jobs in San Francisco in 2004 start at $28,571. For other areas in the United States for which there is no special designation, the locality pay adjustment is 10.9 percent. In addition, overseas jobs have a percentage adjustment.

Full-time federal law enforcement jobs include a Thrift Savings Plan (which is similar to a 401(k) plan); Federal Employees Health Benefits Program (FEHB), which is medical insurance with no required physical exam, no waiting periods, and no restrictions based on age or physical condition; and Federal Employees Group Life Insurance. With some variation, in addition to 10 paid holidays per year, federal employees receive at least 13 days of sick leave and start with about 13 days of vacation. There are also arrangements for working parents, such as flexible work schedules, telecommuting, family-friendly leave policies, part-time and job-sharing positions, child and elder care resources, and child support services.

Another great benefit available for some federal positions is a recruitment or relocation bonus for positions that have been difficult to fill. These bonuses can be up to 25 percent of your basic annual salary. A federal agency may even opt to pay off your student loans on your behalf.

Law Enforcement Availability Pay, or LEAP, is a form of premium pay for criminal investigators who are required to work, or must be available to work, substantial amounts of unscheduled overtime duty based on the needs of the agency. Availability pay is fixed at 25 percent of the adjusted rate of basic pay.

But because they're so appealing, and because the economy has been in a downturn for the past few years, many unscrupulous individuals and groups have come out of the woodwork offering listings of federal jobs "you can't get anywhere else" for a "small fee." Even if the fee is just $25, you're paying too much. Here's why.

The Office of Personnel Management

By law, agencies with "competitive service" job openings that are seeking candidates outside of their current workforce are required to post their openings with the Office of Personnel Management, which lists them on its USAJOBS Web site and distributes them for posting with the State Employment Service Offices. The OPM also offers listings and information by telephone at (703) 724-1850 or, for the hearing impaired, TDD (978) 461-8404.

What are competitive service jobs? They are those positions that are subject to civil service laws that ensure fair and equal hiring practices. This differs from jobs at "excepted service agencies," like the FBI and the CIA, which are not subject to the same laws. Individual positions at various agencies may also be deemed excepted by the OPM or by law.

USAJOBS

The motto at the Office of Personnel Management's USAJOBS Web site is "Working for America." As the official job site of the United States federal government, www.usajobs.opm.gov is a great tool for prospective candidates. The pool of open positions is quite large. A recent look at USAJOBS turned up 17,897 federal jobs in their database—all at your fingertips.

As a candidate, you can search the available jobs for those that suit you personally. You can limit your search by specific department, salary range, geographical location, keyword, and many other factors. Not only that, once you've established a career account with USAJOBS, you can sign up to receive e-mail notification of new vacancies that meet your criteria. You can even tell them how often to send such notification.

USAJOBS works for you from the other direction, too, allowing you to post your résumé (one version or several) on the site for review by the people doing the hiring. This résumé-posting feature includes the option to revise your résumé at any point after it's been posted. This would be useful if you wanted to add a new certification you'd received, for instance, or to change your contact information if you've moved. Personnel managers can search the database of résumés for people who meet their criteria, and get in touch with you either directly or through the Web site (depending upon whether you allow your contact information to be viewed in this way) even if you have not applied for the job they're hoping to fill.

Perhaps most important, you can often apply for specific positions online. You can select which résumé you want to use if you have more than one posted, attach your cover letter, and your application is on the way. If this option isn't available for the position you're interested in, you'll be directed to information about how to apply. Contact information for each position is provided, as is a history of your application.

In addition to being a useful database and link between candidates and agencies, USAJOBS acts as a sort of virtual career counselor, offering information to help you decide what sort of work within which federal agency would best suit your interests and qualifications. One way they do this is through their Career Interest Guide. Here, you can complete their Interest Guide Questionnaire to determine which careers make sense for you based on what your interests are. To follow are some of the duties from this questionnaire that a candidate for a career in law enforcement might indicate interest in:

- Help prison parolees find jobs and adjust to society.
- Guard property against theft.
- Search for legal regulations in a library.
- Patrol a border to detect illegal entry.
- Watch over prison inmates.
- Investigate employment practices to enforce EEO laws.
- Investigate and arrest persons suspected of illegal drug use.
- Detect and prevent smuggling.
- Arrest traffic violators.

The Web site uses your responses to direct you to groups of agencies that fit your interests.

If you already have an interest in a specific field, you can look at jobs related to that field by exploring USAJOB's Career Interest Areas. If you're a candidate for a career in law enforcement, you might opt to look into the "Protective" Career Interest Area, which includes agencies with positions in law enforcement and investigation.

Beyond its Internet presence, the Office of Personnel Management brings job opportunities to the public in a variety of ways. It conducts job fairs in cities around the country, bringing knowledgeable representatives to your community to discuss openings and career paths in the federal government.

Minimum/Maximum Ages

For most positions, applicants must be at least 21 years old and not yet 37. There are exceptions, including excepted transfer applicants, who may be older than 37 in some instances. And in some cases, the maximum age is lower, as with some Department of the Interior law enforcement positions for which individuals over the age of 31 are not eligible.

Veterans

A veteran is someone who was honorably or generally discharged from the armed forces after three years of continuous active duty. By federal law, veterans must receive hiring preference when they are applying for positions for which they meet the job requirements. Veterans who served during certain military campaigns or time periods, like World War II or any 180-day period from January 31, 1955, through October 15, 1976, and veterans who are disabled are entitled to preference over other veterans. Also, hiring preference must be given to unmarried surviving spouses of certain deceased veterans, mothers of veterans who died in service or are totally disabled, and spouses of veterans who are totally disabled from service-related injuries.

Preference does not equal entitlement. Though the federal government has by law instituted an affirmative action program for veterans, jobs are not guaranteed to them. However, there is a process by which veterans may receive appointments to certain positions. A Veterans' Recruitment Appointment (VRA) is a discretionary appointment by a federal agency of a veteran to a position without competition. This means there are no other candidates brought in and a veteran is appointed absent competition. Veterans who are disabled, served in an official war, who earned the Armed Forces Service Medal, or who left active duty within the last three years are eligible for VRAs and must have the qualifications for the position being filled in order to qualify.

Women

As stated by Women in Federal Law Enforcement (WIFLE), until 1971, women were not allowed to have certain federal positions that required carrying a firearm. I know when I started, the FBI was very much still a male-dominated agency, but the number of women grew steadily throughout my career, to the great advantage of the Bureau. As of 2001, according to the Department of Justice Bureau of Justice Statistics, about 14.4 percent of federal law enforcement officers were women, with an average increase annually since 1996 of about 0.4 percent.

That's a small increase, but it's an increase. Federal agencies are keenly interested in bringing in more women. I hope the number of women applying for these jobs continues to grow, and I believe they will continue to represent a greater percentage of law enforcement officers.

Minorities

All federal agencies are bound by federal antidiscrimination laws as enforced by the EEOC, as mentioned earlier. More importantly, perhaps, all federal agencies are interested in and dedicated to reflecting America's diverse population in their workforces. Each agency approaches the challenge of reflecting the "faces of America" differently, but there are some across-the-board federal initiatives.

For example, the Hispanic Employment Initiative has a motto: "Creating a Government That Looks Like America." Its goals are to recruit, advance, and retain qualified Hispanic candidates in the federal workforce by a variety of measures. These include developing mentoring programs for Hispanic youths that introduce them to careers with the federal government, recruiting from schools and colleges with large Hispanic enrollment, and offering internships to Hispanic college students. In addition, the Bilingual/Bicultural Authority offers opportunities in professional and administrative positions for which Spanish language and cultural familiarity are an asset.

Noncitizens and Federal Employment

As more noncitizens look to long-term residence in this country, it stands to reason more noncitizens will look to employment with the federal government. Briefly, I'll touch on the restrictions on hiring noncitizens that are not already in the civil service. First, the government may currently be restricting payment to individuals from certain countries of origin. Second, federal law limits agencies with competitive service job openings to hiring noncitizens only when there are no qualified citizens available. That said, law enforcement positions are restricted to U.S. citizens unless specifically excepted.

Chapter 13

FEDERAL LAW ENFORCEMENT CAREERS BY DEPARTMENT

★

To organize the material on federal law enforcement opportunities, I turned to the Department of Justice Bureau of Justice Statistics. The BJS compiles and analyzes crime and law enforcement statistics of all kinds, from juvenile crimes to school safety to handgun usage to the personnel makeup of law enforcement agencies. The BJS presents its analysis in the form of bulletins or reports, available to the public free of charge, that offer unadulterated facts about the state of the United States' criminal justice system. In my opinion, if you want to understand the dynamics of crime, from prevention to conviction, their publications are great resources. It takes a little more time than a brief sound byte on the news or a glance at CNN, but you'll be able to make your own judgments with such facts at hand.

Depending upon online availability, you can either download these publications directly or order hardcopies from the Web site, www.ncjrs.org, or call (800) 851-3420. U.S. citizens are entitled to two free reports per week. If you order more than two in one week, you will have to pay shipping and handling.

U.S. Department of Justice
Bureau of Justice Statistics
National Criminal Justice Reference Service
www.ncjrs.org
(800) 851-3420

I selected federal law enforcement agencies to profile in this book largely upon the basis of criteria applied by the BJS—federal agencies whose personnel are authorized to make arrests and to carry firearms. This doesn't mean every agent must do either, but that they are authorized to do so if need be. Further, I have included the larger federal law enforcement agencies and representative samples of the smaller ones. For example, there are Offices of Inspectors General other than the Office of Inspector General of the Department of Homeland Security, which is covered in the coming pages. An Office of Inspector General is an important self-regulatory office, inspecting, auditing, regulating, and enforcing laws within the operations of a given department or agency. However, it seemed redundant to include each of these offices, so I have included just the DHS office.

In terms of information presented, I have gone into greater detail about the larger agencies and held back on those that hire few candidates who do not have highly specialized training or education. I hope this presentation provides the information you need to get started investigating a career in federal law enforcement, if that's where your interests lie. Please investigate further each agency that interests you. My goal is to present an overview. Each agency profiled here is much more complex and interesting than I could possibly wholly represent.

All included federal agencies in the coming pages are organized alphabetically by department, then alphabetically within each department. Those outside of cabinet-level departments are listed alphabetically as well.

Department of Agriculture

USDA Forest Service Law Enforcement and Investigations

Headquarters Office
Washington Office
Personnel Management Staff (Rosslyn)
P.O. Box 96090
Washington, DC 20013-6090
Telephone: (703) 235-JOBS or (703) 235-8102
Web site: www.fs.fed.us/lei/jobs_page.html

CAREER QUICK FACTS

Minimum age:	21
Maximum age:	37 (excepting some transfers)
Education:	Accredited baccalaureate (four-year) college degree or one to three years of experience in criminal law enforcement (or combination thereof)
Base salary:	Typically GS-5 ($23,442)
Benefits:	Full federal benefits
Tests:	Extensive background check; physical fitness test; drug screen; firearms test
Academy:	Training at FLETC; one year of field training

Mission Statement

To serve people, protect natural resources and property within the authority and jurisdiction of the Forest Service.

Overview

The Forest Service was established in 1905 and is an agency of the U.S. Department of Agriculture. Its mandate is to manage public lands in national forests and grasslands in the United States, of which there are approximately 191 million acres—equivalent to the size of Texas. The agency protects these lands, and the renewable but vulnerable resources (like timber and water) from wildfires, pests, diseases, theft, vandalism, and other destructive elements.

Law enforcement is key to the agency's mandate, and its need for good people is growing. While the Forest Service might not be the agency you'd think of first when imagining a career in law enforcement on the federal level, if you enjoy and appreciate the outdoors, respect wildlife and natural habitats, and are interested in conserving the same for current and future generations, then it might be a good one for you to consider.

USDA Forest Service Law Enforcement and Investigations

The law enforcement division of the Forest Service is Law Enforcement and Investigations (LE&I). Of the approximately 35,000 employees of the Forest Service, just under 600 are in law enforcement. Though they are a small part of the agency in terms of numbers, they play a very important role in the management of the National Forest System by enforcing federal laws and regulations that protect natural resources, employees of the USDA, and the public who are able to enjoy our public lands. Their motto, "Caring for the Land and Serving People," really reflects what they do. They accomplish this by

- Protecting the public, the employees, the natural resources, and property of the Forest Service;
- Informing visitors to public lands about the laws and regulations pertaining to their use; and
- Investigating violations of those laws and regulations.

There are two types of law enforcement officers in the LE&I, uniformed law enforcement officers (LEO) and special agents.

Uniformed Law Enforcement Officers

Uniformed law enforcement officers are the patrol officers of the Forest Service. The enforcement of laws and regulations governing public lands falls to the men and women on regular patrol of these lands as part of LEO. These are the officers you're likeliest to see as you hike in a national park or fish in a national forest. They carry firearms and defensive equipment, execute warrants and make arrests, complete police reports, and testify in court.

Among the variety of activities and issues addressed daily by the men and women of LEO are timber theft, vehicle accidents (including emergency medical care), search-and-rescue missions, and enforcement of fish and wildlife regulations.

Special Agents

The officers who conduct criminal investigations under the Forest Service are the agency's special agents. They investigate violations within their jurisdiction (i.e., on public lands or connected areas) of criminal provisions of the U.S. Code.

These men and women, like detectives on the local level, are usually plain-clothed and armed with concealed weapons. They investigate crimes, make arrests, and present cases to U.S. Attorneys, who prosecute them. These crimes include starting forest fires, making or distributing illegal drugs, and timber theft. On occasion, special agents will act somewhat like Internal Affairs officers and investigate internal allegations.

Often, special agents will work alone, with little direct supervision. Assignments are usually in rural locations with one special agent per office. While there are undoubtedly positive aspects to any job with the Forest Service in terms of the basic work environment, there is a great deal of travel involved for agents, and the typical caseload per agent is 10 to 15 criminal cases at any given time.

Requirements for Employment as an LE&I Officer

If you would like to become a patrol officer (LEO), you should have a bachelor's degree or one year of experience in criminal law enforcement (or a related field). If you would like to become a special agent, you should have a bachelor's degree or three years of such experience. For this position, the agency will accept experience as equivalent to education based on the formula that nine months of experience equals one year of school.

The minimum age for applicants is 21 and the maximum is 37, except for individuals currently or formerly in federal law enforcement.

As a candidate for either position, you will undergo a background check, physical fitness test, drug screen, and firearms test. Some of these tests will be reapplied throughout your employment. If you are hired, you will be trained at the Federal Law Enforcement Training Center (FLETC) in Glynco, Georgia, followed by a full year of training in the field.

Career Opportunities

Vacancies are typically filled on a regional basis. There is a special agent in charge (or SAC) for each administrative region. Everyone in the region reports to the SAC, either directly or indirectly. The SAC typically advertises open positions in law enforcement and does the hiring him- or herself. If you are interested, contact the Office of Personnel Management (OPM) or the agency directly using the information at the beginning of this section, or visit either Web site, also at the beginning of this section.

LEO and special agents are eligible for all federal benefits and are evaluated for promotions annually.

Department of Defense

Pentagon Force Protection Agency

John Jester, Chief
Pentagon Police Department
9000 Defense Pentagon
Washington, DC 20301-9000
Telephone: (866) 269-1462
E-mail: PFPARecruiting@pfpa.mil
Web site: www.pfpa.mil/employment.html

CAREER QUICK FACTS

Minimum age:	21
Maximum age:	37
Education:	High school diploma or equivalent for entry-level positions; must have honorable discharge if former military
Convictions:	No felony convictions; no domestic violence convictions
Base salary:	$41,201 to $46,257 for police officers
Benefits:	Full federal benefits; overtime available; premium paid for night shifts and Sunday shifts
Tests:	Physical fitness; medical examination; drug test; background check; security clearance check
Academy:	10 weeks at FLETC plus 12 weeks in-house

Mission Statement and Introduction

To provide basic law enforcement and security for the Pentagon and Department of Defense interests in the National Capital Region and to provide protection against the full spectrum of potential threats through robust prevention, preparedness, detection, and response measures.

Formerly the Defense Protective Service (DPS), the Pentagon Force Protection Agency (PFPA) was formed in the aftermath of the September 11th attacks to provide security and protection in the Washington, DC area, including the Pentagon's 280-acre "Reservation," for Pentagon and Defense Department facilities, activities, and interests. The PFPA will ultimately be twice the size in manpower of its predecessor, reflecting the renewed emphasis on security and recognition of terrorist threats since September 11th.

The PFPA includes a police directorate, a chemical/biological/radiological directorate, an antiterrorism/force protection directorate, and a security services directorate. The police directorate has been visibly increased in size, with more than 200 officers added to the police force in 2003. The goal is to add more than 500 uniformed officers to protect the Pentagon and surrounding roadways.

Requirements

A physically demanding job, the police officer position requires that individuals be in very good physical shape, with weight in proportion to height. Candidates must pass medical examinations and a physical fitness test. In addition, you must have at least 20/100 vision that is correctable to 20/20 in each eye and have good hearing.

Career Opportunities

As a PFPA police officer, once you have completed all recruit training and have the required time in that position, there are several specialized positions and assignments with the possibilities of increased salaries, including Field Training officer, K-9 Unit officer, Emergency Response Team officer, and Protective Service Unit officer.

Department of Health and Human Services

National Institutes of Health Police Branch

Al Hinton, Chief
National Institutes of Health
31 Center Drive, MSC 2203
Bethesda, Maryland 20892-2203
Fax: (301) 496-7146
E-mail: careers@box-c.nih.gov

Police branch contact information:

NIH Campus
Building #31, Room B3B17, 31 Center Drive MSC 2012
Bethesda, Maryland 20892-2012
Telephone: (301) 496-5685
Fax: (301) 402-0394

CAREER QUICK FACTS

Minimum age:	21
Maximum age:	37
Education:	Four-year course of study, e.g., in Criminal Justice
or	
Applicable	
equivalent	
experience:	One year
Convictions:	No felony convictions; no domestic violence convictions
Base salary:	According to GS scale and position
Benefits:	Full federal benefits
Tests:	Written exam; medical examination; drug screen; background check
Academy:	Eight weeks at FLETC

Mission Statement

The NIH Police Branch Mission Statement was written with the entire NIH population in mind. It says, "To work in partnership with the citizens of the NIH in providing courteous, competent, and effective delivery of law enforcement service in a manner sensitive to our diverse and multi-cultural community." The Branch's Value Statement sets high standards for all officers in accomplishing the mission by requiring them, " To maintain exemplary personal traits of honesty, morality, self-restraint, courage, obedience to the law, and respect for the rights and liberty of all persons."

Overview

The National Institutes of Health is an agency of the Department of Health and Human Services. It is one of the world's foremost centers for the advancement of health and medical research. The goal of the NIH is to use the information garnered from a wide array of science and research projects to improve the quality of healthy lives and reduce the negative effects of disease, illness, and disability.

The National Institutes of Health was founded in 1887 as the Laboratory of Hygiene. From the very beginning, the NIH has tried to create an environment for researchers that will maximize their abilities to make discoveries and apply knowledge in such ways as will help to improve the health of the entire U.S. population. Protecting the citizenry from disease, enhancing the national scientific research community, and supporting the ideas of accountability and integrity in the scientific community are all part of the National Institutes of Health mission.

National Institutes of Health Police Branch

In 1953, the NIH assumed control of the property that is now the NIH Campus. At that time, security was provided by a uniformed force, but all criminal activities occurring on the campus were investigated by the FBI. At the behest of the Department of Health and Human Services, this security force was transitioned into the NIH Police Branch beginning in 1969. The NIH Police Branch became responsible for all law enforcement activity within its exclusive jurisdiction, the NIH Campus in Bethesda, Maryland.

Like a police officer in any other jurisdiction, the NIH police officer discharges the traditional law enforcement duties. An officer will respond to any emergency situation, conduct investigations, and offer testimony in court. The primary differences are the specificity of the jurisdiction and the specialized nature of the NIH Campus.

Requirements

To qualify for the NIH police officer position, one must be a U.S. citizen with a valid driver's license. The applicant must have at least one year of specialized experience—usually in the law enforcement field or a closely related field—or have completed a four-year course of study at a resident school beyond the high school level. A B.S. degree in Criminal Justice, for instance, would be acceptable.

The applicant must submit to and pass a complete background investigation, drug screen, physical examination, and personal interview. Selected applicants must then pass the eight-week course at the Federal Law Enforcement Training Center in Glynco, Georgia. They must also qualify with issued firearms and maintain that status throughout their time with the NIH Police Branch. Officers typically undergo at least 40 hours of in-service training each year.

Career Opportunities

Opportunities within the Police Branch are available in the following divisions.

General Duties   Full-time security is provided on the NIH Campus. This includes emergency response, foot and vehicle patrols, special-events security, and 24-hour escorts by uniformed police officers.

Investigations   Largely staffed by plainclothes detectives, the Investigations Section of the NIH Police Branch conducts any and all criminal investigations on the campus. The Investigations Section also works in concert with any number of other federal, state, or local agencies.

Traffic Unit   The NIH Police Traffic Unit enforces all traffic laws on the NIH Campus. They employ radar speed detectors and vehicular and bicycle patrols to this end. The Traffic Unit issues citations and tows vehicles, as well.

Canine   The NIH Police maintain a canine unit for the detection of explosives. The highly trained unit has often helped other state and local agencies, also.

Department of Homeland Security

Tom Ridge, Secretary of Homeland Security
Washington, DC 20528
Web site: www.dhs.gov

Mission Statement and Introduction

> *Prevent terrorist attacks within the United States,
> reduce America's vulnerability to terrorism, and minimize the damage
> from potential attacks and natural disasters.*

Formed in the aftermath of September 11th, the Department of Homeland Security is a cabinet-level department made up of all or part of 22 existing federal agencies. Charged with coordinating U.S. efforts in defense of the homeland and in response to disasters, DHS has a combined force of more than 180,000 employees and a budget for 2004 of more than $36 billion, including $11 billion for border security and $6 billion to defend against bioterrorism. In the way it was formed, DHS likens itself to the Department of Defense, which was formed in 1947 through the consolidation of the branches of the armed forces.

Please note the Department of Homeland Security is still evolving. It is a massive endeavor to bring together the agencies and parts of agencies that make up DHS. I have presented the information as it is currently available, but the organization and some facts about DHS may well change in the next few years. Please investigate these agencies on your own if you are interested in a career with DHS.

The agencies now under the DHS are divided into five directorates: Border and Transportation Security, Emergency Preparedness and Response, Science and Technology, Information Analysis and Infrastructure Protection, and Management. These are the missions of the directorates other than Management, along with some primary agencies within each, with law enforcement agencies covered in greater detail in the coming pages.

Border and Transportation Security

This agency includes major border security and transportation operations of Immigration and Naturalization Service, U.S. Customs Service, and Transportation Security Administration (TSA).

TSA is responsible for the security of civil aviation, maritime, railroad, and other modes of transportation. One of TSA's main responsibilities is security at U.S. airports. Since the formation of DHS, TSA has become a high-profile agency, as airport security has become an issue of paramount importance. TSA agents investigate suspicious luggage and parcels and may detain passengers for questioning and/or prevent them from boarding an airplane. They do so with an emphasis on safety while endeavoring not to impede the flow of travelers.

Although the Federal Air Marshal Service was within the TSA, it was transferred to DHS's Bureau of Customs and Immigration Enforcement (ICE) in November of 2003. This is part of the evolution of DHS, as mentioned earlier. Information about the air marshals and ICE is in the coming pages.

TSA has a National Explosives Detection Canine Program to detect explosive devices within the U.S. transportation system, and to deter the same from entering it and endangering us. They investigate suspicious packages, as well as areas identified in bomb threats or where an explosive is suspected. The TSA also has an Explosives Unit to immediately deploy assistance on a national level in any explosives situation related to modes of transportation. The Explosives Unit helps plan countermeasures and investigate blasts when they occur.

An initiative of TSA concurrent with the establishment of DHS and evolving since then is the Federal Flight Deck Officer Program. This program requires that the TSA train selected volunteer passenger and cargo air carrier pilots and other flight-crew members to defend their flight decks. Federal flight deck officers (FFDOs) are deputized for five years unless suspension or revocation is deemed necessary sooner. FFDOs are federal law enforcement officers for the limited purposes of carrying firearms and using force, including lethal force, as trained to defend the flight deck of an aircraft from piracy or criminal violence. They are not given arrest authority, nor can they execute warrants.

Another initiative is the Computer Assisted Passenger Prescreening System (CAPPS II) program, which is not yet implemented as of this writing, pending testing and the meeting of congressional requirements. In short, it will prescreen passengers, authenticate their identities, and perform risk assessments on those who may pose a terrorist threat and/or those for whom there are outstanding state or federal warrants for violent crimes. Law enforcement officers will be notified when a passenger raises such a red flag.

Emergency Preparedness and Response

This agency includes domestic disaster preparedness training and government disaster response coordination of the Federal Emergency Management Agency (FEMA).

FEMA gained attention for its efforts following the attacks of September 11, 2001. Prior to that, the agency was well known mostly to the citizens and communities its efforts had benefited.

FEMA, headquartered in Washington, DC, offers emergency management services to communities throughout the country. FEMA partners its efforts with state and local management agencies, other federal agencies, and the American Red Cross.

Among the many functions FEMA performs are

- Helping Americans prepare for natural disasters, through planning, training, exercises, and information and preparedness programs;
- Responding to disasters, mobilizing immediately upon request from state and local government to provide equipment, get citizens out of danger, provide food and water, provide medical services and temporary shelter, and provide financial resources;
- Assisting in disaster recovery, including rebuilding efforts in infrastructure and essential services for communities and individual financial and emergency housing assistance for citizens;

- Mitigating the effects of disasters, including management of the National Flood Insurance Program and initiatives for structural integrity in floodplains, along fault lines, in tornado zones, and in coastal areas subject to hurricanes; and
- Reducing the risk of loss by helping prevent those disasters, like fires, when they can be prevented.

Science and Technology

This agency includes utilization of all scientific and technological advantages when securing the homeland (Countermeasures Programs).

Information Analysis and Infrastructure Protection

This agency includes analysis and evaluation of intelligence and information from other agencies (including the CIA, FBI, DEA, and NSA) involving threats to homeland security and vulnerabilities in the nation's infrastructure (National Communications System).

The Secret Service and the Coast Guard, as well as the Federal Law Enforcement Training Center (FLETC), are also now within the Department of Homeland Security.

Department of Homeland Security

Federal Law Enforcement Training Center

Connie L. Patrick, Director
Multiple facilities

Mission Statement

> To serve as the Federal government's leader for and provider of world-class law enforcement training. We prepare new and experienced law enforcement professionals to fulfill their responsibilities in a safe manner and at the highest level of proficiency.
>
> We also ensure that training is provided in the most cost-effective manner by taking advantage of economies of scale available only from a consolidated law enforcement training organization.

Overview

An overview of the Federal Law Enforcement Training Center (FLETC) is useful, as so many agencies use the facility and its curriculum to train their officers. FLETC is an interagency law enforcement training center and organization, and it is the largest law enforcement training center in the United States. FLETC is responsible for the training of most federal agents, with more than 75 federal law enforcement agencies, including the U.S. Secret Service and Marshals Service, training their officers at FLETC. In addition, a great many local, state, and even some international agencies utilize the facility. About 50,000 individuals graduate from FLETC each year.

To accomplish consistency in training and skills across federal agencies, training as many agents as possible in the same manner and in the same facility makes good sense, and it is cost-effective as well. Training with new or experienced individuals from other agencies gives trainees great exposure to what the other agencies do, which opens their horizons and helps them understand how best to cooperate with those other agencies. Agencies have input via curriculum and policy reviews, and shape the mission of FLETC by their needs and observations.

Brief History

The need for FLETC became clear in the late 1960s and early 1970s. The extent and quality of training had historically differed from agency to agency, and it became clear that agencies were spending money building and outfitting facilities that were, in a sense, redundant. It became apparent that the federal government could better spend that money in making a joint facility that was world-class, with up-to-date technology, quality instructors, and a curriculum that would guarantee consistent preparedness among federal agents trained there.

Curriculum: Basic Training

One of the main functions of FLETC is to provide basic training to law enforcement officers. There are three primary programs within basic training: Criminal Investigator Training Program (CITP), the Land Management Training Program (LMTP), and the Mixed Basic Police Training Program (MBPTP).

CITP is appropriate for most federal agents. LMTP is designed for individuals in agencies with expansive land-based governance, like the National Park Service. MBPTP is designed for officers of security agencies, like the U.S. Secret Service.

You might imagine training at FLETC to be a lot of gun-shooting and obstacle-course running. That happens, and both are important. But there is a great deal of classroom instruction and simulation exercises reinforcing and testing the student's grasp of that classroom instruction.

In basic training and advanced training, there are more than 100 agency-specific programs, including the Bureau of Prisons Basic Training and the U.S. Customs Service Undercover Operatives School.

Curriculum: Agency-Specific Training

Upon completion of basic training at FLETC, many new agents will go on to add-on programs specifically designed by and with their agency. For example, after the nine-week Basic Criminal Investigator's course, agents of the Department of the Navy's Naval Criminal Investigative Service (NCIS) undergo six weeks of NCIS-specific training.

Curriculum: Areas of Instruction

Training at FLETC includes, but is not limited to, five main areas of instruction: Behavioral Science, Firearms, Driver Education, Physical Techniques, and Legal Instruction. There are also many specialized areas of instruction offered to specific agencies.

There is advanced training offered in areas including Law Enforcement Photography, Wildfire Investigation, and Antiterrorism Management, as well as Physical Security Management.

Training for State and Local Officers

Part of FLETC is the National Center for State and Local Law Enforcement Training, which trains officers from state and local law enforcement agencies in areas for which training does not exist in their own facilities. Trainees get the benefit of federal expertise and quality instruction. Such areas of instruction include, but are not limited to, Crisis Management, Fraud and Financial Investigations, Explosives Investigative Techniques, and Environmental Crimes.

Training for International Agents

The International Programs Division of FLETC offers training to officers of foreign law enforcement agencies. This serves two purposes: It helps those agencies fight crime on their own soil, and it helps protect American interests on that soil as well. There are three main areas of instruction: the U.S. government's Law and Democracy Program, the Antiterrorism Assistance (ATA) Program, and the International Law Enforcement Academy (ILEA), with operations around the world.

Facilities

FLETC's main facility is a city (Glynco, Georgia) unto itself—much like a military base. In fact, FLETC's Glynco campus covers about 1,500 acres near Georgia's Atlantic coast, at the site of the former Glynco Naval Air Station. Glynco features classrooms, computer centers, residence halls, firearms ranges, a driver training center, physical training facilities, a library, laboratories, and a 34-building complex for practical exercises. There are tennis courts, swimming pools, basketball courts, and many other recreational facilities. Glynco is so large and inclusive it has a post office, a bank, and a convenience store.

There are also locations in Artesia, New Mexico, and Cheltenham, Maryland, and a satellite training center for border agents in Charleston, South Carolina. The Office of Artesia Operations provides advanced training for border and immigration officers, and the Bureau of Indian Affairs Indian Police Academy is located there. The Cheltenham complex, formerly the Naval Communications Detachment facility, is primarily for firearms and automotive operations retraining for federal agents, especially those in the Washington, DC area, and training of the U.S. Capitol Police. The Charleston satellite facility, at the former Charleston Naval Base, is being used temporarily to accommodate overflow that occurred as a result of increased recruitment mandated by the President and Congress.

Department Of Homeland Security

Customs and Border Protection

Robert C. Bonner, Commissioner of Customs
CBP Headquarters
1300 Pennsylvania Ave. NW
Washington, DC 20229
Quality Recruitment Hotline: (202) 927-3955
Web site: www.cbp.gov/xp/cgov/careers/

CAREER QUICK FACTS

Minimum age:	21
Maximum age:	37
Education:	Four years of college (in some cases, a college degree) or three years of work experience or a combination thereof (requirements increase per GS level)
Base salary:	According to GS and position plus possible 25 percent on top of base salary (Law Enforcement Availability Pay, or LEAP)
Benefits:	Full federal benefits
Tests:	Written and medical exams; background check; drug screen
Academy:	According to position (i.e., 17 weeks for special agents)

Mission Statement

The priority mission of CBP is to prevent terrorists and terrorist weapons from entering the United States. CBP also is responsible for appre-hending individuals attempting to enter the United States illegally, stemming the flow of illegal drugs and other contraband; protecting our agricultural and economic interests from harmful pests and diseases; protecting American businesses from theft of their intellectual property; and regulating and facilitating international trade, collecting import duties, and enforcing U.S. trade laws.

Overview

In March of 2003, Customs and Border Protection was officially established as the single, unified border agency of the United States. Remember, the United States borders are land, sea, and air, and include the Atlantic and Pacific coasts, the land borders with Mexico and Canada, and the borders around our peninsular and island states and territories.

Part of the newly established Department of Homeland Security, CBP has a workforce of more than 40,000 employees combined from the Department of Agriculture, the Immigration and Naturalization Service, the Border Patrol, and the U.S. Customs Service. The goal of unifying all these employees, including Border Patrol agents, inspectors, and support staff, with their various responsibilities, under one agency was to improve the way the U.S. borders are managed by the government. As a result, instead of four agencies under three departments overseeing U.S. borders, one agency within one department handles that job. So every individual crossing U.S. borders is met with a unified set of rules and enforcement procedures.

CBP states a unified goal for itself: to facilitate legitimate trade and travel while utilizing all of the resources at our disposal to protect and defend the United States from those who would do its population harm. To achieve this goal, CBP employs several strategies, including improving the gathering of intelligence about people and materials (including illegal drugs) coming into the United States, using advanced technology and increased staff to secure the borders, and working with other governments (which includes the placement of CBP agents at foreign ports), other U.S. government agencies, and the private sector to accomplish its goal.

The men and women of Customs and Border Protection are committed to a critical mission, dedicated to keeping America safe, and proud to serve their country with integrity and honor.

Requirements

Entry-level positions at GS-5 require four years of college or three years of work experience or a combination thereof. For GS-7 positions, academic honors, some graduate school, or law enforcement experience is helpful in satisfying the requirements. For the position of criminal investigator (special agent), a college degree is required. Among the recommended majors for those interested in special agent positions are criminal justice, international finance, and computer science.

The first step, once you've decided which position you're interested in and found out there are vacancies, is to obtain an application by calling the Quality Recruitment Hotline at 202-927-3955. Complete the application carefully and submit all requested materials in a timely manner. For example, CBP has strict requirements pertaining to your medical condition and will require a medical exam. They will want medical records from your doctor, and you should be vigilant in making sure these records are sent by your doctor, or just obtain and send them yourself.

Note: The process, from application to hiring, can take about eight months, so be sure to plan ahead. Begin applying while you are still in school, or employed at another job. Throughout the process, you may contact the Quality Recruitment Hotline with questions about your status and to obtain information about the next steps for you to take.

Career Opportunities

Two main law enforcement positions with CBP are canine enforcement officer (CEO) and criminal investigator (special agent).

Canine Enforcement Officer   Dogs are important personnel in the fight to keep illegal drugs out of this country. A canine enforcement officer works with a drug-detector dog to find narcotics en route to the United States in cars, mail parcels, luggage, and other places.

CEO is not by any means an easy position. There are endless hours on your feet, there is often a great deal of strenuous work—when searching through heavy cargo, for instance—and you must always be ready to make quick decisions.

Fifteen weeks of law enforcement and canine-handling training are required to become a CEO. In addition, CEOs are required to undergo firearms training and are regularly tested with their firearms.

Criminal Investigator (Special Agent)   As a special agent for CBP, your mission will include investigating trade fraud, money laundering, illegal drug and weapons trafficking, child pornography, and smuggling via the Internet (cyber-smuggling). The criminals could be money launderers, drug dealers, or even terrorists. There are more than 400 laws actively enforced by CBP, and a special agent must understand these laws and be 100 percent devoted to their enforcement.

Often, crimes investigated by CBP are planned and carried out by a network of criminals. Therefore, as a special agent you will not be going after just the individual who may be caught with contraband— you will be going after his or her network. The mantra: Disrupt and dismantle criminal organizations. Not an easy job, and not one with a lot of instant gratification. Mental clarity, self-motivation, integrity, accountability, problem-solving ability, patience, and dedication are qualities that would suggest you as a good candidate for special agent.

The requirements for special agents are somewhat stricter than for other positions. Candidates must have a college degree, for instance, and are required to undergo about 17 weeks of specialized training at FLETC

Getting Started Early

If you are between 14 and 21 (and if you are, I congratulate you on getting started early), you might be interested in the CBP's Explorer Program. The Explorer Program seeks to build character, good citizenship, and fitness for young people while exposing them to careers that protect the U.S. borders. Participants receive training in law enforcement and criminal justice, as well as on-the-job experience.

Some examples of activities participants take part in are processing passengers at airports, observing surveillance operations, and observing searches.

The requirements are that you must be in high school or college with at least a "C" average and you must obtain permission from your parents. It goes without saying you should have an interest in law enforcement careers. As an explorer, you may discover that a career with CBP is just what you want—or you may decide it is not. Either way, you will have gained valuable experience and knowledge that will prepare you for other careers, in law enforcement or in other areas.

After a year, participants in the Explorer Program may go on to the Explorer Academy. Though it lasts less than two weeks, the academy provides real training that can prepare you for a career in law enforcement. Focusing on laws, history, values, and enforcement techniques, instructors take candidates who are not yet age-eligible for most law enforcement careers and give them a head start on qualifying when they are of age.

Department of Homeland Security

U.S. Immigration and Customs Enforcement

Michael J. Garcia, Assistant Secretary
425 I Street
Washington, DC 20536
Telephone: (800) 944-7725
Web site: www.ice.gov/graphics/careers/index.htm
Job listings: www.usajobs.gov

CAREER QUICK FACTS

Minimum age:	21
Maximum age:	37
Education:	Four-year college degree or equivalent experience
Criminal record:	No felony convictions; no misdemeanor conviction of domestic violence; any prior convictions may prevent acceptance
Base salary:	GS-5 with 25 percent on top of base salary (Law Enforcement Availability Pay, or LEAP)
Benefit:	Full federal benefits
Academy:	Four to five months

Mission Statement

As the largest investigative arm of the Department of Homeland Security, U.S. Immigration and Customs Enforcement (ICE) brings a unified and coordinated focus to the enforcement of federal immigration laws, customs laws, and, as of November 2003, air security laws. ICE brings to bear all of the considerable resources and authorities invested in it to fulfill its primary mission: to detect vulnerabilities and prevent violations that threaten national security.

ICE works to protect the United States and its people by deterring, interdicting, and investigating threats arising from the movement of people and goods into and out of the United States, and by policing and securing federal government facilities across the nation.

Vision

To be the nation's preeminent law enforcement agency, dedicated to detecting vulnerabilities and preventing violations that threaten national security. Established to combat the criminal and national security threats emergent in a post 9/11 environment, ICE combines a new investigative approach with new resources to provide unparalleled investigation, interdiction, and security services to the public and to our law enforcement partners in the federal and local sectors.

ICE Core Values

Integrity

We will adhere to the highest standards of honesty and conduct.

Courage

We will be accountable for our actions; we will do the right thing even when it is not the easy thing; and we will always fulfill our duties with courage.

Excellence

We will strive for excellence in all things, aspiring to the highest standards of performance, professionalism, and leadership.

Overview

When the Department of Homeland Security was established and the disparate border security agencies were combined under its auspices, U.S. Immigration and Customs Enforcement was formed. The largest investigative bureau within the department, ICE is the result of a combination of resources from the U.S. Customs Service, the Immigration and Naturalization Service, the Federal Protective Service, and the Federal Air Marshals Service. ICE enforces immigration and customs laws, protects certain federal buildings, and performs other national security functions.

ICE is part of the department's Border and Transportation Security Directorate (BTS), which employs more than 100,000 people, of which more than 15,000 work for ICE.

ICE is organized as follows.

Office of Investigations   The Office of Investigations investigates crimes in the following areas, among others:

- Smuggling, of narcotics, contraband, and/or humans
- Fraud and financial crimes, including money laundering
- Child pornography and exploitation
- Immigration crime and immigration fraud
- Human rights violations
- Illegal arms exports.

The office of Investigations also protects segments of the U.S. infrastructure that are potential targets of sabotage or other attacks. There are four divisions within the Office of Investigations. National Security Investigations Division protects national security by preventing acts of terrorism and the import or export of illegal arms. The Financial Investigations Division oversees the investigation of financial crimes, including money laundering, cash smuggling, and counterfeit goods trafficking, working closely with individuals and companies in the financial sector to efficiently and thoroughly investigate such crimes. The Smuggling/Public Safety Division identifies and dismantles criminal organizations that smuggle contraband and human beings into the United States, often in violation of human rights laws, which this division investigates as well. The Investigative Services Division includes several specialized investigative support branches, including the Cyber Branch, specializing in use of the Internet, and the self-explanatory Undercover Branch.

To assist and to cooperate with law enforcement agencies on all levels of government, the Office of Investigations offers two major centralized resources. The Law Enforcement Support Center (LESC) provides immigration and identity information on aliens who are suspected criminals. The Forensic Document Laboratory provides investigative support in the analysis of documents, fingerprints, and other such evidence.

Office of Detention and Removal   This office is responsible for the removal or deportation of illegal aliens in accordance with U.S. immigration law. This office works with the U.S. Customs and Border Protection and the U.S. Citizenship and Immigration Services to identify, detain, and ultimately remove high-risk illegal aliens as necessary and warranted by law. These aliens may include fugitives and individuals in violations of multiple laws in addition to immigration laws.

Subject to a removal proceeding before an immigration judge, aliens may be removed for reasons of health, criminal activity, economic status, risk to national security, and other reasons. When it is determined that an alien must be removed, this office works with the foreign government to coordinate travel and transport, sometimes even escorting the individual.

Among the Office of Detention and Removal's primary programs is Fugitive Operations, which captures and removes aliens who have not complied with removal orders. The ICE's Most Wanted program provides information to the public on those 10 fugitives most wanted by ICE.

Detention is a function of this office as well, with facilities in the United States and Puerto Rico. ICE also will utilize local and state facilities to house detainees.

Office of Federal Air Marshal Service   This department deploys federal air marshals on U.S. flights and in airports to protect passengers and others from potential acts of violence or terrorism targeting air travel. Restoring confidence in the safety of flight is part of their mission. Formerly part of Transportation Security Administration (TSA), the air marshals were brought under the aegis of ICE in November of 2003. ICE FAMS Mission Operations Center (MOC) is located in Herndon, Virginia. Its capabilities were recently enhanced by bringing in the Secret Service as a partner in FAMS efforts.

The Federal Air Marshal Service includes an Explosives Unit, formed from the Aviation Explosives Security Program. This unit can be deployed quickly to investigate suspected explosives on flights and other modes of transportation, to investigate blasts where a bomb is the suspected cause, and to conduct other operations to ensure transportation safety with regard to the threat of explosives. This unit conducts missions for the U.S. government and other governments around the world.

Office of Air and Marine Operations   This department is responsible for protecting the U.S. population and borders from dangerous crimes like smuggling and acts of terrorism. With its air and marine operations working as a double-pronged force, this office also provides support to departments and agencies at all levels of government in similar efforts against smuggling and terrorism. In addition, the Office of Air and Marine Operations develops policy and advises government on regulations concerning air and marine security.

Office of Federal Protective Service   This office polices and secures federal facilities nationwide, of which there are more than 8,800. More than 1 million people either work in, live in, or visit these federal facilities each day. The Office of Federal Protective Service provides uniformed security for these facilities, investigates incidents and emergencies, enforces laws, detains and arrests violators, and provides security during demonstrations or protests and during natural emergencies, including lending its substantial support to the Federal Emergency Management Agency (FEMA).

Among the special programs of this Office are the National Weapons of Mass Destruction (WMD) Program, which responds to threats potentially involving such weapons, and the Hazardous Response

Program, which responds to threats potentially involving chemical, biological, or nuclear weapons.

Office of Intelligence   This department collects, analyzes, and distributes information and data in the interests of national security and public safety. Such information may relate to suspected terrorists, smugglers, money launderers, arms and drug dealers, cybercriminals, and others, either as individuals or as part of larger criminal organizations. The Office of Intelligence shares this information with and gathers information from other departments and agencies on the state, local, and federal level, and beyond.

Career Opportunities

Criminal investigators, or special agents, carry out investigative functions in the preceding operations and initiatives. Special agents may be assigned throughout the country and in 24 countries around the world, in both temporary and long-term tours of duty.

Immigration enforcement agents carry out the enforcement functions for the special agents. Assignments may be in field offices or at correction facilities.

Deportation officers detain and/or deport individuals in close liaison with foreign governments.

Aviation enforcement officers and marine enforcement officers, with extensive training, enforce laws at our borders in airborne and marine operations.

All law enforcement activities are managed by region by Special-Agent-in-Charge (SAC) offices. In addition, there are subordinate Resident Agents-in-Charge field offices. Both are offices to which agents can aspire to rise.

Requirements

Applicants for law enforcement positions within ICE must possess at least a four-year college degree or equivalent work experience. Degrees common to special agents are in criminal justice, foreign languages, computer science, and international finance. Prior law enforcement experience is preferred but not required. ICE emphasizes that it seeks in applicants such intangibles as self-motivation, integrity, honesty, accountability, assertiveness, tenacity, and patience. Other requirements are per position and the Office of Personnel Management.

Training

Special agents and immigration enforcement agents undergo between four and five months of specialized training at FLETC, which houses the ICE Law Enforcement Academy. Further training may be required per position and advancement.

Department of Homeland Security

Office of Inspector General

General Clark Kent Ervin, Inspector General
Washington, DC 20528
Telephone: (202) 254-4100
Web site: www.dhs.gov/dhspublic/display?theme=89

Mission Statement

> *To serve as an independent and objective inspection, audit, and investigative body to promote effectiveness, efficiency, and economy in the Department of Homeland Security's programs and operations, and to prevent and detect fraud, abuse, mismanagement, and waste in such programs and operations.*

Overview

The Office of Inspector General (OIG) is responsible for conducting investigations, inspections, and audits when warranted into various programs and operations of the Department of Homeland Security. The Inspector General is appointed by the President and is subject to Senate confirmation.

OIG polices DHS for waste, fraud, abuse, and mismanagement in any of its programs and initiatives, and recommends improvements. OIG is required to report semiannually to Congress on the activities of DHS. OIG was formerly under the Federal Emergency Management Agency (FEMA), which it continues to oversee, as it does all DHS agencies.

Career Opportunities

Special agents of OIG conduct investigations into crimes such as fraud, theft, bribery, smuggling, and any other violations of laws relevant to the performance of DHS duties by or involving any of its employees, officers, programs, or agencies. Recent cases include the arrest of 19 people, including one individual who worked in a Department of Homeland Security Customs and Border Patrol office, in an automobile export bribery scheme.

Department of Homeland Security

U.S. Secret Service

W. Ralph Basham, Director
U.S. Secret Service
Personnel Division
245 Murray Drive
Building 410
Washington, DC 20223
Telephone: (202) 406-5800
Web site: www.secretservice.gov/opportunities.shtml

CAREER QUICK FACTS

Minimum age:	21
Maximum age:	37
Education:	Special agent: four-year course of college study
or	
Equivalent experience:	Three years (or combination thereof)
Base salary:	According to GS and position
Benefits:	Full federal benefits
Tests:	Written, medical, polygraph exams; drug screen; background check
Academy:	Nine weeks at FLETC

Mission Statement

The United States Secret Service is mandated by statute and executive order to carry out two significant missions: protection and criminal investigations. The Secret Service protects the President and Vice President, their families, heads of state, and other designated individuals; investigates threats against these protectees; protects the White House, Vice

President's Residence, Foreign Missions, and other buildings within Washington, D.C.; and plans and implements security designs for designated National Special Security Events. The Secret Service also investigates violations of laws relating to counterfeiting of obligations and securities of the United States; financial crimes that include, but are not limited to, access device fraud, financial institution fraud, identity theft, computer fraud; and computer-based attacks on our nation's financial, banking, and telecommunications infrastructure.

Vision

Building on a Tradition of Excellence and Meeting the Challenges of the Future.

History

When most people think of the Secret Service, they think of dark suits, earpieces, and the willingness to jump in front of the President in the event of an attempt on his life. There is, however, much more to the Secret Service than this idea alone. Until recently, the Secret Service was a part of the Treasury Department. With the restructuring of several agencies in the wake of the events of September 11th, the Secret Service was made part of the new Department of Homeland Security in 2003. The duties of the Secret Service still reflect its time spent in the Treasury Department, however. In addition to the more familiar duties of protecting the President, Vice President, President-elect, Vice President-elect, and their spouses and children, the Secret Service is designated as the primary agency for the protection of federal financial institutions. This latter duty involves the investigation of the counterfeiting of U.S. currency and the forgery or theft of federal bonds, checks, and securities.

The Secret Service was founded on July 5, 1865. Its initial charge was to investigate the problem of widespread counterfeit currency in the United States. In these first years, the role of the Secret Service in the fledgling federal law enforcement community was expanded to include the authority to investigate any instance of or attempt to defraud the federal government. This broad responsibility saw the service working against the Ku Klux Klan, smugglers, and numerous individuals involved in land and mail fraud. In 1883, the U.S. Secret Service was formally organized as a part of the Treasury Department.

The Secret Service's most well-known duty began with the informal, part-time protection of President Cleveland in 1894. After President McKinley was assassinated in 1901, Congress requested that the Secret Service provide presidential protection, again informally. Two Secret Service agents were assigned to full-time duty at the White House in 1902, and the Secret Service began its protection of the President. Beginning in 1908, the Secret Service started protecting the President-elect as well. It was also in that same year that President Roosevelt used eight Secret Service agents to form a special investigative unit within the Department of Justice. These eight agents were the beginnings of what would come to be the FBI. In 1913, Congress mandated the permanent protection of the President and issued the official authorization for the protection of the President-elect. Four years later, these protective services were expanded to include the President's immediate family. Congress made it a federal violation to threaten the President in 1917. In 1922, President Harding requested the creation of the White House Police Force.

After the 1950 attack on President Truman by Puerto Rican nationalists at the Blair House (during which a White House Police officer was killed), Congress further codified the protection of the President and his family, the President-elect, and the Vice President (at his discretion). In 1961, this protective coverage was extended to include former Presidents and, in 1962, the Vice President and the Vice President-elect were added to this policy of mandatory protection.

Responding to President Kennedy's assassination in 1963, Congress granted protection to Mrs. John F. Kennedy and their children for two years. Congressional authorization for the protection of former Presidents and their spouses for life and their minor children (until they reached age 16) was granted in 1965. After the assassination of Robert F. Kennedy, the duties of the Secret Service expanded to include protecting prominent presidential and vice presidential candidates.

The White House Police Force was renamed the Executive Protective Service in 1970 and was charged with protecting diplomatic missions in Washington, DC. Secret Service protection was granted to visiting dignitaries and heads of state the following year. In 1975, the Executive Protective Service took over the security and protection duties at foreign diplomatic missions throughout the United States and its territories. The Executive Protective Service was renamed the Secret Service Uniformed Division in 1977.

During the 1980s, the fraudulent use of credit and debit cards became a federal crime and the investigative responsibility of the Secret Service. The U.S. Treasury Police were incorporated into the Secret Service Uniformed Division in the decade as well. In 1990, the Secret Service was authorized to conduct any investigations pertaining to federally insured financial institutions as a joint effort with other applicable Department of Justice personnel and agencies. The protective duties and responsibilities of the Secret Service were changed once again, in 1994, to stipulate that Presidents elected after 1997 will receive Secret Service protection for 10 years after the end of their time in office. Also during the 1990s, the Secret Service saw more involvement in the investigation of crimes like telemarketing fraud and identity theft, as Congress passed laws dealing with these issues in the federal forum.

With the passage of the Patriot Act in 2001, the Secret Service was given greater responsibility for combating fraud cases that involve computers. The Secret Service can establish special task forces to assist other law enforcement agencies and members of the private sector with problems arising from computer crimes. Investigating the potential role of financial institutions and practices in terrorist events was also made a major duty of the Secret Service under the Patriot Act. In March of 2003, the U.S. Secret Service was designated as one of the agencies of the new Department of Homeland Security.

Today, the U.S. Secret Service is made up of approximately 2,100 special agents, 1,200 uniformed division officers, and 1,700 various technical and support staff in more than 125 offices. The current director is W. Ralph Basham.

Career Opportunities: Special Agent

The primary arm of the U.S. Secret Service, the special agent operates in both protective and investigative capacities. As with many federal law enforcement positions, the U.S. Secret Service special agent faces a challenging and rewarding career.

Requirements   The applicant must be a U.S. citizen between the ages of 21 and 37 (at time of appointment). A bachelor's degree from an accredited college or university or three years of substantive experience in the field of law enforcement or criminal investigation is required. Certain combinations of education and experience may be accepted as well.

Uncorrected vision not worse than 20/60 (binocular), corrected to 20/20 in each eye is a minimum. Corrective eye surgeries are acceptable if the applicant passes specific visual tests one year after the surgery in question (three months in the case of Lasik surgeries). A medical exam, a drug screen, and a polygraph are all required. The applicant must pass the Treasury Enforcement Agent Examination or the U.S. Marshals Enforcement Examination (both written tests) and an interview also.

Frequent travel, reassignment, and transfer throughout the United States and foreign countries must be accepted as part of this position. Special agents are often required to travel with protectees. Undercover assignments are also understood to be part of the position.

Training   U.S. Secret Service special agents undergo training in the Criminal Investigator Training Program (CITP), a nine-week course, at the Federal Law Enforcement Training Center (FLETC) in Glynco, Georgia, or Artesia, New Mexico. This is followed by the Special Agent Training Course, another 11 weeks of agency training at the Secret Service Training Academy in Maryland. In addition to the physical fitness, firearms, and personal defense programs, special agents are trained in investigative procedures pertinent to the agency's goals: Banking, telecommunications fraud, and financial institution fraud are just a few examples of some of the areas in which an agent may train. Special agents in the Secret Service also experience ongoing training opportunities over the course of their careers, from simulations and requalifications to updating their training with new information or techniques.

Career Opportunities: Secret Service Uniformed Division

The Secret Service Uniformed Division is a security force that provides protection for the White House Complex, the Main Treasury Building and Annex, and other presidential offices. The President (and his family), the Vice President (and his family), and foreign diplomatic missions in the Washington, DC area are the primary protectees of the Secret Service Uniformed Division. Like any protective or police force, the Uniformed Division is divided into various specialties: foot patrols, canine units, and countersnipers being but a few.

Requirements To be considered for a position with the Secret Service Uniformed Division the applicant must be a U.S. citizen between the ages of 21 and 37 (upon appointment). A high school diploma is required, but many of the officers have college degrees as well. The applicant must pass a written test, background check, and an in-depth interview. A polygraph, drug screen, and physical examination are all required and must be passed. The applicant's vision must be 20/60 (binocular) correctable to 20/20 in each eye.

Training The new Secret Service uniformed division officer will follow a rigorous training course at the Federal Law Enforcement Training Center (FLETC) in Glynco, Georgia, followed by more specific training at the Secret Service Training Academy in Maryland. The training consists of firearm and self-defense instruction as well as psychology and situational logic programs. The job will likely require relocation to the Washington, DC area.

Career Opportunities: Technical Positions

As is the case with other federal law enforcement agencies, the U.S. Secret Service has an important need for talented men and women with a wide variety of skills and aptitudes. The technical positions in the Secret Service include computer experts, engineers, photographers, various analysts, fingerprint specialists, and telecommunications experts, among others.

These positions require the necessary experience in the respective field, or in many cases, a college degree in the field in question. Travel may be required based on the position. Anyone interested in applying his or her specific technical talents to one of the Secret Service's missions must be a U.S. citizen, pass a drug screen, and (depending on the position) pass a polygraph examination.

Career Opportunities: Professional and Administrative Positions

Professional positions with the U.S. Secret Service may mean any number of jobs, such as accountant, architect, engineer, psychologist, nurse, analyst, or contracts specialist. As with the technical positions in the preceding section, these roles typically require specific education or work experience equivalent to a bachelor's degree or higher.

Administrative positions in the Secret Service can range from personnel managers to facilities management specialists. These positions don't require a specialized background, but they do typically require the knowledge and skills that can be obtained through college education or several years of progressively responsible experience.

Anyone hoping to fill a professional or administrative position with the U.S. Secret Service must pass a drug screen, submit to a polygraph, and be a citizen of the United States.

Department of the Interior

National Park Service

Frances P. Mainella, Director
U.S. Park Police
United States Park Police Personnel Office
1100 Ohio Drive SW
Washington, DC 20242
Telephone: (202) 619-7056
Web site: www.nps.gov/uspp

National Park Service, Division of Ranger Activities
1849 C Street NW
Washington, DC 20240
Telephone: (202) 208-6843
Web site: www.nps.gov

Mission Statement

The National Park Service preserves unimpaired the natural and cultural resources and values of the national park system for the enjoyment, education, and inspiration of this and future generations. The Park Service cooperates with partners to extend the benefits of natural and cultural resource conservation and outdoor recreation throughout this country and the world.

History and Overview

In 1872, Congress designated Yellowstone National Park as the first national park. Responsibility for the newly created park was assigned to the secretary of the interior. Various parks and protected monuments were assigned to different federal agencies and bureaus as they were designated over the next few decades. Legislators and citizens both began to realize the importance of preserving these areas for future generations, and the need to organize their administration under one agency became clear. To that end, the National Park Service was created in 1916 when then-President Woodrow Wilson signed an act creating a new bureau within the Department of the Interior to protect the national parks and monuments.

The National Park Service still follows this original mandate and has expanded its efforts to include increased roles in cultural preservation and global advocacy for environmental efforts in many forms.

The vast National Park System spans more than 83 million acres in 49 states and many U.S. territories. Each protected area is determined by Congress, but the President can designate national monuments on lands that are already under federal jurisdiction.

The National Park Service has two major arms with law enforcement responsibilities, the United States Park Police and the Park Rangers.

United States Park Police

Originally called Park Watchmen when they were created by George Washington in 1791, the United States Park Police (USPP) are the oldest uniformed federal law enforcement agency. They were founded to maintain order and perform any other necessary duties in the parks and public areas of Washington, DC. In 1882, they were given the same authority as the city's Metropolitan Police. In 1919, Congress changed the name of the Park Watchmen to United States Park Police.

The Park Police saw the beginnings of jurisdictional expansion when, between 1928 and 1930, officers were assigned to the newly constructed Mount Vernon and George Washington Memorial Highways. This authority was defined by Congress in 1948 as being specific to the federally controlled lands in Washington, DC and the surrounding counties of Maryland and Virginia. Newly established areas such as Gateway National Recreation Area in New York City and Golden Gate National Recreation Area in San Francisco clouded jurisdictional boundaries, and in 1976, the USPP authority was clearly defined by Congress as extending to all areas within the National Park System.

The U.S. Park Police defines its primary duty as protecting lives, though the scope of its responsibilities mirrors that of any major urban police department. Investigating crimes of all sorts, offering emergency aid, making arrests, and serving in a crowd control capacity are just some of the duties that the U.S. Park Police carry out on a daily basis. The majority of USPP officers operate out of the Washington, DC area, where all new hires are first assigned. Officers can be sent to any site within the National Park System temporarily, but they typically operate out of the urban offices such as San Francisco or New York City.

Following are the United States Park Police divisions and their organization.

Patrol Branch   USPP officers mainly patrol the Washington, DC metropolitan area.

- **Horse Mounted Unit.** Established in 1934, the Horse Mounted Unit has, in addition to its regular enforcement and protection duties, provided training to the military and other federal law enforcement agencies.

Criminal Investigations Branch

- **Major Crimes.** Officers of the Major Crimes division are stationed in all jurisdictions. They investigate all serious incidents, such as death or sexual assault.
- **Identification.** Identification officers document crime scenes and record and maintain all seized drugs.
- **Special Investigations.** These officers maintain intelligence and serve as the liaisons with other federal law enforcement agencies. They also handle all youthful offenders.
- **Narcotics and Vice.** USPP Narcotics and Vice officers are stationed primarily in Washington, DC and the surrounding areas, where they seek to eradicate drug trafficking on federally controlled lands.
- **Asset Forfeiture.** This division handles all assets confiscated or forfeited as part of criminal activity in USPP jurisdiction.

Special Forces Branch

- SWAT team
- Motorcycle Unit
- Aviation Unit
- Canine Unit
- Special Events Unit
- Community Relations Unit

The Special Forces Branch officers all have highly specialized training in keeping with the skills needed for any of the preceding duties. These officers often work closely with the Secret Service and other federal law enforcement organizations to protect the President, Vice President, and other heads of state, and to secure the areas in which public appearances by these figures are to take place.

Requirements

Jobs with the U.S. Park Police are administered by the Office of Personnel Management in Washington, DC. Those interested in USPP jobs should check with the OPM periodically to see when USPP testing is being offered.

Applicants must be U.S. citizens between the ages of 21 and 31 in possession of (or able to obtain) a valid driver's license. Vision of 20/100 correctable to 20/20 with glasses or contacts is necessary, as is a high school diploma. Two years of education beyond high school, two years of honorable active duty military service, or two years of progressively more responsible work experience is required. Certain combinations of education and work experience may also be qualifying.

The U.S. Park Police values initiative, responsibility, social and communication skills, adaptability, and maturity in candidates for the police officer position. Physical strength and endurance are both necessary to carry out the potentially exacting duties that a U.S. Park Police officer may face.

All applicants must first take a three-part written test administered by the OPM. The test involves name and number recognition, reading comprehension, and mathematical reasoning. A full background check will be conducted on each applicant. Each candidate must successfully complete an oral interview before a panel of U.S. Park Police officers.

The physical tests that must be passed include the following:

- Body Composition
- Body Weight Pushed Standard (chest press)
- Trunk Flexion Standards
- Agility Run Standards
- 1.5-Mile Run Standard

If hired, the new U.S. Park Police officer recruit must complete all required training. All successful candidates are hired on a one-year probationary basis.

Park Rangers

The duties of a park ranger are almost unparalleled in their scope. While most park rangers wear uniforms and enforce laws, they also must be prepared to serve in very important administrative capacities. They manage parks, oversee the use of park resources, prevent and control forest fires, lead tours, operate campgrounds, and perform search-and-rescue missions. They also enforce federal laws and park regulations, carry firearms, conduct criminal investigations, and apprehend violators.

Park rangers work at park sites throughout the United States. A love for the outdoors is important for a park ranger, but managerial tasks and other indoor duties are also a part of the job.

Requirements

A candidate may apply for vacant park ranger positions through the Office of Personnel Management Administrative Careers with America Program under Group VI, Law Enforcement.

The applicant must be a U.S. citizen and cannot have reached his or her 37th birthday. To qualify at the GS-5 level, a bachelor's degree from an accredited institution or one year of specialized experience is required. Degrees with major study in the fields of natural resource management, natural sciences, history, archaeology, anthropology, park and recreation management, law enforcement, or another discipline that would prepare the candidate for the protection of natural and cultural resources is required. Specialized experience that is qualifying includes time spent at a position equivalent to GS-4 federal service in the areas of fish and wildlife management, as a park guide or a tour leader, or in law enforcement. In certain cases, a combination of education and experience can be qualifying.

At the GS-7 level, the applicant must meet the preceding qualifications, as well as demonstrate Superior Academic Achievement (SAA), have completed one full year of graduate level study, or have at least one year of experience (as defined previously) equivalent to the GS-5 level in federal service. Superior Academic Achievement is defined by a GPA of 3.0 or higher on a 4.0 scale, graduation in the upper third of one's class or major subdivision, or membership in a nationally recognized scholastic honor society (freshman honor societies excluded). Graduate study should be in one of the related fields mentioned. Again, certain combinations of experience and education requirements may suffice.

The applicant must pass a preemployment medical examination, a drug screen, and a background investigation.

Training

Newly hired rangers receive a great deal of site-specific training, but it is often supplemented by other courses. The Horace M. Albright Training Center at Grand Canyon National Park, Arizona, or the Stephen T. Mather Training Center at Harpers Ferry, West Virginia, provide training for duties that are specific to the National Park Service.

Department of Justice

Bureau of Alcohol, Tobacco, Firearms and Explosives

Edgar Domenech, Acting Director
Personnel Division
Employment Branch
650 Massachusetts Avenue NW, Room 4100
Washington, DC 20226
Telephone: (202) 927-8610
or (202) 927-5690—agent applicants only
Web site: www.atf.gov/jobs/index.htm

CAREER QUICK FACTS

Minimum age:	21
Maximum age:	37
Education: or	Four years of college (in some cases, a college degree)
Equivalent experience:	Three years of work experience or a combination thereof (requirements increase per GS level)
Base salary:	According to GS and position plus possible 25 percent on top of base salary (Law Enforcement Availability Pay, or LEAP)
Benefits:	Full federal benefits
Tests:	Written, physical fitness, medical, polygraph exams; background check; drug screen
Academy:	According to position

Mission Statement

The Bureau of Alcohol, Tobacco, Firearms and Explosives (ATF) is a law enforcement organization within the United States Department of Justice with unique responsibilities dedicated to reducing violent crime and protecting the public.

Vision

> *Working for a Sound and Safer America . . . Through Innovation and Partnerships*
>
> *The Bureau of Alcohol, Tobacco, Firearms and Explosives (ATF) must respond to the public outcry against crime, violence, and other threats to public safety. We must also continue to do our part to maintain the economic stability of the country. Our vision will help us chart the course to change the way we serve the public and achieve new levels of effectiveness and teamwork.*

> "More than ever, the success or failure of a Federal agency will be determined by the value it brings to the American public. If we continue to become a better, faster, and more effective organization, ATF will thrive and the American public will benefit."
>
> **—Bradley A. Buckles, December 1999**

History

The U.S. Bureau of Alcohol, Tobacco, Firearms and Explosives (ATF) is, relative to some of the other federal agencies covered in this book, a young agency. Created as a splinter from the Internal Revenue Service in July of 1972, the ATF is charged with the tax-collecting duties of the U.S. Department of the Treasury, including enforcement and regulatory action.

Though taxation has long been an issue of debate, particularly in this country (it having been one of the central motivating forces behind the open rebellion that gave birth to the United States), the establishment of taxes on imported spirits in 1789 marked the beginning of this practice under the new, independent government. Beginning in 1862, the Treasury Department, which had been initially responsible for the collection of taxes and the enforcement of tax laws, was supported by the newly created Internal Revenue Service. It wasn't long before the need for an investigative component was filled by the hiring of detectives, attorneys, and even laboratory staff.

The Bureau of Internal Revenue (as it was then called) experienced a massive increase in its duties with the passage of the Volstead Prohibition Act of 1919. The Prohibition Unit was formed the following year and was to weather a rocky and bureaucratically winding path before the ultimate repeal of Prohibition in 1933. To steer the country through the transition from Prohibition status to the legal production and sale of alcohol, several agencies arose that have since been dissolved, as their primary functions became unnecessary, or incorporated into other agencies. By 1940, the Alcohol Tax Unit (ATU) had merged with the Federal Alcohol Administration (FAA), for example.

Following the passage of two Firearms Acts in the 1930s, the Miscellaneous Tax Unit of the Bureau of Internal Revenue sought to handle the fee-related aspects of these laws. The enforcement of the laws was the responsibility of the ATU. In 1952, these duties were consolidated into the mandate of the Alcohol Tax Unit, along with tobacco tax responsibilities. A steady passage of laws and restructuring of internal responsibilities throughout the 1960s (including passage of the Gun Control Act in 1968) culminated with the formation of the Alcohol, Tobacco and Firearms division of the Internal Revenue Service. In 1970, explosives responsibilities were given to the ATF as part of the Organized Crime Control Act.

As the functions of the ATF evolved away from the daily operations of the Internal Revenue Service, the Treasury Department defined it as a discrete agency: the U.S. Bureau of Alcohol, Tobacco and Firearms. The ATF added arson to its growing responsibilities in 1982, when the Anti-Arson Act defined certain forms of arson as federal crimes. In January of 2003, the ATF's law enforcement functions were transferred to the Department of Justice (DOJ), and the ATF became the Bureau of Alcohol, Tobacco, Firearms and Explosives.

Career Opportunities: Criminal Investigator (Special Agent)

When most people think of the ATF, the first position that comes to mind is the criminal investigator (special agent). These agents are responsible for directly enforcing federal laws assigned to the ATF's jurisdiction. Surveillance, participating in raids, interviewing suspects and witnesses, making arrests, obtaining search warrants, and searching for physical evidence are just some of the important tasks performed in the daily work of ATF agents. Agents are also expected to generate case reports and testify in court or before grand juries.

Requirements   To become an ATF criminal investigator (special agent), one must be a U.S. citizen between the ages of 21 and 37 (at the time of appointment) in possession of a valid driver's license. The applicant must fill out the ATF questionnaire, take and pass the Treasury Enforcement Agent Examination, complete a field panel review (including a writing sample), pass polygraph and background examinations, and pass a medical examination. The applicant must remain in compliance with the ATF drug policy, as well.

Because certain felony convictions (and some misdemeanors) prohibit the possession of a firearm or ammunition, applicants who have been convicted of these offenses will not be eligible for the position of criminal investigator (special agent).

The applicant will undergo the following physical tests: the 1.5-mile run, the bench press, and the agility run. The successful candidate must achieve a rating of 25 percent, or higher in each of these categories. These tests are administered at the Federal Law Enforcement Training Center (FLETC) in Glynco, Georgia.

Educational requirements for Grade-5 agents are a bachelor's degree from an accredited college or university or three years of general experience in the investigative or law enforcement fields (preferably with increasing responsibility). A combination of work experience and education is acceptable and 30 semester hours (or 45 quarter hours) are equivalent to nine months of work experience.

For Grade-7 qualifiers, all of the above qualifications must be met with the addition of proof of Superior Academic Achievement (SAA). Superior Academic Achievement is defined by a rank in the upper third of the candidate's graduating class, a minimum grade point average (GPA) of 2.95 out of 4.0 over four years of education or in the final two years of the curriculum, a major GPA (in courses directly related to the candidate's field of study) of 3.5 or higher, or membership in a nationally recognized honor society. Also acceptable for the GS-7 position is the completion of one year of graduate study or one full year of specialized experience in a field related to the investigation of criminal violations.

The Grade-9 position requires that the applicant meet all of the previous qualifications and have attained a postgraduate degree or have two years of progressively higher-level graduate education. One full year of specialized experience, at least equivalent to the GS-7-level requirements, will also suffice.

Career Opportunities: Inspector

Though perhaps less glamorous than the criminal investigator, the ATF inspector performs many of the agency's regulatory duties. By examining the records and inventories of firearms dealers, alcoholic beverage producers, and explosives businesses, the inspectors generate a great deal of information that initiates or supports other investigations. The role of the inspector as a deterrent to crime is not to be overlooked, either.

While inspectors spend much of their time verifying that tax records and activities are in order for the businesses subject to ATF jurisdiction, they also help to ensure that the markets in question are free of practices restricting free trade or competition. Helping to verify that new entrants into these markets meet the regulatory requirements and educating the firearms industry on the best ways to prevent improper sales and identify trafficking are further duties of the ATF inspectors.

Requirements   Like the criminal investigator (special agent) position, the inspector position is divided into three potential entry levels: GS-5, GS-7, and GS-9. To qualify for consideration as Grade-5, the candidate must demonstrate three years of progressive general experience (experience that involves analyzing and solving problem, organizing work, and strong oral and written communication skills), hold a four-year degree from an accredited college or university, or present a combination of education and experience similar to the one mentioned for the criminal investigator.

Grade-7 qualifications are similar, except that the applicant must demonstrate specialized experience instead of the generalized experience mentioned for the GS-5 position. Specialized experience is defined as work in which the candidate will have gained specific knowledge or skills in an area that would help him or her perform the duties of the ATF inspector. Knowledge of and experience with the federal laws regarding alcohol production, transportation, and sale would be acceptable, as would auditing or accounting experience, as just two examples. The completion of one full year of graduate study or the demonstration of Superior Academic Achievement (SSA) (see definition in the Criminal Investigator section) will qualify the candidate for Grade-7 entry.

Grade-9 determinations may be made if the candidate holds a graduate degree, has successfully completed two progressive years of graduate education, or has specialized experience at least equivalent to that required at the GS-7 level.

Career Opportunities: Other Positions
The ATF, like most of the other federal agencies covered in this book, has any number of openings available to people with the special skills required to help the agency enforce federal laws in an increasingly high-tech world. The ATF maintains some of the most advanced laboratories in the world—particularly in the areas of ballistics, explosives, and fire debris. Additionally, much of the work requires knowledge of accounting or the law. These are just a few examples of areas in which the ATF has a need for qualified and dedicated people.

Department of Justice

Drug Enforcement Agency

Karen Tandy, Administrator
Drug Enforcement Headquarters
Special Agent Recruitment
Drug Enforcement Administration
700 Army Navy Drive
Arlington, Virginia 22202
Telephone: (800) DEA-4288
Web site: www.dea.gov

CAREER QUICK FACTS

Minimum age:	21
Maximum age:	37
Education:	Special agent: Bachelor's degree with a 2.95 GPA
or	
Equivalent experience:	Three years of work experience may be accepted in place of the minimum GPA
Base salary:	According to GS and position plus possible 25 percent on top of base salary (Law Enforcement Availability Pay, or LEAP)
Benefits:	Full federal benefits
Tests:	Written, physical fitness, medical, psychological, polygraph exams; background check; drug screen
Academy:	According to position

Mission Statement

The mission of the Drug Enforcement Administration (DEA) is to enforce the controlled substances laws and regulations of the United States and bring to the criminal and civil justice system of the United

States, or any other competent jurisdiction, those organizations and principal members of organizations, involved in the growing, manufacture, or distribution of controlled substances appearing in or destined for illicit traffic in the United States; and to recommend and support non-enforcement programs aimed at reducing the availability of illicit controlled substances on the domestic and international markets.

Overview

Operating within the Department of Justice, the administrator of the DEA is appointed by the President of the United States and confirmed by the U.S. Senate.

In 1915, the United States first passed legislation that can be regarded as antidrug. Federal drug law enforcement, in one form or another, has been going on since that time. The Bureau of Narcotics and Dangerous Drugs was the immediate predecessor to the modern DEA, which was officially formed in 1973. That first year, the DEA employed 2,775 total employees and operated with a budget of 65.2 million dollars. In 2003, the DEA employed 9,629 total employees and utilized a budget of approximately 1.9 billion dollars. The DEA has 237 offices in the United States and 80 foreign offices in 58 countries.

The DEA is responsible for enforcing U.S. controlled-substances laws. Within this mandate fall duties such as the following:

- Gathering and disseminating intelligence, in cooperation with local, state, and other federal agencies, about drug-related activities, involving both illicit drugs and legal but illegally distributed (i.e., prescription) controlled substances
- Investigating and preparing for the prosecution of criminals, gangs, and major violators of U.S. drug laws operating within the U.S. and internationally (and cooperating with foreign governments and law enforcement agencies, like Interpol, on their counterpart investigations and programs), including the seizure of materials used (or to be used) in violating those same laws

- Working with local, state, and other federal agencies on techniques to limit the amount of illegal drugs available and marketable in the United States, through programs like crop substitution

Career Opportunities: Special Agents

When most people think of the DEA, they think of the special agents. They are the frontline of the agency's efforts to stop drug trafficking. Highly trained, the special agents conduct surveillance, make arrests and confiscations, go under cover inside drug trafficking organizations, and gather evidence using all manner of sophisticated methods. As is the case with many other law enforcement positions, DEA special agents also testify in court cases.

Requirements   Individuals hoping to become special agents must be

- Between 21 and 36 years old;
- Citizens of the United States;
- In possession of a valid driver's license; and
- Able to obtain a Top Secret security clearance.

The applicant has to be in top physical condition, have good hearing, have uncorrected vision no worse than 20/200 that is correctable to 20/20 in one eye and 20/40 in the other, and be able to pass heavy-lifting tests and carry 45 pounds or more. Radial keratotomy, hearing aids, and color blindness are not acceptable for special agents.

Special agent candidates must have a college degree with a minimum overall GPA of 2.95. Obviously, degree programs that are more applicable to the needs of the DEA (criminal justice, various business degrees, engineering, computer science, and certain foreign languages) will receive more weight. In some cases where an applicant has a bachelor's degree with a lower GPA, three years of previous law enforcement experience (or experience in a related professional field) can qualify him or her as well.

Applicants must pass written and oral tests, a variety of medical and physical examinations, a polygraph test, and a psychological examination. Of course, a full disclosure of any previous drug use and a drug screen are required.

Career Opportunities: Intelligence Research Specialists

Though not as likely to be profiled in movies and on TV, the intelligence research specialists are integral to the success of DEA operations. They play an important part in collecting and distributing information about drug manufacturing, trafficking routes, smuggling methods, and drug organizations. Not only is this information crucial to the DEA, but it is often used to help coordinate interagency efforts against the narcotics trade and to aid other federal, state, and local law enforcement organizations with their own ongoing investigations and initiatives. Intelligence research specialists organize and present information that goes toward helping individual, local investigations, as well as shape national and international policy in the war on drugs.

Requirements   Applicants hoping to become intelligence research specialists will have to be willing to relocate to any number of potential postings in the United States and abroad. They must pass a drug screen both before being hired and periodically throughout their tenure with the DEA. After being hired, intelligence research analysts participate in a six-week training program followed by a mentoring program in which they are placed with a more experienced analyst until they are able to assume full duties.

Individuals interested in the intelligence research analyst position can visit local DEA field offices or send their resumes to

DEA Headquarters
ATTN: NPMS
2401 Jefferson Davis Highway
Alexandria, Virginia 22301

Career Opportunities: Forensic Chemists

Highly specialized members of the DEA team, forensic chemists are extremely important in helping the DEA in its effort to understand and halt drug manufacture and trafficking. Individuals wishing to become DEA forensic chemists must be U.S. citizens, able to pass certain physical tests, and able to clear a thorough background investigation. Entry-level qualifications are a college degree from an accredited four-year university with a major in science or engineering, with a concentration in chemistry. Graduate work and professional experience in chemistry or another related field is favored.

Applicants must pass a drug screen and be willing to accept a posting anywhere in the United States or abroad. Certification by the Office of Personnel Management is required. New hires submit to a one-year probationary period.

Career Opportunities: Diversion Investigators

Since the passage of the Controlled Substances Act (CSA) in 1970, it has been the role of diversion investigators (DIs) to investigate incidents involving the diversion of controlled substances and regulated chemicals from the pathways that have been set up to oversee their legal handling and distribution. The DIs help the pharmaceutical and chemical companies comply with various laws, treaties, and conventions, as well as help to ensure that organizations licensed to handle and dispense these controlled substances are doing so in ways that are legal and safe. There are more than 500 DIs working in more than 80 offices throughout the United States and abroad.

Diversion investigators conduct scheduled investigations of outlets for controlled substances such as pharmaceutical and chemical companies, pharmacies, doctors, and veterinarians, among others. By verifying records and security at these outlets, the diversion officer can prevent violations before there is a chance for them to occur. The energies of diversion investigators are often turned toward scrutinizing the practices of companies and organizations with a documented history of violations. They work closely with special agents and officers from state and local agencies, as well as with attorneys and prosecutors at every level of the legal system.

Often, diversion investigators work to help law-abiding handlers of controlled substances comply with the increasingly complex laws regarding these substances. One recent concern has been the regulation of the selling of narcotics and other controlled substances over the Internet.

Requirements   A candidate for the diversion investigator position must be a U.S. citizen with a valid driver's license who is able to pass a medical examination to determine both physical and mental fitness. Vision of 20/40 at distances and 20/25 for close range (can be corrected with glasses or contact lenses) and a hearing test (hearing aids are acceptable) are required. Color blindness and depth-perception problems are disqualifying. A panel interview helps to determine the candidate's temperament, personal characteristics, and fitness for the position. A polygraph examination may also be administered.

A bachelor's degree is required. In addition, the candidate must meet one of the DEA's Superior Academic Achievement Provisions. These include criteria such as a minimum GPA of 3.0, a major GPA of 3.5, or graduation in the top third of your class, among others. Certain combinations of education and specialized experience may be acceptable also. Candidates with experience or knowledge pertaining to chemistry, pharmacy, accounting, law enforcement, and other pertinent fields will be given extra consideration, as will those demonstrating proficiency in a foreign language.

A 12-week basic training program is conducted at the Justice Training Center, the DEA's training facility located at the FBI Academy in Quantico, Virginia. Candidates selected for Diversion Investigator positions will accept employment on condition of a one-year probationary period. Diversion investigators, like many other DEA personnel, must be willing to relocate to any number of locations across the United States or abroad. Travel can also be a big part of the DI's job.

Two new programs for recruiting diversion investigators have been implemented to help find individuals with specialized skills. These are the Veterans' Readjustment Act (VRA) and the Federal Career Intern

Program (FCIP). The VRA is for candidates who have received an honorable discharge from active duty in the U.S. military in the last 10 years and served at least 180 consecutive days during that time. The FCIP has not yet taken effect but is planned to be two-year training program for prospective federal employees. It will offer benefits and promotion opportunities. Candidates who are selected to become diversion investigators through either of these programs will experience a two-year probationary period upon acceptance of employment.

For information regarding diversion investigator openings, contact the Diversion Investigator Recruitment and Hiring Call Center at (202) 307-8846 or

DEA Headquarters
ATTN: ODAS
(DI Hiring)
Washington, DC 20537

Career Opportunities: Investigative Technology Program

Like most of the other federal law enforcement agencies covered in this book, the DEA is always looking for the right people to help them meet the challenges of law enforcement in a high-tech world. Engineers, computer scientists, telecommunications specialists, and other individuals with technological backgrounds are good candidates for the DEA's Investigative Technology Program.

Investigative technology specialists focus on issues of surveillance, from telephone taps to the vanguard of modern information-gathering techniques, as well as the development and security of the IT systems that are key to the operations of the agency.

Requirements Interested candidates need the applicable special skills and must be able to pass a battery of physical and psychological examinations in addition to drug screens and background checks.

Department of Justice

Federal Bureau of Investigation

Robert S. Mueller, III, Director
J. Edgar Hoover Building
935 Pennsylvania Avenue NW
Washington, DC 20535-0001
Telephone: (202) 324-3000
Web site: www.fbijobs.com

CAREER QUICK FACTS

Minimum age:	23
Maximum age:	37
Education:	Special agent: bachelor's degree
Base salary:	According to GS and position plus possible 25 percent on top of base salary (Law Enforcement Availability Pay, or LEAP)
Benefits:	Full federal benefits
Tests:	Written, physical fitness, medical, psychological, polygraph exams; background check; drug screen
Academy:	16 weeks at Quantico

Mission Statement and Introduction

The Mission of the FBI is to uphold the law through the investigation of violations of federal criminal law; to protect the United States from foreign intelligence and terrorist activities; to provide leadership and law enforcement assistance to federal, state, local, and international agencies; and to perform these responsibilities in a manner that is responsive to the needs of the public and is faithful to the Constitution of the United States.

Obviously, the Bureau gets some extra attention from me. Through good and bad times, the Bureau was my home and calling for 25 years. I highly recommend an FBI career to those who know what they're signing up for. Read on.

The FBI is the primary investigative unit of the Department of Justice. Charged with a wide variety of law enforcement duties, the FBI takes the lead on any of the crimes for which it is designated as the primary agency as well as supports various state and local agencies in any number of ways.

The FBI is a catchall agency in the federal law enforcement community—at least in the sense that it has the jurisdiction to investigate all federal crimes not specifically detailed as duties of one of the other 31 federal law enforcement agencies. This gives the FBI a very broad scope of responsibilities—and one that is always being redefined and changed to correspond with the creation of new laws, new crimes, and new agencies.

That said, the FBI divides its primary areas of investigative function into the following categories:

- Applicant matters
- Civil rights
- Counterterrorism
- Foreign counterintelligence
- Organized crime/drugs
- Violent crimes and major offenders
- Financial crime

History

The agency that has come to be known as the FBI was founded in 1908 when Charles J. Bonaparte, the attorney general, appointed a small group of agents as a separate entity within the Department of Justice. These 34 men reported to Chief Examiner Stanley W. Finch. Prior to World War I, the Bureau of Investigation operated within relatively narrow parameters. The earliest federal offenses investigated by the fledgling FBI included enforcing the Mann Act, which specifically made it illegal to transport women across state lines for immoral purposes but also helped to establish crossing state lines to avoid state and local law enforcement as a means to investigate criminals who had not specifically violated federal laws. Bank fraud, antitrust, and the interstate shipment of liquor also kept the Bureau busy in its earliest days.

As Chief Finch was succeeded by A. Bruce Bielaski in 1912, the Bureau adopted a number of new duties, including the investigation of enemy aliens (with the Department of Labor), suspicions or acts of sabotage or espionage, and enforcement of the Selective Service Act. The Bureau grew to nearly 300 agents and 300 support staff during this time.

In 1919, former Secret Service head William J. Flynn took over as new director. The Bureau of Investigation settled back into the role it had occupied before World War I—enforcing the existing federal laws. The passage of the National Motor Vehicle Theft Act expanded the Bureau's ability to crack down on criminals who were crossing state lines in their efforts to stay one step ahead of local and state authorities.

Under President Harding, the attorney general replaced Flynn with William J. Burns. A friend of the attorney general, Burns ran the Burns Agency, a powerful detective agency known for its strike-breaking during labor disputes. As the Coolidge administration took over, some changes were due. As part of a pledge to weed out corruption in the federal government, the new attorney general, Harlan Fiske Stone, asked Burns to resign and, in 1924, appointed J. Edgar Hoover the new director of the Bureau of Investigation.

I am sure you've heard any number of things about J. Edgar Hoover. He is certainly one of the more divisive topics in American history, not just law enforcement. Trying to remove the man himself from his accomplishments is difficult, so forcibly did he inject his personality into the Bureau. Though some of his later policies ranged from unusual to counterproductive, his work in the earliest days of his tenure helped to give the Bureau the character of professionalism and efficiency that are its hallmarks even today.

Hoover began his efforts to transform the Bureau almost immediately. Upon his appointment, he took over a force of nearly 650 people, 441 of whom were special agents. He set up a system of standards for agents, instituted the idea of a regular review process for them, and fired everyone he considered unqualified. He also abolished the seniority-based system of promotion then in place. He organized inspections of the headquarters and field offices, developed and implemented new hiring standards, and established a formal training course within the agency for new agents. In 1932, the agency's official name was changed to the United States Bureau of Investigation.

Hoover's directorship saw the establishment of the Identification Division—the FBI's repository of fingerprint records collected from sources throughout the United States and centrally administered by the Bureau in Washington, DC. This became an increasingly useful tool to American law enforcement officials at every level. Another newly created resource under the umbrella of the rapidly developing agency was the Technical Laboratory. First established in 1932, this facility ushered in and codified the Bureau's involvement in the scientific aspects of crime-fighting. This aspect of the Bureau has grown from a small research facility into the FBI's world-famous laboratory and forensic capability.

The year 1934 saw the passage or amendment of several laws that expanded the scope of the Bureau's duties. In the wake of the Lindbergh baby case, Congress passed a kidnapping statute that was amended to further define the offense and allow for federal intervention in specified capacities. Also, President Roosevelt, in a crime reduction effort, passed a series of laws defining many federal crimes and specifying the Bureau's enforcement of these laws. Among them were extortion involving interstate commerce, killing or assaulting a federal officer, and kidnapping without a ransom demand. In 1935, the agency was officially named the Federal Bureau of Investigation, and the FBI National Academy was established to train police officers from all over the United States.

Just before the advent of World War II, the FBI's ability to investigate individuals and groups suspected of subversive activities, already a responsibility of the agency, was significantly expanded. A series of social and economic factors, the continuing Depression among them, combined to create a sense of discontent that lead to burgeoning membership in organizations such as the American Communist Party and, conversely, several fascist groups. All of these were seen as threats to the federal government. A Presidential Directive of 1939 was augmented by the passage of the Smith Act in 1940—an act outlawing the violent overthrow of the government. The prewar fear that gripped America meant that the FBI was busier than ever. With the onset of hostilities, the FBI began to locate draft evaders, aid other agencies in the collection and analysis of intelligence information, investigate sabotage attempts, and work to uncover spies and other threats to national security. In an unprecedented overseas operation for the FBI, the Special Intelligence Service (SIS) was set up to monitor Axis activity in Latin America. Some members of the active German and Japanese population in South America were believed to be providing a conduit for Axis intelligence and activity. The SIS identified these rings and sought to destroy them. Because of the successful work of the SIS, there was very little open support for the Axis cause in the region by 1944.

The FBI ranks swelled during wartime, largely because of the agency's taking in many of its National Academy graduates in an effort to keep up with the expanding duties mentioned. Total FBI personnel increased by nearly 50 percent, to approximately 13,000, by the end of 1943. Of course, the FBI continued to maintain its normal duty workload, as well.

The events of World War II had changed America's perception of its role in global affairs. A fear of Communist expansion, not limited to Russia's immediate neighbors or even just Europe, helped to create an environment of anti-Communist hysteria. Following the precedent of several previous directives, Truman and Eisenhower both charged the FBI with investigating "subversive activities." Conducting background checks and responding to the glut of tips from the concerned American public became important Bureau duties. By the end of the Korean War, the Bureau fielded some 6,200 agents. In 1950, the FBI's well-known "Ten Most Wanted Fugitives" list was first disseminated.

The passage of new laws regarding civil rights violations meant that the FBI had specific jurisdiction in more incidents than ever before. Many civil rights violation investigations had already occurred, but the 1964 murders of voter registration workers Michael Schwerner, Andrew Goodman, and James Chaney in Mississippi became a case in which the FBI took a decisive role. Working on the case for several years, the 1966 prosecution of the seven people responsible helped the FBI establish its efficacy in enforcing civil rights violation laws. The assassination of Dr. Martin Luther King, Jr. and the murder of Medgar Evers prompted other high-profile FBI investigations.

Racketeering and gambling laws were changing in the late 1960s and early 1970s to make it possible for the FBI to identify and investigate the nebulous underworld of America's organized crime families. Starting as early as 1957, the Bureau had been aware of the true interstate nature of the Mafia, but the structure of then-current laws made it difficult for the Bureau to pursue the crime families. After several important breakthroughs, including the testimony of mob informant Joseph Valachi, the FBI took full advantage of such new laws as the Omnibus Crime Control and Safe Streets Act (1968) and the Racketeer Influenced and Corrupt Organizations Statute (RICO, 1970) to deploy their full forces, including the increased use of undercover agents. The outcome of these ongoing investigations was the incarceration of a great many underworld figures and the ultimate dissolution of many of the major crime families during the 1980s. The end of the 1960s saw the FBI employing roughly 16,000 total personnel.

The late 1960s and early 1970s were characterized by social unrest, most commonly in the form of opposition to the Vietnam War, and the continuing efforts of the civil rights movement. The FBI investigated any number of high-profile incidents during the era, including the shooting deaths of four Kent State University students by National Guardsmen and the University of Wisconsin-Madison Army Math Research Center bombing that claimed one life. It was during this period that the Bureau began its controversial counterintelligence programs ("Cointelpro") that used wiretapping and other clandestine methods to create sometimes voluminous files on individuals deemed suspicious or seditious. The Cointelpro initiative was abandoned in 1971, and some specific episodes in the program's history have been seen as unconstitutional. In 1972, Hoover, in his 47th year as the director of the FBI, died. He was succeeded by L. Patrick Gray as acting director.

Gray's time was short-lived. Before he could be considered by the Senate (the second step, after presidential appointment, to becoming the director), he resigned in the wake of rumors of his involvement in the just-breaking Watergate scandal. After the brief acting director-ship of William Ruckleshaus, Clarence Kelley, former FBI agent and Kansas City police chief, took over as new director of the FBI. He served until 1978 and was responsible for many efforts to rebuild the esteem of the Bureau in the eyes of many Americans.

William H. Webster became the director of the FBI in 1978. Respond-ing to new law enforcement challenges, Webster placed emphasis on counterterrorism measures and on the investigation of several high-profile espionage incidents, the John Walker spy ring and the case of NSA employee William Pelton among them. The concern over the increasing drug trafficking problem, both internationally and in the United States, gave rise to the combination of FBI and DEA jurisdic-tions in an effort to maximize efficiency in the new war on drugs. Webster made white-collar crime a Bureau priority and met with much success in weeding out corruption in business as well as in gov-ernment at various levels, from state legislatures up to Congress. Investigating bank and savings-and-loan failures became an impor-tant initiative for the Bureau.

While acting as lead agency for security at the Los Angeles Olympics in 1984, the FBI pioneered new methods of working with local and state agencies and announced its Hostage Rescue Team (HRT) as a new force ready to respond to domestic hostage situa-tions. The year 1984 also marked the establishment of the Com-puter Analysis and Response Team (CART), which as the name suggests, would work to help the Bureau recover and analyze evi-dence from computers.

Webster resigned in 1987, going on to become director of the Cen-tral Intelligence Agency. After the brief acting directorship of John E. Otto, William Steele Sessions became the new director of the FBI. Sessions was famous for his crime prevention and educational pro-grams. In 1998, the Bureau fielded 9,663 special agents and 13,651 support staff employees. The conclusion of the Cold War marked an important shift in most government agencies, and by 1992, the FBI shifted its emphasis from counterintelligence efforts to violent crime here in America's borders, reassigning 300 agents. White-collar crimes, the application of DNA evidence technology, and new initiatives in national security were defining issues during the transition from the 1980s to the 1990s.

Louis J. Freeh took over as director of the FBI in 1993. Freeh was determined to focus on a great many joint initiatives—expanding the Bureau's role in the international community, working with other agencies to combat drug trafficking and terrorism, and attacking organized crime. Working to improve emergency response and repair public relations damage, the FBI formed the Critical Incident Response Group (CIRG) to help prevent situations like the ones that had arisen in Waco, Texas, at the Branch Davidian compound, and in Ruby Ridge, Idaho, at the home of Randy Weaver.

The FBI also began to combat crime in the world of computers with a continually expanding role for the Computer Analysis and Response Team (CART), and the formation of the Computer Investigations and Infrastructure Threat Assessment Center (CITAC), a team charged with keeping the U.S. infrastructure safe.

The current director of the Bureau is Robert S. Mueller, III. His efforts to secure America's computer infrastructure and improve the FBI's security and counterintelligence efforts were put on the back burner, as the events September 11, 2001 changed the mandate of the FBI. Large-scale investigation of the incidents themselves and general counterintelligence work have been the focus of an increasingly large amount of the Bureau's time. Today the FBI employs as many as 27,000 total personnel (special agents and support staff) in 56 field offices throughout the United States.

Career Opportunities: Special Agent

Certainly the FBI's most well-known position, the special agent is the frontline officer for the Bureau. The position is rigorous and challenging, but ultimately rewarding. Changing times and changing laws mean that the FBI's duties are diversifying to a dizzying degree. Some of the special skills that the Bureau looks for when considering individuals for a special agent position include the following:

- A background in the law, engineering, computer science, accounting/finance, or foreign languages

- Law enforcement experience
- Military experience
- Intelligence experience
- Chemistry, biology, or physics education or experience

Requirements To become a special agent, the applicant will need to be able to pass a standardized physical fitness test (PFT) before being admitted into a New Agent Training (NAT) class. The test is made up of one minute of sit-ups, a 300-meter sprint, maximum push-ups, and a 1.5-mile run. The results are tabulated on a scale that awards points for predetermined levels of accomplishment. The scale is different for males and females, but everyone hoping to become a special agent must take the same physical fitness test.

In addition to passing the physical fitness test, the applicant must be a U.S. citizen (or a citizen of the Northern Mariana Islands) between the ages of 23 and 37 (upon appointment), in possession of a valid driver's license, and willing to be assigned to any duty station within the Bureau's jurisdiction. Uncorrected vision no worse than 20/200 and corrected to 20/20 in one eye and not worse than 20/40 in the other eye is also necessary. All applicants are required to pass a color vision test. Those hoping to become special agents must pass a hearing test as well.

All special agent applicants must hold a four-year degree from a college or university accredited by a regional or national institutional association recognized by the United States secretary of education.

The applicant must submit to and pass a background check. This is a relatively comprehensive check ranging from your bank records, school transcripts, and other pertinent records to personal interviews with your friends, family, and previous employers.

Like most other federal agencies, the FBI requires that the candidate pass a drug test and will use this information and a consideration of your history with illegal drugs (provided in the polygraph exam) to make their final assessment in this category. Again, as with other agencies, the type of drug and degree of abuse is important. The use of marijuana in the previous three years is a disqualifier, as is the use of any other illegal drug in the last 10 years.

The polygraph exam is used by the Bureau primarily to establish criminal and drug history, but also to begin to establish a sense of the applicant's integrity and personality.

The applicant will have to take a written test that is composed of three parts: a personal assessment test, a cognitive ability test, and a situational judgment test. If the candidate passes the three-part written test, a panel interview and an essay test are the next step. The interview is conducted by active special agents who have received some additional training specifically in the questioning and evaluation of new candidates. The written section at this stage is an essay test that challenges the applicant to be clear, articulate, and creative.

Training　As can be imagined from the preceding list of tests and trials, it's a long and difficult process to become a special agent of the FBI. Once the candidate has cleared all of these hurdles, it's just the beginning, really. Accepted on a two-year probationary basis (one year for preference eligible veterans), the new agent must travel to the FBI Academy in Quantico, Virginia, to undergo an extensive, 16-week training program. It is here that the new hires receive top-notch instruction in everything from esoteric points of law to how to disarm a would-be attacker.

Career Opportunities: FBI Profilers

Over the past eight years or so, many people have become interested in a career in profiling. The Bureau gets scores of requests from people wanting to know how to become a profiler and asking what the requirements are for the position. I should straighten out some of the confusion here, since I am at least partially responsible for the media attention given to folks like me, my colleagues, and our successors.

As the Bureau will tell you, there is no job specifically referred to as a "profiler." It's a term that everyone uses, but it's not written on anyone's business card or door. Supervisory special agents at the National Center for the Analysis of Violent Crime (NCAVC) at Quantico perform behavioral support investigative functions. This includes examining evidence and information, from crime scene photographs to witness accounts to victimology, and developing profiles of UNknown SUBjects (UNSUBs). Profiles are used to help investigators narrow the search for violent criminals in unsolved cases, to determine when attacks may have been committed by a serial criminal, and to assist prosecutors in determining motive—a critical element in most prosecutions.

Such special agents work extremely long days. I took my job home with me every night and every weekend, so you might say the days don't end. There are always multiple open cases, and they are all high priority, because you're dealing with violent criminals. It is a rewarding but difficult job—and it's becoming a more and more difficult job to get.

Requirements   As a new special agent, you cannot immediately become a profiler. You must first serve at least three years as a special agent. Then, because the positions are so competitive, it may take up to 10 years for you to reach that position, if you are selected.

The selection process is complicated. An education in Behavioral Science or Forensic Science is preferred. Investigatory experience in violent crime is a real must, so a special agent's experience with the Bureau should include homicide, rape, and other such cases. But it is a subjective process and, as I mentioned, highly competitive. If your hope is to become a profiler, you should be certain that being a special agent in another capacity would be as satisfying to you, as such an assignment is far from guaranteed.

I don't mean to discourage anyone. The field needs good people. If you understand the requirements and believe you have what it takes to work cases from that side of things, please work toward that goal. There's nothing like hard work to get you where you want to go, no matter what the odds tell you.

Training   Upon receiving the assignment to NCAVC, special agents undergo more than 500 hours of structured training.

Career Opportunities: Other Positions

The FBI is one of the most complex, diverse, and technically advanced law enforcement agencies in the world. As such, it needs a great many people with highly specialized skills. As new crimes occur (and are defined by law), the FBI will continue to find ways to stop them. Following is a list of just some of the other positions at the Bureau:

- Forensic scientist
- Intelligence analyst
- Investigative analyst
- Surveillance specialist
- Linguist
- Information technology specialist
- Accountant
- Automotive worker
- Various clerical and support positions

Department of Justice

Federal Bureau of Prisons

Harley G. Lappin, Director
Federal Bureau of Prisons Central Office
320 First St. NW
Washington, DC 20534
General information: (202) 307-3198
Web site: www.bop.gov

CAREER QUICK FACTS

Minimum age:	No minimum, but see educational requirement below
Maximum age:	37
Education:	Four-year course of college study
or	
Equivalent	
experience:	Three-years (or combination thereof)
Base salary:	According to GS and position
Benefits:	Full federal benefits
Tests:	Physical fitness, medical exams; background check; drug screen
Academy:	Three weeks

Mission Statement

It is the mission of the Federal Bureau of Prisons to protect society by confining offenders in the controlled environments of prisons and community-based facilities that are safe, humane, cost-efficient, and appropriately secure, and that provide work and other self-improvement opportunities to assist offenders in becoming law-abiding citizens.

Goals

The Bureau of Prisons (BOP) seeks to reduce escapes and prison disturbances to none, eliminate any unsafe conditions for inmates within the facilities, prepare inmates for law-abiding lives upon release, utilize cost-effective methods of operation, and provide safe and discrimination-free workplaces for their employees and staff.

History

Established in 1930, the Federal Bureau of Prisons was originally created to standardize operations at the 11 federal prisons then in existence. In keeping with its original aims, the bureau strives for consistency and unification of purpose in the methods of administration in place throughout its extensive network of facilities.

The inmates in federal prisons have been convicted of federal crimes or are awaiting trial and/or sentencing in federal matters. As of 1997, the Federal Bureau of Prisons also handles all the inmates convicted for the commission of felony crimes in the District of Columbia.

The bureau helps to protect public welfare by maintaining the security and safety of federal correctional facilities. Institutions operate at four security levels—minimum, low, medium, and high—to accommodate prisoners of varying needs. There is one maximum-security facility in operation. Open interaction between staff and inmates is an important tool in maintaining and improving both security and morale of the prison population.

In an effort to help federal inmates lead law-abiding lives after their sentences have been served, the BOP encourages participation in constructive programs and activities that can help to rehabilitate the offenders. Work programs, vocational training, various levels and types of education, substance abuse treatment and counseling, and a wide array of therapies help the inmates to make better choices and lead fuller, crime-free lives upon release. These initiatives also lead to safer, more secure prisons as well.

Prison population growth is a challenge at all levels of law enforcement, but it is, of course, the primary concern for the Bureau of Prisons. The bureau is charged not only with operating secure and humane facilities, but doing so in a manner that is cost-effective. By the end of 1930, the BOP consisted of 14 correctional facilities and 13,000 inmates. Growth reached a plateau of 24 facilities and roughly 25,000 inmates for the entire period from 1940 to 1980. Various changes and additions to existing federal sentencing laws beginning in the 1980s radically changed the face of the BOP system, marking the beginning of a period of explosive growth. Recent statistics show the BOP to be operating 103 facilities and housing 172,315 inmates. Without question, the administration and oversight of this system requires a great many employees. There were approximately 34,000 employees in the BOP system, according to 2003 statistics.

Career Opportunities: Correctional Officer

The correctional officer is the core of the BOP workforce. Having daily direct contact with the individuals incarcerated in the BOP system can be both difficult and rewarding. The successful candidate should be prepared for a career in which he or she will both assist and oversee the prison population, balancing strict enforcement with understanding. Like many other careers in law enforcement, correctional officers often work unusual shifts, holidays, and weekends.

Requirements General qualifications for BOP positions require that the applicant be a U.S. citizen, but waivers are occasionally granted for certain positions. There is no minimum age requirement, but the maximum is 37 years.

A preemployment physical is conducted which includes a drug screen. At the BOP training facility at the Federal Law Enforcement Training Center (FLETC) in Glynco, Georgia, a physical ability test assesses the following:

- Walking/standing for up to an hour
- Seeing a human figure at certain distances
- Hearing and detecting movement
- Using firearms
- Performing self-defense movements

- Running an extended distance
- Climbing stairs
- Lifting, dragging, and carrying objects
- Smelling smoke and drugs

Background checks including references, previous employers, and a criminal record check must be cleared. Candidates who have a family member in prison can apply, but all information regarding incarcerated relatives must be disclosed. A review of the candidate's financial history will be conducted also.

There are two levels of correctional officers: GS-007-05 and GS-007-06. To qualify for the GS-007-05 level, the candidate will need a full four-year course of study from an accredited school or a bachelor's degree, three years of full-time applicable experience, or a combination of undergraduate education and experience equal to three years of full-time experience.

Applicable experience can be loosely defined as teaching, counseling, social work, nursing, or any number of other occupations in which responsibility levels are high and successful interaction with others is paramount. Certain sales positions qualify as well.

Candidates hoping to become GS-007-06 correctional officers need 9 semester hours or 14 quarter hours of graduate study in academic areas such as criminal justice, social science, or other similar fields. One year of full-time experience in a field where the candidate is responsible for inmates (mental health facility, etc.) or for apprehending and arresting offenders in an official law enforcement organization is also acceptable. Various combinations of the preceding are also acceptable and can be evaluated on a candidate-by-candidate basis.

Training   New hires at the BOP receive Institution Familiarization Training to teach them the nature of their duties at the facility where they will be employed. All correctional officers (and other individuals working at a correctional facility) undergo a three-week Introduction to Correctional Techniques program. This training occurs at the Federal Law Enforcement Training Center (FLETC) in Glynco, Georgia.

It includes the physical test mentioned as well as numerous written exams. Certain positions require further, specialized education.

Career Opportunities: Other Positions

The complex nature of the work carried out by the Bureau of Prisons demands a wide array of specialties among BOP employees. There are many opportunities for individuals with special skills. For instance, the BOP employs doctors, psychologists, nurses, accountants, attorneys, teachers, computer specialists, mechanics, carpenters, and food service employees, to name but a few of the important members of the BOP's diversified workforce.

BOP-HIRES

BOP-HIRES is an online application method for individuals interested in the following positions:

- Correctional officer
- Psychologist
- Medical officer
- Physician's assistant
- Nurse practitioner

Visit the BOP Web site at www.bop.gov for more information.

Department of Justice

U.S. Marshals Service

Benigno G. Reyna, Director
Human Resources Division
Law Enforcement Recruiting
Washington, DC 20530-1000
Web site: www.usdoj.gov/marshals/careers/career.html

CAREER QUICK FACTS

Minimum age:	21
Maximum age:	37
Education:	Four-year college degree
or	
Applicable equivalent experience:	Three years
Convictions:	No felony convictions; no domestic violence convictions
Base salary:	$27,000 to $34,000 or higher depending upon GS scale and position
Benefits:	Full federal benefits
Tests:	Written, physical fitness, and medical examination; background check
Academy:	10 weeks at FLETC

Mission Statement

The mission of the United States Marshals Service is to protect the Federal courts and ensure the effective operation of the judicial system.

History

When you think of the U.S. Marshals, you probably think of Tommy Lee Jones chasing Harrison Ford in *The Fugitive*. But if you're like most Americans, you don't have a clear idea of what the marshals do. Tracking and apprehending fugitives is what they're known for, but it's only part of the job of the U.S. Marshals.

The U.S. Marshals Service has the distinction of having been created as part of the Judiciary Act of 1789, an act that set up the federal judicial system. The first marshals were appointed by George Washington. These initial marshals held positions of extraordinary responsibility within their respective judicial districts. They handled all arrests, prisoners, service of court documents, and monetary disbursements. Almost every conceivable detail of court proceedings, from arranging for courtrooms and prisoner detention facilities to hiring and paying staff, was a part of the duties of the first marshals.

The most important function of the fledgling Marshals Service, however, was to serve as the representative for the federal government in the furthest reaches of the growing country. As the nation has grown and changing times have yielded new law enforcement challenges, the U.S. Marshals Service has adapted its methods to suit modern law enforcement while retaining the principles that have always been at the core of the organization.

Marshals Service Missions

Either the President or the attorney general appoints the director, the deputy director, and 94 United States Marshals to administer the 95 district offices and nearly 350 total locations throughout the United States and its holdings. Arlington, Virginia, is home to the U.S. Marshals Service Headquarters.

The staggering array of activities performed by the Marshals Service means that they are involved in the vast majority of federal law enforcement programs on one level or another. Following are some of the more prominent missions of the Marshals Service.

Fugitive Investigations   Easily their most well-known role, the U.S. Marshals are responsible for investigating probation, parole, and bond default violators; fugitives from warrants relating to drug investigations; and, most famously, escaped federal prisoners.

Domestic Investigations

- **"15 Most Wanted" Fugitive Program.** Since 1983, the Marshals Service has compiled and maintained a list of the "15 Most Wanted" fugitives. Based on information taken from Marshals Service cases, cases handled by other federal agencies with the aid of the marshals, and serious state and local cases where the authorities in the appropriate jurisdiction have solicited the aid of the Marshals Service, this list represents the most dangerous of America's criminals. Out of the 167 people who have made this list, 159 have been apprehended.
- **Major Case Fugitive Program.** Designed as an augmentation to the "15 Most Wanted" program, major cases within the agency highlight offenders and incidents that are to receive greater attention and resources.
- **District Fugitive Task Forces.** U.S. Marshals operate in 132 cooperative task forces around the country, taking the lead in roughly half of them. This continues the long-standing tradition of assisting other agencies on a wide variety of levels in the law enforcement community. Most of the task forces are full-time efforts, though some are temporary and designed around the apprehension of specific offenders.

  The Investigative Services Division also oversees the Regional Fugitive Task Forces. Established by the Presidential Threat Protection Act of 2000, these forces work to apprehend the most dangerous fugitives on the eastern and western seaboards from their offices in New York City and Los Angeles.

International Investigations   The Marshals Service is responsible for capturing fugitives wanted for crimes in foreign countries and suspected of being in the United States. They also handle the tracking and extradition of criminals wanted in the United States who are captured in other nations.

Technical Operations Group

- **Electronic Surveillance Unit.** As the name implies, the Electronic Surveillance Unit (ESU) is one of the most advanced surveillance forces in all of federal law enforcement. Not only do they provide the evidence that helps to bring in fugitives for both the Marshals Service and other agencies, but they help to train federal, state, and local agencies in the fine and ever-changing art of electronic surveillance. They also testify in various court settings.
- **Air Surveillance Operations.** The Aviation Support Unit is the aerial surveillance and support force of the U.S. Marshals Service. They provide information and track fugitives.
- **Operational Wireless Communications Support.** The Operational Wireless Communications Support (OWCS) is a highly specialized subgroup of the Marshals Service. The communication and information technology experts of the OWCS ensure the security of the agency's communications systems. They support the entire breadth of the service in the apprehension of fugitives and various other activities with radio, satellite, and power equipment to aid in the communications aspects of Marshals Service operations, often at a moment's notice.

Analytical Support Unit   The Analytical Support Unit is a team of tactical and strategic experts who analyze information and provide recommendations to the service on almost all operations. They also collect and interpret data about any threats to federal judicial employees. Among the most important of their duties is the maintenance of the Marshals Service database, the Warrant Information Network.

Judicial Security

The Marshals Service Judicial Security section maintains a safe environment for the federal courts and those served by the judicial system, including jurors.

Court Security   Senior inspectors, deputy marshals, and contracted court security officers (CSOs) are the front line for security in federal courts at more than 800 locations in the nation. These officers see that jurors and others conducting business at federal courts can do so in a safe environment. They also investigate threats against judges and other members of the federal judiciary, often providing 24-hour protection for those in danger.

Judicial Security Systems   The Marshals Service's Judicial Security Systems (JSS) is responsible for developing and implementing the complex, and hopefully unobtrusive, electronic security systems at federal courts. They also employ bullet-resistant glass and explosive-detection materials in their efforts to keep the courts safe.

Prisoner Services

The Marshals Service handles all prisoners arrested by federal law enforcement agencies from the time of arrest until they are acquitted or incarcerated.

Prisoner Custody   More than 42,000 detainees are handled by the U.S. Marshals Service each day. From the time an individual is arrested or detained, brought before a judge, and made to stand trial for a federal offense, he or she is the responsibility of the U.S. Marshals Service. If a person is convicted and sentenced, the Marshals Service provides or arranges for the prisoner's transport to the designated facility.

Witness Security Program

The safety of all witnesses for the government in federal cases who may have reason to fear for their lives is the responsibility of the Marshals Service. The organized Crime Control Act of 1970 (furthered by the Comprehensive Crime Control Act of 1984) initialized the Witness Protection Program. To date, more than 7,500 witnesses and 9,500 immediate dependents have been part of the program. The Marshals Service relocates these individuals and gives them new identities: sanctioned documentation, career training, housing, and even stipends in certain cases.

Second only to the actual apprehension of fugitives, the Witness Protection Program is well known from its frequent portrayal in movies and books, and on television. The agency is proud of the fact that no one in the Witness Protection Program has ever been killed or injured while following security protocols and being under the direct supervision of the Marshals Service.

Asset Forfeiture Program

The aforementioned Crime Control Act of 1984 granted federal prosecutors the ability to sell seized and otherwise forfeited assets and use the funds for expanding and improving federal law enforcement agencies. The Marshals Service plays an important part in this process; they serve as the temporary custodians of the property and see to its disposal through auction or another approved outlet.

Special Operations and Programs

Special Operations Group   The Marshals Service maintains what they call the Special Operations Group (SOG), an emergency response team that is always ready to respond to a wide variety of emergency situations anywhere within the Marshals Service area of operation. Something like a SWAT team, the SOG is made up of marshals serving in regular duty elsewhere who are prepared to assemble at any time. The Marshals Service Tactical Operations Center at Camp Beauregard, Louisiana, is the home to a smaller SOG whose members are stationed there in a dedicated capacity. The volunteers and full-time SOG members must pass a difficult battery of physical and mental tests and participate in special training in the fields of weaponry and tactics, among others.

The SOG is deployed in situations where the Marshals Service faces extraordinary challenges performing their normal security, transport, or apprehension duties.

Special Assignments The Office of District Affairs is an arm of the Marshals Service that can be implemented by order of the U.S. attorney general to help a district office encountering unusual or extenuating circumstances due to any number of causes: natural disaster, highly publicized security or protection situations, or any instance in which the SOG is in the field.

Career Opportunities: Deputy U.S. Marshall

The wide range of duties performed by a deputy U.S. Marshal is indicative of the broad scope of the agency's imperatives as a whole. They are responsible for court security, prisoner transport, prisoner custody in court situations, jury protection, and many other duties in keeping with the needs of this extremely wide-ranging agency.

Requirements for the Position of Deputy U.S. Marshall

Qualification Requirements. A candidate for the deputy U.S. Marshal position must be a U.S. citizen between the ages of 21 and 36 in excellent physical condition with a bachelor's degree or three years of applicable experience. Certain combinations of education and experience are acceptable. Accepted combinations of education and experience will be determined by the Marshals Service at the time of application. The candidate must have a valid driver's license and a good driving record and submit to a background check.

Deputy U.S. Marshals must pass a written examination, an agency interview, and a structured interview. A candidate who successfully completes these stages will attend the 10-week basic training program at the agency's academy in Glynco, Georgia.

General Experience Requirements (GS-5). At least three years of experience (paid or responsible volunteer) or a four-year degree from an accredited college or university is required. Experience in the fields of law enforcement, corrections, classroom instruction, or journalism would be acceptable, among others. Experience is often evaluated on a case-by-case basis.

Specialized Experience (GS-7 only). To qualify as GS-7, one must meet all the preceding requirements as well as have one year of substantive law enforcement experience. The ability to interact with the public, coworkers, and prisoners/suspects is essential, as is demonstrated proficiency with a firearm and the ability to make arrests.

Substitution of Education for Specialized Experience (GS-7 only). Superior academic achievement by a candidate may be acceptable for classification as GS-7 in lieu of the preceding experience requirements. Superior academic achievement can be defined as a bachelor's degree with any one of the following four conditions: a grade point average (GPA) of 3.0 or higher overall, for major classes or for the last two years of study; a ranking in the upper third of the candidate's undergraduate class; membership in a (nonfreshman) Honor Society as recognized by the Association of College Honor Societies; a graduate degree in a field related to law enforcement or at least one year of graduate education in a field defined as such.

Medical Qualifications. A deputy U.S. Marshal has to be prepared for the physical rigors that may present themselves during the course of duty. A medical or physical condition that could create an unsafe environment for coworkers, the public, or anyone else can be disqualifying. Some potentially disqualifying conditions include problems of mobility, strength, or flexibility; heart disease; and color blindness or eye surgery.

A successful candidate must have 20/20 vision (correction with lenses is acceptable, as is corrective surgery, in some cases). Uncorrected vision must test at 20/200 or better in each eye. Basic color vision and depth perception are both required. The candidate must pass a hearing test.

Physically, the deputy U.S. Marshal candidate must pass tests of flexibility, push-ups, sit-ups, and a 1.5-mile run.

Compensation and Benefits

Compensation. A deputy U.S. Marshal at the GS-5 level can expect a salary of $27,000 to $34,000. The GS-7 level deputy U.S. Marshal salary ranges from $31,000 to $39,000. Geographic location, among other factors, determines the successful candidate's salary.

After one year, a candidate starting at GS-5 can be promoted to GS-7. A deputy Marshal at GS-7 is eligible for promotion to GS-9 after one year. A three-year process can lead from GS-9 to GS-11.

Benefits. Deputy U.S. Marshals enjoy a pension plan, social security, and the equivalent to a 401(k) called the Thrift Savings Plan. Retirement eligibility begins after 25 years of service. Retirement is available after 20 years of service if the individual is over 50 years of age. Retirement is mandatory at 57 years of age.

The U.S. Marshals Service offers an optional health benefit plan that features shared costs and broad choices. The same is true of the life insurance program.

Like many other federal law enforcement agencies, the Marshals Service offers the Employee Assistance Plan (EAP)—a confidential resource for federal employees to get help resolving family, personal, and job-related issues.

The Application Process

The U.S. Marshals Service did not offer public testing in 2003. All open positions were filled from the existing register of eligible candidates. The agency creates a register to reflect, in score order, the candidates who have passed the written exam and are slated for the interview process should applicable positions become available. Veterans are awarded preference points. As positions open, candidates are contacted to attend structured interviews in a number of cities.

The interview, before a panel of senior deputy U.S. Marshals, helps to determine the candidate's suitability for the high-pressure deputy U.S. Marshal position. Decision-making, integrity, and teamwork are but a few of the important qualities the interviewers seek to discern in the prospective deputy Marshal.

After giving a successful interview, the candidate must pass the background examination, drug test, medical examination, and fitness tests. Upon satisfactory completion of these tests, the candidate undergoes a final review before two U.S. Marshals and a representative from the training academy.

Candidates who have completed all of the preceding will receive an offer of employment based on openings and duty needs in the agency. When an applicant is offered a position, the duty station is assigned. If the applicant declines the offer, he or she will not be eligible for another position/opening. After acceptance and posting to the duty station, the applicant must complete the 10-week Basic Deputy U.S. Marshal training program at the U.S. Marshals Service Training Academy in Glynco, Georgia.

Professional Credential Services

Professional Credential Services (PCS) is the agency that processes applications and administers and reports the scores of the Deputy U.S. Marshal GS-082 Written Examination.

Currently, disabled and recently discharged military personnel may submit their information to

PCS/USM
Post Office Box 198748
Nashville, Tennessee 37219-8748
(877) 887-9727
(615) 880-4275
usmarshalcord@pcshq.com
www.pcshq.com

Disabled veterans must submit an "official document" (dated within the last year) from the Veterans Administration verifying their disability. Military personnel within 120 days of ETS or EAS may submit a letter from the military personnel office confirming their separation date. Those within a 120-day window after their ETS or EAS should submit a copy of form DD-214.

All correspondence should include return address information (including telephone number and e-mail address). If designated as eligible, PCS will send the required information to the prospective candidate via the United States Postal Service.

Department of the Navy

Naval Criminal Investigative Service

Special Agent David L. Brant, Director
Naval Criminal Investigative Service Headquarters
716 Sicard St. SE, Suite 2000
Washington Navy Yard, DC 20388-5380
E-mail: jobs@ncis.navy.mil
Web site: www.ncis.navy.mil/careers.html

CAREER QUICK FACTS

Minimum age:	21
Maximum age:	37
Education:	Accredited baccalaureate (four-year) college degree
Base salary:	According to GS and position plus 25 percent on top of base salary (Law Enforcement Availability Pay, or LEAP)
Benefits:	Full federal benefits
Academy:	Total of 15 to 16 weeks at FLETC

Mission Statement

The Naval Criminal Investigative Service (NCIS)—the Department of the Navy's (DoN's) primary law enforcement arm— is in the midst of a transformation. No longer is the traditional reactive law enforcement model adequate given the complex and increasingly blurred terrorist, intelligence, and criminal threats to our Navy and Marine Corps.

To counter the evolving threats, NCIS has implemented a new, proactive strategic plan which emphasizes the following priorities: Prevent terrorism and related hostile acts against DoN forces and installations; Protect DoN systems and information against compromise; and Reduce criminal activity and mitigate its impact on Navy and Marine Corps operational readiness.

Overview

The NCIS is under the Department of the Navy, but you do not have to be in the military or even have any military experience to be a candidate. In fact, of the 2,300 NCIS employees, most are civilian, and of the special agents, nearly half are civilian. Agents may be assigned to work in locations in 140 locations across the globe, in addition to potential "afloat" duty on ships and carriers.

It's worth mentioning that the NCIS has a few special public service programs I think are really good and that provide information to the public. These include their Identity Theft program, which informs people about how to protect themselves against identity theft, Safekids program, which helps parents and their children avoid being victimized by computer criminals, and Wanted Fugitives and Missing Persons program, which invites people with information about fugitives or missing persons to come forward with that information.

NCIS Then and Now

During World War I, what is now NCIS emerged out of the Office of Naval Intelligence (ONI), which was established in 1915 to investigate espionage and sabotage. In 1966, the Naval Investigative Service was designated as the name for what is now NCIS, setting it apart from the rest of the ONI. In 1982, the agency became Naval Security and Investigative Command (NSIC) and became responsible for the Navy's Law Enforcement and Physical Security Program. In 1983, a 24-hour a day intelligence/operational center, Navy Antiterrorist Alert Center (ATAC), was established after the bombing of Marine barracks in Beirut.

The agency's name was changed twice more, to Naval Investigative Service Command (NISCOM) in 1988 and to its current name in 1992. In 1994, NCIS was reorganized as a federal law enforcement agency. In 1995, the Cold Case Homicide Unit was established. In 1999, Marine Corps CID was integrated into NCIS, and in 2000, NCIS civilian special agents received congressional authorization to execute warrants and make arrests. In 2002, in response to growing terrorist threats, ATAC became the Multiple Threat Alert Center (MTAC).

NCIS is responsible for many types of operations through its directorates and major programs, as outlined in the following.

Criminal Investigations Directorate

Within the Criminal Investigations Directorate, crimes that pose serious threats, from acts of violence to white-collar felonies to drug offenses, are investigated. Loosely, these three types of crimes are the focus of NCIS in the form of the following:

- **General Criminal Investigations.** Crimes including homicide, child abuse, rape, burglary, robbery, and theft of government property
- **Procurement Fraud Investigations.** Economic crimes, especially fraud, bribery, arson, and property theft
- **Counterdrug Program.** Narcotics crimes, especially trafficking
- **Cold Case Squad.** Unresolved homicide cases (the oldest case of the 44 solved by the Cold Case Squad dated back to 1968)
- **Criminal Intelligence Department.** Supports investigations with systems for and analysis of data
- **Technical Services.** Provides investigative support in the form of surveillance installation, remote sensors, homing devices, firearms, body armor, polygraph examinations, and other services

In addition, the Criminal Investigations Directorate administers the Navy's Law Enforcement and Physical Security Program, which is responsible for policy about weapons security, antiterrorism, and other matters of security. It also manages, among others, the Master-at-Arms Program, electronic security systems, crime prevention and reporting, security force training, Military Working Dog Program, and the Naval Reserve Security Program.

Of these law enforcement programs, two of the largest are Master-at-Arms Program and the Military Working Dog Programs. A Master-at-Arms (MA) is a "sheriff of the sea" or "sea corporal." There are about 1,800 MAs in the Navy today. Theirs are sea-intensive law enforcement jobs, though they also serve ashore and operate as handlers in the Military Working Dog Program (MWD). The MWD program trains and provides dogs for patrol duty and for the detection of bombs and narcotics. The MWD provides support to other agencies, including U.S. Secret Service, U.S. Marshals Service, and Drug Enforcement Administration.

Counterterrorism Directorate

The Counterterrorism Directorate is charged with some awesome responsibilities, especially of late. Within the directorate are the Counterterrorism Department, the Multiple Threat Alert Center (MTAC). The Counterterrorism Department investigates and prevents terrorist acts against Navy and Marine Corps personnel, installations, and assets. The MTAC monitors and provides warnings of threats to the Navy and Marine Corps on a 24-hour basis.

Protective Operations

Certain special agents are selected for collateral duty with Protective Operations. They undergo training specific to the assignment, as well as defensive driving, evasive maneuvers, and special weapons. Protective Operations are undertaken when certain important individuals require special protection, as they are potential targets for criminals and terrorists. Such individuals might include the secretary of the navy and visiting heads-of-state.

Special Agents Afloat

A rigorous but prestigious duty with NCIS is in the Special Agents Afloat program. In this program, certain special agents are assigned to aircraft carriers or other large ships. In so doing, NCIS can provide investigative support to deployed commanders. A special agent afloat is assigned to a carrier or ship for one year. A special agent afloat must be ready to prevent crimes aboard the ship and to evaluate crime scene and other evidence, and he or she must be skilled in proactive and investigative techniques in order to solve crimes. In addition, the special agent afloat will support the commander in counterintelligence and antiterrorism matters.

Requirements for NCIS Candidates

There are many positions within NCIS, but as a law enforcement candidate, you would be applying for a position of special agent. The minimum age for candidates is 21 years and the maximum is 37. The maximum age limit is fixed. You must be a U.S. citizen to apply. You must have a baccalaureate (four-year) college degree. You cannot be color-blind.

NCIS conducts a very thorough background check, going back 15 years or to your 18th birthday, whichever is shorter.

As I mentioned, there is no military experience prerequisite for NCIS, but related work experience would make you a more attractive candidate, as would foreign language fluency, certain advanced degrees, and/or computer skills.

Training and Opportunities

If you are hired, you will undergo 15 to 16 weeks of training at the Federal Law Enforcement Training Center (FLETC), which includes the nine-week Basic Criminal Investigator's Course , as well as six weeks of NCIS-specific training. Special agents carry firearms, so this training includes firearm instruction. During their careers, special agents must qualify quarterly with their service weapon.

New special agents are then assigned to field training offices. For the first several years, they are exposed to a wide range of investigations. They then begin specializing in one of four fields: General Criminal Investigations, Procurement Fraud Investigations, Foreign Counterintelligence, or Technical Services, as detailed previously.

Of note, special agents in General Criminal Investigations may qualify for a one-year graduate course that will lead to a master's degree in Forensic Science. So if you think forensic science is an area you'd like to go into within law enforcement, but you don't already have the education, this might be a route you could take to attain your goal—if you qualify. Likewise, special agents in Foreign Counterintelligence may qualify for graduate-level programs in history, religion, culture, and economy as pertains to their role in counterintelligence.

NCIS special agents must expect to be assigned around the world. In fact, they are required to sign a Mobility Agreement. While an agent's preference of assignment is taken into account, the needs of the agency are the most important factors. This is a great opportunity if you're willing to uproot and take on the challenge. For all overseas tours of duty, families go with the special agents. The only exception is the Special Agents Afloat program, which, for obvious reasons, does not allow families to join the agent in his or her assignment.

Getting Started Early

NCIS offers unpaid internships to those interested in learning about NCIS from within in order to make an informed decision about whether to apply when the time comes. For more information, e-mail jobs@ncis.navy.mil.

Department of State

Bureau of Diplomatic Security

Ambassador Francis X. Taylor, Assistant Secretary of State for Diplomatic Security and Director of the Office of Foreign Missions
Department of State
Attention: Recruitment Office
2401 E Street NW, 5th Floor
Washington, DC 20037
Telephone: (202) 261–8941
E-mail: DSRecruitment@state.gov
Web site: www.state.gov/m/ds/

CAREER QUICK FACTS

Minimum age:	21
Maximum age:	37
Education:	Four-year college degree
Convictions:	No felony convictions; no misdemeanor conviction of domestic violence
Base salary:	$33,763 to $46,736 plus 25 percent on top of base salary (Law Enforcement Availability Pay, or LEAP), depending upon position, education, and experience; danger pay for some assignments;
Benefits:	Full federal benefits
Tests:	Written and medical (including vision and hearing) exams; physical fitness test; background check; drug screen
Academy:	Six months (at FLETC and Diplomatic Security Training Center)

Mission Statement of the Department of State

Create a more secure, democratic, and prosperous world for the benefit of the American people and the international community.

Overview

The mandate of the Department of State's Bureau of Diplomatic Security is the provision of a safe and secure environment for the conduct of American diplomacy. The men and women who are special agents of the Diplomatic Security Service are sworn federal law enforcement officers, and they protect more dignitaries than any other agency in the U.S. government.

Department of State special agents perform law enforcement functions around the world, and as such a substantial portion of a special agent's career is spent living and working abroad. In foreign assignments, special agents advise ambassadors on all security issues and coordinate security programs. In the United States, special agents are armed and have arrest authority. They provide security for the secretary of state, the U.S. ambassador to the United Nations, and visiting foreign dignitaries; investigate passport and visa fraud; and conduct personnel investigations.

A current Department of State special agent assignment is the protection of the President of Afghanistan, Hamid Karzai, and the training of an Afghan force to ultimately take over the responsibility of so guarding their president. Protection details and other assignments keep special agents at work an average of 10 hours per day, and their responsibilities extend into evenings, weekends, holidays—basically around the clock, all year long. It is a demanding job, but a rewarding one, as the work of special agents facilitates the efforts of diplomats and cooperation among governments.

Requirements

Applicants must possess a four-year college degree and must be at least 21 years old but not yet 37. Foreign language skills are desirable but not required. Applicants must be in good physical condition, be good communicators, be able to handle firearms and to perform in very demanding physical conditions, and be willing to relocate for long periods to foreign countries.

In addition, applicants and all immediate family members must be U.S. citizens. This is because of the requirements of the level of security clearance special agents must obtain to perform their jobs.

Testing

Applicants must undergo a stringent medical examination and physical fitness test. Qualified applicants undergo a written test that includes essay writing. Those who pass the written test move on to an oral interview. There is also a thorough background investigation and qualification for Top Secret clearance.

Training

Six months of training include basic and specialized training at the Federal Law Enforcement Training Center (FLETC) in Glynco, Georgia, then the training continues at the Diplomatic Security Training Center near Washington, DC. Training includes personal protection techniques, criminal law and investigation, background investigations, first aid, firearms, and defensive driving. There is also instruction in arson investigation, advanced firearms techniques, and medical assistance.

Career Opportunities

Special agents are initially hired for a four-year probationary period. To begin their service, special agents are often first assigned to one of eight domestic field offices for a duration of one to two years. They may perform domestic security functions, including background investigations on personnel, investigation of passport and visa fraud, counterintelligence, and other criminal investigations. They may also be assigned to security detail with the secretary of state and/or visiting foreign dignitaries. There may also be temporary foreign assignments within this initial two years of employment.

After one to two years in a domestic assignment, special agents spend much of their careers in foreign assignments at diplomatic posts. They are given a great deal of responsibility early in their careers, along with opportunities for promotions. Special agents may first serve as diplomatic security officers, or DSOs, under the supervision of other special agents who have reached the level of regional security officers, or RSOs, at U.S. embassies and consulates anywhere in the world. These special agents plan and implement security programs for the protection of U.S. citizens, property, information, intelligence, and other assets. RSOs also supervise the operations of U.S. Marine Security Guards.

Special agents can attain supervisory positions in the United States after significant foreign service, supervising efforts at field offices or in Department of State headquarters.

Department of Treasury

Internal Revenue Service Criminal Investigation

Nancy J. Jardini, Chief, Criminal Investigation
1111 Constitution Ave. NW
Room 2527
Washington, DC 20224
E-mail: cishr@ci.irs.gov
Web site: www.jobs.irs.gov/mn-LawEnforcement.html

CAREER QUICK FACTS

Minimum age:	21
Maximum age:	37
Education: or Equivalent experience:	Four-year college degree with accounting and finance study
	Certified Public Accountant certification
Convictions:	No felony convictions; no misdemeanor conviction of domestic violence
Base salary:	According to GS pay scale and position, plus 25 percent on top of base salary (Law Enforcement Availability Pay, or LEAP)
Benefits:	Full federal benefits
Academy:	26 weeks at FLETC

Mission Statement

To serve the American public by investigating potential criminal violations of the Internal Revenue Code and related financial crimes in a manner that fosters confidence in the tax system and compliance with the law.

Overview

It's been said that nobody likes the IRS. Well, I'll agree that nobody likes to pay taxes. But we should all have a healthy respect for the work the IRS does, as the government does depend upon taxes to stay afloat. Within the IRS, Criminal Investigations special agents investigate violations of IRS code as well as other financial crimes. Special agents locate and investigate earned income, legal and illegal, which may be involved in other crimes within their jurisdiction, such as tax, money laundering, and Bank Secrecy Act laws.

Special agents are also involved in cross-agency counterterrorism efforts, including the FBI's Joint Terrorism Task Force. Special agents investigate the sources of financing for terrorist groups and individuals. They also investigate potential criminal violations within their jurisdiction, including money laundering and tax evasion, by suspected persons or groups.

IRS Criminal Investigation dates back to 1919, when it was established as the IRS Intelligence Unit. Most famously, special agents brought down Al Capone for income tax evasion. The Intelligence Unit began with six officers. There are now approximately 2,900 special agents within IRS Criminal Investigation.

Violations of the IRS Code are solely under the jurisdiction of IRS Criminal Investigation. When individuals and corporations deliberately violate IRS Code, they may face an audit, which is a civil procedure, or a criminal investigation. Such an investigation might result in prosecution and even in the service of jail time. Throughout the history of IRS Criminal Investigation, the conviction rate for federal tax prosecutions has never been less than 90 percent.

Requirements

Not everyone can become an IRS Criminal Investigation special agent. IRS special agents are considered to be our government's premier financial investigators. If you are looking for an entry-level law enforcement career, this may not be it for you unless you have an accounting or finance background as outlined in the requirements for a given open law enforcement position.

Because of the sophisticated financial nature of these agents' investigations, you must have an accounting background and a high level of skill in accounting. For the most basic position, you must not only have a four-year college degree; your education must include at least 15 semester hours of study in accounting and nine additional semester house in either finance, economics, business law, tax law, or money and banking. Equivalent experience may be accepted in lieu of the educational minimum requirements or in combination with partial satisfaction of educational minimum requirements. Also, certification as a Certified Public Accountant is considered equivalent to the educational minimum.

Testing

In addition to Office of Personnel Management requirements, and those determined by the level of the job desired, each qualified candidate will undergo an intensive interview to determine his or her suitability for the demands of the job.

Training

In-residence training for 26 weeks at the Federal Law Enforcement Training Center (FLETC) in Glynco, Georgia, is required. Special agents are trained in IRS statutes and jurisdiction, complex financial investigative techniques, Internet investigation, self-defense, firearm use, arrest techniques, and other areas as required. In addition to having finely tuned financial investigative skills, special agents are highly trained in the recovery of computer evidence, including getting past encryption, password protection, and other electronic protections hiding criminal activity.

Career Opportunities

The career of an IRS special agent goes wherever the investigations take him or her. As mentioned, they investigate earned income, legal and illegal, which has potential involvement in crimes within their jurisdiction. Special agents must be available for temporary assignments and permanent reassignments as determined by the workload and needs of the IRS. They may be relocated at any time, and for any length of time.

Some work may involve locating and investigating criminals and potential criminals in other countries, using the Internet, computer records, document "paper" trails, and other means. Special agents of the IRS often work in cooperation with other federal agencies, including the DEA, FBI, and ATF. They also may be required to work on undercover investigations.

Special agents may be involved in three main programs within Criminal Investigation's strategic plan: Legal Source Tax Crimes, Illegal Source Financial Crimes, and Narcotics Related Financial Crimes.

Department of Treasury

U.S. Mint Police

Bill Daddio, Associate Director for Protection/Chief, U.S. Mint Police
United States Mint Police
Recruiting Division, 8th Floor
801 Ninth St. NW
Washington, DC 20220
Telephone: (202) 354 7300
Web site: www.usmint.gov/about_the_mint/mint_police/

CAREER QUICK FACTS

Minimum age:	21
Maximum age:	37
Education:	Four-year college degree in related degree field
or	
Equivalent law	
enforcement	
experience:	Three years
Convictions:	No felony convictions; no misdemeanor conviction of domestic violence
Base salary:	$34,324
Benefits:	Full federal benefits
Tests:	Medical (including vision and hearing) exam; background check; drug screen
Academy:	10 weeks at FLETC and five weeks at a field office

Mission Statement of the U.S. Mint

The United States Mint applies world-class business practices in making, selling, and protecting our Nation's coinage and assets.

Overview

No doubt you've heard and might have even used the expression, "as secure as Fort Knox." But you have probably never wondered where it came from. Who do you think secures Fort Knox? It's the U.S. Mint Police, the sworn federal law enforcement officers responsible for protecting the more than $100 billion in Department of Treasury and other government assets held in facilities in Fort Knox (of course), San Francisco, Denver, West Point (New York), Philadelphia, and Washington, DC.

The U.S. Mint Police are among the oldest law enforcement agencies in the nation, having been established in 1792. Operating now for more than 200 years, the U.S. Mint Police protect life and property, safeguard the nearly 3,000 U.S. Mint employees and many thousands of visitors to mint facilities, collect evidence, make arrests, and enforce applicable laws.

Requirements

Applicants must have a four-year college degree in police science, criminal justice, or a comparable degree program, or have three years of creditable law enforcement experience.

Testing

Applicants undergo a medical evaluation with a drug screen. Applicants must be physically able to meet the demands of the job. Communication ability will be observed and evaluated through written and oral questions.

Training

Training includes 10 weeks at the Federal Law Enforcement Training Center (FLETC) in Glynco, Georgia, and five additional weeks at a U.S. Mint field office. Trainees are assigned to a field-training officer for additional training. General training topics that are stressed include professionalism, the law, public relations, firearm proficiency, and physical fitness. More specifically, trainees must learn U.S. Mint Policy and Procedures and Jurisdiction, applicable federal, state, and local laws, report writing, computer network functions within the U.S. Mint system, and radio communication.

Career Opportunities

After two years of service, U.S. Mint Police officers are eligible for promotions within the U.S. Mint Police organization. Specialized assignments for U.S. Mint Police officers are available, including

- **Bike Patrol,** which includes a two-week bicycle patrol training program at FLETC. Bike Patrol officers are visible security in and around U.S. Mint facilities and are able to maneuver easily in downtown assignments in locations within the U.S. Mint Police jurisdictions. Bike Patrol officers may assist local police departments where U.S. Mint facilities are located and may respond to calls.
- **Special Response Team (SRT)** is made up of specially selected officers in excellent physical shape who are highly motivated. These officers must pass a series of tests before being given an SRT assignment and then must be certified in Special Weapons and Tactics. A recent SRT assignment was during the Republican National Convention in Philadelphia.

Officers may also become instructional trainers, either as firearms instructors or field training officers. These instructional trainers ensure that U.S. Mint Police officers are fully trained and proficient with firearms and in the principles and techniques necessary for the performance of U.S. Mint Police duties.

United States Capitol Police

Terrance W. Gainer, Chief
Recruiting & Investigations Section
119 D St. NE
Washington, DC 20510-7218
Telephone: (202)224-9819, employment information
Fax: (202)228-5764
E-mail: Recruiting@Cap-Police.Senate.Gov
Web site: www.uscapitolpolice.gov/

CAREER QUICK FACTS

Minimum age:	21
Maximum age:	37
Education:	High school diploma or equivalent (GED)
Convictions:	No felony convictions; no pending charges
Base salary:	$43,166
Benefits:	Full federal benefits
Testing:	Written, physical, psychological, and polygraph exams; extensive background check
Academy:	Eight weeks at FLETC plus 10 weeks in Washington, DC

Mission Statement

Our mission is to protect and support the Congress in meeting its Constitutional responsibilities

Overview

The U.S. Capitol Police were created in 1828 by the U.S. Congress to provide security for the Capitol Building. Their mission is now broader and includes police services to the congressional community and the thousands of visitors to the U.S. Capitol. U.S. Capitol Police officers protect members of Congress, officers of Congress, and their families not only within the Capitol complex but throughout the country.

U.S. Capitol Police officers patrol, protect life and property, investigate criminal acts, and enforce laws, including traffic laws, within their jurisdiction. This jurisdiction includes the U.S. Capitol complex of congressional buildings, parks, and thoroughfares.

You may be familiar with the U.S. Capitol Police through their recent work securing the Senate office buildings that were apparently targets for contamination with ricin powder and previously with anthrax. Obviously, it can be a dangerous job in unpredictable conditions.

Requirements

You must be at least 21 years of age but not yet 37. You must have a high school diploma or equivalency certificate (GED). If you have a felony conviction, or if you are involved in any pending criminal charges, you will not be considered. If you served in the military, you must have been honorably discharged.

The U.S. Capitol Police also stress the importance of certain intangibles: maturity, responsibility, self-direction, and an interest in assisting members of Congress.

Testing

The entry-level police officers' examination includes questions designed to test your reading comprehension, math, writing, grammar, punctuation, and spelling skills. There is also a personal interview, polygraph examination, psychological examination, and medical examination, including vision testing. Applicants must meet certain height/weight and body fat requirements as well.

Training

Trainees receive full pay and begin training immediately upon hire. Following a week-long orientation at the U.S. Capitol Police training center near Washington, DC, you undergo eight weeks of intensive training at the Federal Law Enforcement Training Center (FLETC) in Glynco, Georgia, or Artesia, New Mexico. Training includes police procedures, criminal law, arrest procedures, search and seizure, psychology, self-defense, and other relevant topics.

After training at FLETC is complete, trainees return to the Capitol Police Training Academy for 10 weeks of additional training.

Career Opportunities

Upon completion of their training, officers are assigned to a field training officer. After one or two years of field experience, they may specialize in areas including Dignitary Protection, Criminal Investigations, Intelligence, Threats, Containment and Emergency Response Team, K-9, Communications, Motorized and Mountain Bicycle Patrol, Hazardous Devices and Electronic Countermeasures, and other units.

Additionally, after three years with the department, officers may be promoted to the rank of sergeant.

United States Postal Service

United States Postal Inspection Service

Lee R. Heath, Chief Postal Inspector
U.S. Postal Inspection Service
Security Investigations Service Center
ATTN: Recruitment
225 N. Humphreys Blvd., Fourth Floor
Memphis, Tennessee 38161-0001
Telephone: (866) 648-7472.
Web site: www.usps.com/postalinspectors

CAREER QUICK FACTS

Minimum age:	21
Maximum age:	37
Education:	Four-year college degree
Convictions:	No felony convictions; some felony charges without conviction disqualify; no misdemeanor conviction of domestic violence
Base salary:	According to GS level and position
Benefits:	Full federal benefits
Tests:	Written exams (business writing and cognitive abilities tests); medical (including vision and hearing) and polygraph exams; background check; drug screen
Academy:	13 weeks for postal inspectors; 10 weeks for postal police

Mission Statement and Introduction

The mission of the United States Postal Inspection Service is to protect the U.S. Postal Service, its employees and its customers from criminal attack, and protect the nation's mail system from criminal misuse.

The United States Postal Inspection Service is among the most interesting law enforcement agencies in the country. The mission of the more than 2,000 U.S. postal inspectors is straightforward, but their investigations are diverse. Postal inspectors are federal law enforcement agents, and they are charged with the enforcement of more than 200 federal laws related to the United States Postal Service and the mail it carries.

The Postal Inspection Service secures the system upon which American businesses and citizens depend for the safe exchange of money, securities, correspondence, and much more. You are probably most familiar with the Postal Inspection Service as a result of the anthrax scare following the September 11th attacks. Postal inspectors are responsible for the protection of the mail, the postal employees who process it, and, as recipients of the mail, us. With anthrax and other potential chemical and biological weapons, as well as more traditional weapons like small explosives, distributable within the mail, postal inspectors are on the front lines of the fight against terrorism. Don't forget that the Unabomber, Ted Kaczynski, sent multiple bombs through the mail.

In addition to protecting the mail and mail facilities in terms of physical security, the U.S. Postal Inspection Service also protects children from exploitation by leading the federal government's battle against child pornography and protects citizens from identity fraud. Its jurisdiction is covered in more detail in the following.

Brief History

The U.S. Postal Inspection Service was founded by in 1772 by our first postmaster general, Benjamin Franklin. Originally called "surveyors," U.S. postal inspectors were designated special agents in 1801, and their mandate increased with the enaction by Congress of a Mail Fraud Statute in 1872 in response to a Reconstruction-era rash of mail confidence scams. In 1880, special agents were redesignated as inspectors.

Some of the operations of the U.S. Postal Inspection Service are legendary. In 1926 postal inspectors brought in the three notorious D'Autremont brothers, who had killed four people in their detonation of a railroad train mail car, which they wrongly thought was carrying a half million dollars' worth of gold. In 1937, they planned and carried out the transfer of the country's gold reserve from New York to Fort Knox, a staggering feat which took 500 train cars and several years. The transfer went off without a hitch. Even the Hope Diamond has been successfully sent through the mail—in 1958, to the Smithsonian Institution. In 1991, postal inspectors dismantled a global art fraud organization responsible for selling fake Dali, Miro, and Picasso paintings around the world.

The U.S. Postal Inspection Service is a progressive agency. Their investigative methods were advanced in 1940 with the establishment of the first Postal Inspection Service Crime Laboratory. They also stood on the cutting edge of gender diversity by being among the first federal law enforcement agencies to admit women, beginning in the 1970s. And their jurisdiction was expanded in 1984 to include not only those who deal in child pornography but those who receive it through the mail.

Jurisdiction

One thing U.S. postal inspectors cannot do is open first-class letters and parcels without first obtaining a search warrant, as such action is prohibited by the Fourth Amendment. Other types of mail do not enjoy such protection.

The jurisdiction of U.S. postal inspectors includes the following types of crimes:

- Assaults against U.S. Postal Service employees while on duty or related to their jobs
- Bombs sent through the mail or at postal facilities
- Burglary or robbery of U.S. Postal Service facilities, employees, and contractors
- Child exploitation in materials sent through the mail and, in certain situations, over the Internet
- Controlled substances sent through the mail or at postal facilities
- Counterfeit stamps and postal money orders

- Destruction, obstruction, delay, or theft of mail, as prohibited by federal statute
- Electronic crimes, including fraud schemes
- Embezzlement of postal funds
- Extortion, when threats and/or demands are sent through the mail
- Identity theft, which often involves a theft of someone's mail or use of the mail
- Mail fraud, including schemes involving health care, insurance, and consumer fraud
- Money laundering
- Obscenity sent through the mail

Occasionally, U.S. postal inspectors will participate in investigations outside their normal jurisdiction, per the request of the U.S. Department of Justice or a U.S. Attorney.

Career Opportunities

U.S. postal inspectors may work in a variety of positions and facilities. In addition to the investigation of crimes outlined previously, the conduction of internal audits and inspections, and other duties, inspectors may specialize further.

The agency's Forensic & Technical Services Division (F&TSD) includes more than 100 U.S. postal inspectors who may work at one of the agency's five forensic crime laboratories. At these labs, inspectors analyze evidence with the assistance of scientists and specialists. Their findings are used to identify suspects and aid in the prosecution of the same and are presented by inspectors in expert trial testimony. Analysis units include the following:

- **Questioned Documents Unit,** which analyzes handwriting, ink, paper, fingerprints, and other document evidence to determine authenticity, origin, and other factors
- **Fingerprint Unit,** which looks at fingerprints, visible or latent, on evidentiary materials

- **Physical Sciences Unit,** which performs physical and chemical examinations and processes crime scene evidence, including bomb debris, explosive devices, firearm and tire impressions, controlled substances, and other types of evidence
- **Polygraph Services,** which includes specially trained U.S. postal inspectors who perform polygraph examinations

In addition to employing postal inspectors, the U.S. Postal Inspection Service maintains a security force of uniformed postal police officers, who currently number about 1,400 nationwide. These officers provide security and escort services to facilities and high-value shipments, in addition to providing other protective services.

Requirements

As with other federal law enforcement jobs, applicants must be at least 21 years old and no more than 37. You must have a four-year college degree, be in sound physical condition, and meet all vision and hearing requirements, as well as height-weight requirements. You must be able to communicate well in English.

If you have ever been convicted of a felony, you will not be considered. If you have a misdemeanor domestic violence conviction, you will not be considered. In addition, certain felony or misdemeanor charges without conviction may disqualify you.

Applicants are required to take two written tests, a business writing test and a cognitive abilities examination. There is a medical examination, including a drug screen, and a polygraph examination. And all applicants undergo a thorough background check.

There are several special tracks to employment as a U.S. postal inspector, for which there are special requirements:

- **The Language Skills Track** is ideal for those with fluency in a foreign language for which such skill is sought by the agency. Some of these languages are Arabic, Cantonese, Farsi, French, German, Korean, Russian, Turkish, and Vietnamese. Applicants on this track must pass a formal proficiency test.

- **The Specialized Postal Experience Track** applicants must have at least one year of experience with the U.S. Postal Service.
- **The Specialized Nonpostal Skill Track** applicants must possess a law degree.
- In addition, a fourth specialized track is for applicants with advanced degrees or advanced work experience.

Training

Upon hire, employment is probationary for six months. U.S. postal inspectors are trained in residence at the William F. Bolger Center for Leadership Development in Potomac, Maryland, for 13 weeks. This training includes investigative techniques, defensive tactics, firearms, legal matters, search and seizure, arrest techniques, court procedures, postal operations, and a detailed study of the U.S. Postal Inspection Service's jurisdiction. You must pass practical exercises in academic areas and with firearms to graduate. After graduation, training continues in the field for four to six months.

Postal police officers undergo a 10-week basic training course at the Federal Law Enforcement Training Center (FLETC) in Glynco, Georgia.

Department of Veterans Affairs

Office of Security and Law Enforcement
Police and Security Service

John H. Baffa, Deputy Assistant Secretary for Security and Law Enforcement
William B. Harper, Director of Police and Security Service

Visit any VA Medical Facility for employment information
Web site: www.va.gov/osle/programinfo.htm

CAREER QUICK FACTS

Education:	Two or four year degree
or	
Law enforcement	
experience:	Per OPM requirements
Convictions:	No felony convictions; no misdemeanor conviction of domestic violence

Mission Statement

Provides guidance, consultation, investigations and direct operational support for all elements of the Department of Veterans Affairs.

Overview

With jurisdiction over all facilities and grounds owned by or used by the Veterans Administration (VA), the Police and Security Service is the element of the Office of Security and Law Enforcement responsible for the protection of life and property and the maintenance of order. Most VA police do not carry firearms, but wider implementation of firearms is being undertaken.

The Police and Security Service is organized as follows:

- **Police and Security Inspection Program** conducts on-site inspections of VA Medical Centers to determine whether the security and law enforcement operations at each are operating properly.
- **Program Guidance and Planning** determines security plans for medical centers, taking into consideration the safety of staff, patients, and visitors.
- **Criminal Investigation** conducts criminal investigations of offenses that occur on property of the Veterans Administration or property used by it. Criminal Investigation officers in the Office of Security and Law Enforcement have arrest authority for such offenses.
- **Secretarial Protection** provides security and protection for the secretary of veterans affairs. As a member of the President's cabinet, he or she receives an appropriate level of executive protection.
- **Liaison with Other Federal Law Enforcement,** just as it sounds, works with federal law enforcement agencies on joint efforts from training to information sharing and policy development.

Requirements

Candidates must have a two- or four-year degree in a criminal justice field or required experience in law enforcement. Applicants are subject to a thorough background investigation.

Training

Upon hire, VA police officers receive training at the VA Law Enforcement Training Center (LETC) in North Little Rock, Arkansas. This facility is also utilized by other departments and agencies in basic training and specific mission training. Basic programs include criminal law, search and seizure, patrol techniques, and many other law enforcement–related subjects. Given the nature of the facilities the VA police officers will be assigned to, special emphasis is given to verbal skills and methods for effectively and compassionately dealing with individuals of diminished capacity.

Appendix A

ALBUQUERQUE (NEW MEXICO) POLICE DEPARTMENT CADET WRITTEN ENTRANCE EXAMINATION

Test Guide

This study guide has been developed by the Testing Division of the Human Services Department to assist you in preparing for the Albuquerque Police Department's entry level Police Cadet examination. This information is intended to help you familiarize yourself with the types of questions that will be administered, as well as the various types of material that will be covered in the examination.

It is suggested that you read the entire study guide as soon as possible. This will help you identify areas in which you anticipate problems. If you find that you are weak in one or more areas, your local librarian should be able to assist you in locating materials, which will help you do in-depth studying.

If you are able to answer all questions in the study guide easily and correctly, you will probably do well on the actual examination. **If you cannot answer all of the questions correctly, you would be well advised to study before the test.** Your study efforts will help you on the test, and later, on the job, if you are hired.

This study guide consists of six sections:

- The first section provides an overview of the information, which will be covered in the examination.
- The second provides information on how to take the test and how to record your responses on the answer sheet.
- The last four sections of this study packet contain information and sample test items for each of the following:
  Observation and Recall/Cognitive Abilities
  Personal Maturity and Integrity
  Technical Skills
  Written and Oral Communications

Section 1: Overview

The Albuquerque Police Department City of Albuquerque written examination consists of five sections:

- <u>**OBSERVATION AND RECALL:**</u> Measures your ability to make detailed observations on the basis of written, oral and visual data and recall the data clearly and accurately.

- **COGNITIVE ABILITIES:** Measures your ability to think toward a good conclusion.
- **PERSONAL MATURITY AND INTEGRITY:** Measures your ability to handle situations requiring strong personal ethics as well as the ability to make mature calm decisions in difficult situations.
- **TECHNICAL SKILLS:** Measures your skill in writing, making basic mathematical calculations, reading and interpreting charts, and basic map reading skills. A calculator may be used for this section of the written exam.
- **WRITTEN AND ORAL COMMUNICATION:** Measures your ability to use proper grammar, spelling and punctuation in preparing written documents. It also measures your ability to read textbooks, statutes, and procedural orders commonly found in the job setting.

These test sections measure knowledge skills and abilities necessary to succeed in the field of law enforcement. The minimum qualification score for this 100 question multiple-choice test is 70 or better. Scores of 69 or below do not meet our minimum requirements in order to continue in our process. The applicant who does not meet our minimum requirements, must wait for the next cadet class recruitment process before they can re-test.

Section 2: General Instructions
Examination Answer List

All items on the written examination are in multiple-choice format. During the exam you will record your answers on the separate answer sheet which will be provided for you at the beginning of testing. **You will not make any marks in the test booklet.** Your answers will be recorded by darkening the circle on the answer sheet, which corresponds to both the question number in the test booklet and the answer you have selected as the **best answer. Check frequently to ensure that the number next to your answer is the same as the number of the question you are answering.**

Mark only one answer per test question. Questions for which more than one answer have been marked will be scored as **incorrect** even if one of the answers is correct. If you decide to change an answer, erase your first answer completely, then darken the space corresponding to the answer you feel is the **best answer.** Avoid making any stray pencil marks on the answer sheet.

Your score on the examination is based on the number of correct responses. If you do not know an answer and cannot make an educated or informed choice then simply guess on an answer. It is better to guess than to leave a question blank.

Sample Question:

Question as it will appear in the text booklet:

1. To record an answer on the Albuquerque Police Cadet entrance exam, you darken

   A: One circle
   B: Two circles
   C: Three circles
   D: Four circles

Item as it would appear on the answer sheet:

A B C D E
1. ● ○ ○ ○ ○

"A" is the right answer. Remember, you may darken only one answer. If you darken more than one answer, the item will be incorrect.

Section 3: Observation and Recall Cognitive Abilities
Part 1: Test Questions

1. You will have the opportunity to view a photograph for 60 seconds. After the time allotment is complete, you will be required to answer questions relating to the photograph.

2. You will study a "wanted" poster for 60 seconds. You will also be required to answer specific questions relating to your observations.

3. You will be required to read through three brief passages in a three-minute time frame and answer questions relating to the content of the passages.
4. You will listen to a statement read by the City Human Resources test giver and answer related questions.
5. You will complete a map reading exercise. While instructions are read, you will be looking at a map.

Each group of questions is designed to measure your ability to observe and recall details. Your study efforts should focus on **recalling visual information (seeing), auditory information (hearing) and written information (reading)**.

We have included two exercises to help you study for this portion of the testing. Continue practicing these exercises until you can accurately respond to the questions asked.

Part 2: Observation and Recall

Exercise I

1. You will require the assistance of another person. Have your study partner select a photograph.
2. Have your partner allow you to study this photograph for **60 seconds.**
3. Have your partner ask you <u>specific</u> questions about the photograph.
4. In responding to the questions <u>**do not**</u> look at the photograph. Rely only on your memory of the photograph. Continue practicing with different photographs until you can accurately respond to the questions being asked.

Exercise II

1. Have your study partner select a news article (5 to 7 columns).
2. Have your partner carefully read the article out loud for two minutes.
3. Your partner should then ask you specific detailed questions about the article.

The observation and recall cognitive abilities section of the City Police Entrance exam should be easy for you if you practice each of the two ways described above.

Part 3: Cognitive Abilities

The questions contained in the second half of the cognitive abilities of the City Police Written examination are designed to measure your ability to separate speculation from fact and to draw logical conclusions. It also is designed to measure your ability to prioritize information and discern patterns, trends and similarities.

In some of the questions, you will be given several pieces of information and asked to draw factual conclusions based on the information. In other questions, you will be given a series of numbers or letters and asked to determine the next item in the sequence based on the recognition of the pattern.

Once you understand how an answer is obtained, it will be easier to determine the correct answer on future questions. A study partner can assist you by preparing similar questions.

Note: Drawing or listing information can be <u>very helpful</u> in determining the correct answer.

Q: Mary has two sons. Their names are Bill and Joe. Joe's stepfather is named John and his father is named Dick. Joe's stepmother is named Lillian. Which of the following is a definite statement of fact.

A. Dick is, or was at one time, married to Lillian.
B. Mary and Dick are now divorced from each other.
C. Bill's stepfather is named John.
D. Bill's father is named Dick.

Correct answer: A

Explanation: If Lillian is Joe's stepmother, she had to have been married to Joe's father at one time or another so sentence A is a fact. Mary and Dick produced a child, but there is no definite statement that they were married. Sentence B is possible, but not a definite fact. Sentences C and D are wrong for the same reason since it has not been established that Bill and Joe share the same father.

Section 4: Personal Maturity and Integrity

In the Personal Maturity and Integrity section, you will be presented with a variety of situations for which you must select the best course of action. You should select the best or most correct answer taking into consideration personal ethics, honesty, and integrity. The situations are designed to also examine your level of maturity in handling sensitive issues of various kinds. Several sample questions follow:

Q: You are in your car and in line at a traffic light. The traffic is very heavy and you have already sat through three red lights. A driver several cars behind you has become very impatient and is trying to jump to the front of the line, by pulling into the a parking lot on the right hand side of the street and driving in the parking lot until he is even with the first car in line. When the light changes, he begins to move his vehicle back into the street from the parking lot in a very aggressive manner. The other drivers refuse to allow him in and as you watch him, he becomes more and more agitated and careless as he tries to push his way into line. You are the next vehicle in line. What would you do?

A. Let him in the line of traffic.
B. Block his vehicle and then get out and explain what a hazard he is presenting to other drivers.
C. Let him wait his turn like everyone else.
D. Get his license number and report the matter to the Police.

Correct answer: A

Explanation: Answers B and C will just escalate the situation. Answer D is inappropriate because the police cannot do anything since a crime has not occurred. Answer A is the best way to remove the hazard immediately.

Q: You witness a shooting in a parking lot (you are a civilian, not a police officer). You are alone, but you have a weapon in your vehicle. The person doing the shooting is in a car with two other men and the vehicle is leaving the parking lot. What do you do?

A. Help the victim as soon as the vehicle leaves.
B. Fire at the tires of the vehicle to keep it from leaving the area.

C. Leave the area to avoid becoming involved. Call the police as quickly as possible.
D. Follow the vehicle to get its license number and then report the matter to the police.

Correct answer: A

Explanation: Answer B is not correct because it would escalate the situation and possibly lead to other injuries. Answer C and D are incorrect because they fail to provide immediate assistance to the victim. Answer D is also incorrect because it puts you in unnecessary danger. Answer A is the best answer of those provided.

Section 5: Technical Skills

Section five is based on your basic technical skills. This section is designed to measure your ability to make accurate mathematical calculations. Calculators will be allowed during the examination, but you must bring your own if you plan to use one. **Calculators will not be provided.** This section of the test will also measure your ability to read maps, but sample questions are not provided.

The math questions are presented in a word-problem format. You will be asked to add, divide, subtract and calculate averages. If you have difficulty with the math questions provided on this study guide, you may wish to review basic math techniques. Your local library should have fifth grade to eighth grade math books, which will be helpful to refresh your basic math skills. Or, if you have school age children their schoolbooks may provide helpful information.

Q: You are asked for your estimated time of arrival at the scene of an incident. The time is now 10:00 p.m. You are 10 minutes away from the scene and traveling at a rate of 60 miles per hour. Assuming that you are able to maintain this speed. What is you estimated time of arrival?

A. 10:03 p.m.
B. 10:10 p.m.
C. 10:15 p.m.
D. 10:20 p.m.

Correct answer: B

Q: You are told by your supervisor that you will receive a 3% cost of living increase this year. Your current salary (before deductions) is $1,800 per month. What will your salary be after the increase?

A. $54.00
B. $540.00
C. $1,854.00
D. $2,340.00

Correct answer: C

Q: Your supervisor asks you to determine the average number of gallons of gasoline you use each shift based on your usage over the last 10 days. Your daily usage for this period of time (in gallons) was 8, 7, 6, 9, 5, 8, 8, 7, 6, and 6. What was the average number of gallons used each day?

A. 5
B. 7
C. 9
D. 70

Correct answer: B

Section 6: Written and Oral Communications

In this section, you will be instructed to read several passages. After you read the information, you will respond to the question or questions relating to the passage. These passages are taken from materials, which you as a police officer will be required to read and interpret at both the Academy and on the job as an officer. Several sample questions follow:

Q: "The crime of obtaining property by false pretenses always involves misrepresentations by the accused of past or present fact. The accused must be aware that his statement is false whereas the victim believes it to be true. The property must be delivered in reliance on the misrepresentation to the detriment of the victim and the benefit of the accused." According to the information contained in this paragraph, which of the following examples provides the best illustration of obtaining property by false pretenses?

A. Carol asks to borrow her mother's car to go to the mall with a friend. On her way to the mall, she runs into a friend who invites her to a party at her house. Instead of going to the mall, she goes to the party. While the car is parked at the friend's house, it is struck by another vehicle causing $2,500.00 in damage.

B. Tom is selling his car through a newspaper ad. The newspaper mistakenly prints the mileage as 45,000 rather than the actual mileage of 85,000. Tom does not inform a potential buyer of the error.

C. Sue stops Bill as he is leaving a pawn shop after purchasing an expensive piece of jewelry. Sue tells Bill she is a police officer and must confiscate the piece of jewelry as a part of a fencing investigation. Sue is not an officer, but Bill believing she is an officer, turns the item over to her. Sue then sells the item at another pawn shop and keeps the money.

D. Arnold tells his friend Joe that he has a "sure-fire" plan to make $5,000.00. The plan involves a bet at the horse races. Arnold wants Joe to split the $100.00 bet. They both lose their money.

Correct answer: C

Explanation: Choice C is the only situation in which the accused obtains property through a false statement of fact. In situation A, Carol intended to go to the mall at the time she borrowed the car. In situation B, Tom was not the one who made the false statement, he simply failed to correct it. In situation D, Arnold states an option rather than a fact and Joe has the opportunity to assess the information for himself.

Q: "Burglary consists of the unauthorized entry of any vehicle, watercraft, aircraft, dwelling, or other structure, movable or immovable, with the intent to commit any felony or theft therein." Of the following types of structures, which would apply to the type of structure defined in this statute?

A. A houseboat
B. A motor home
C. A storage shed
D. All of the above

Correct answer: D

Explanation A houseboat is a type of watercraft; a motor home is both a vehicle and a dwelling structure; a storage shed is an immovable structure. Although each answer is correct, the BEST answer is (most correct) D.

Q: "Reckless driving is a voluntary act done with a conscious disregard of the consequences." According to this definition of reckless driving, which of the following conditions is not necessary in the crime of reckless driving?

A. The accused must willfully do the act.
B. The accused must consciously do the act.
C. The accused must volunteer to drive instead of letting a more competent driver operate the vehicle.
D. The accused must knowingly fail to consider the consequences of driving carelessly or recklessly.

Correct answer: C

In addition to measuring your reading skills, this section of the City of Albuquerque Written examination is designed to measure ability to correctly identify proper grammar. You will need to read each question carefully for instructions. Some questions will give you four sentences: you are to choose the one sentence which contains no errors. Other questions will ask you to identify a misspelled word. As you make your selection, consider proper spelling, grammar, punctuation, and word usage.

Q: Which of the following words is misspelled?

A. concise
B. deter
C. offendor
D. witnessed

Correct answer: C

Q: Of the following sentences, which is technically correct considering proper spelling, grammar, capitalization, and punctuation?

A. He didn't want to go to there house.

B. He stuttered a lot before he answered the question.

C. He reported the crime at 9:00 a.m. on Saturday.

D. The sergeant, took the report.

Correct answer: C

Explanation: Sentences A uses "there" instead of "their": sentence B uses "a lot," which does not need to be there. Sentence D contains a comma which does not belong in the sentence.

Q: Select the correct sentence from those presented.

A. I want you too know how I feel.

B. Todays society has many problems.

C. John and Tom has a reason to be angry.

D. The supervisors will be meeting on Friday.

Correct answer: D

Explanation: Sentences A misuses "too" (it should be "to"); sentence B omits an apostrophe (it should be "today's"); sentence C lacks verb/noun agreement (it should be John and Tom <u>have</u> a reason to be angry).

We hope that the information contained in this study guide has been beneficial to you. If you are wanting to obtain more information on subject material from this study guide, we suggest contacting your local librarian for a work-book on Police Entrance Exams. We wish all applicants the best of luck with your pursuit in becoming one of Albuquerque's finest, an Albuquerque Police Officer.

Appendix B

AUSTIN (TEXAS) POLICE DEPARTMENT APPLICANT INFORMATION PACKET

Section 5:
Physical Ability Testing

★

Applicants successfully completing the first 4 steps will be required to return for a physical ability test. Each applicant must successfully complete all stages of the physical ability test to remain eligible for employment consideration. The Recruiting Division's staff may require an applicant to submit a letter from his/her personal physician confirming that the applicant can safely perform each and every element of this phase of the testing. If the applicant's personal physician cannot or will not affirm that the applicant can safely perform each and every element of this phase of the testing, the applicant will be disqualified. The following are elements of this phase of testing:

Shotgun

Applicant, in standing position, places the 12-gauge shotgun on his/her shoulder as if to fire. The barrel of the shotgun is placed inside a 6" hole of a wooden test stand. The shotgun must then be dry fired 4 times in a 10 second time limit without letting the barrel of the shotgun touch any part of the wood.

Handgun Trigger Squeeze and Direction Control

Pull the trigger six times within ten seconds—double action with right and left hand. The barrel of handgun cannot have a directional variance of more than 6".

Note: If you do not have strong fingers, you need to start strengthening them at least a month prior to testing.

Driver/Vehicle Compatibility

From a seated position in a standard patrol vehicle, lap-belt tightly secured, you must be able to see over the steering wheel, successfully operate the accelerator and brake, and grip the steering wheel with both hands, looking forward and through the rear window.

1 1/2 mile run

Applicants will have to complete a 1 1/2 mile run. All applicants must complete the run in 15 minutes and 18 seconds. This test will be conducted on the same day as the obstacle course.

Obstacle Course

The following information is designed to describe the physical tasks you will be required to perform for the Austin Police Department's physical ability examination. You will increase your chances of a passing score if you spend a fair amount of time preparing for the test. This includes thoroughly reviewing this information packet, following the specific directions given regarding attire, paying proper attention to your physical well-being before the test and taking care to avoid becoming overly anxious about the test.

A job analysis of police officers in the Austin Police Department revealed that they perform certain essential or important physical functions that are vital to their job duties. Many essential functions identified from this job analysis were included in the physical ability examination described below. Subject matter expert panel meetings composed of law enforcement personnel from this municipality also confirmed that the functions included in the physical ability test were job related and essential for successful performance as an Austin police officer.

The Importance of Core Fitness Components to the Physical Ability Examination

The Physical Ability Examination has been designed to simulate certain essential job tasks common to law enforcement. The successful completion of each "event" in this examination is dependent on the ability of the candidate to perform one or more specific core fitness components. In order to perform well on this examination candidates must have *at least* an average level of physical fitness in the core fitness components. Failure to perform well on any "event" suggests a low level of fitness in one or more of the underlying core physical fitness components. Fitness training and periodic self-assessment will result in improvement.

In Austin, police officers must be able to run (speed and distance), climb through windows, crawl in confined spaces, climb over obstacles (fences, etc.), lift, carry, walk, sit or stand for long periods of time, and arrest resisting individuals. The Austin police officer physical ability examination measures job related physical skills such as these, which

Event	Core Component	Training Fitness Mode	Suggested Self-test
1. Patrol car	None		
2. Physical description	None		
3. Run	Anaerobic power, body composition	Sprinting, high intensity/short intervals	Timed 300m run
4. Incline climb	As above	As above with incline	As above w/ incline
5. Obstacle run I	Anaerobic power, muscular endurance, aerobic endurance	As above, > 1.5 mile run, low back & hamstring strengthening	As above, timed agility run, 1-RM leg press, 1.5 mile run
6. Barrier climb	Absolute strength, muscular endurance	Upper & lower body strengthening	1-RM bench & leg press, 1 min sit-ups/push- or pull-ups
7. Duck under barrier	Agility/flexibility, power	Lower body & abdominal strengthening	1 min sit-ups, 1-RM leg press, vertical jump
8. Wall climb	Absolute strength	Overall strengthening (upper body focus)	Pull-ups
9. Stair climb	Power, leg strength, endurance	Stair climbing, lower body strengthening	Timed 300m run, 1-RM leg press
10. Forced door entry	Strength	Upper & lower body strengthening, sit-ups, push-ups	1-RM bench & leg press.
11. Obstacle run 2	Agility/flexibility, power	Lower body & abdominal strengthening	1 min sit-ups, 1-RM leg press, vertical jump
12. Window climb	Strength, endurance, body composition	Upper & lower body strengthening, sit-ups, push-ups, 1.5 mile run	1 min sit-ups, pull-ups, 1.5 mile run
13. Suspect ID	None		
14. Suspect take-down	Strength/endurance	Upper & lower body strengthening, sit-ups, push-ups, 1.5 mile run	1 min sit-ups & push-ups, 1.5 mile run
15. Suspect move	Strength/ endurance	Upper & lower body strengthening, sit-ups, push-ups, 1.5 mile run	1-RM leg & bench press, 1 min sit ups & push ups, pull-ups

are necessary for successful performance as a police officer. Only those skills that do not require training to become proficient are assessed.

The examination is equally valid for assessing the physical skills of candidates with police experience and those without. For example, one portion of the test requires the applicant to climb a wooden fence. It is not necessary to have prior experience as a police officer to possess the physical ability to climb a fence.

Test Preparation

The following suggestions should help you prepare yourself physically for the test:

- Avoid junk food and concentrate on a well balanced diet for several days before the test.
- Avoid tranquilizers and stimulants such as beverages containing caffeine, especially on the day of the test.
- Get a good night sleep before the test.
- Do not drink a lot of liquids or eat a <u>big</u> meal before the test. The actual ability test will start about 8:00 AM, so eat accordingly and/or bring a snack.
- It is important to stay hydrated, especially during the hot months. Be sure to drink plenty of water for several days before the test, and in moderation the morning of the test.
- Avoid alcohol several days prior to and especially on the day of the test.

On the day of the testing, all candidates are required to wear long pants with belt loops. Belt loops are required because a police utility belt needs to be attached during testing. Sport shoes are highly recommended. Sweatpants or shorts are not allowed for safety reasons.

Description of the Obstacle Course

The test will require an applicant to complete several specified physical tasks in a given sequence within an allotted time frame. An orientation is conducted prior to testing.

To simulate a police officer on duty, applicants will be provided with and will be required to wear police equipment during the physical testing session. This includes items such as a utility belt, handcuffs, a gun in a holster (the gun will be real but inoperable) and two magazine pouches containing two magazines. All of this equipment will be provided to you by the Austin Police Department at the time of testing.

Criteria for Passing the Exam

- Candidates must complete all events in 3 minutes and 8 seconds or less.
- Candidates must complete all events in the specified amount of time in the required sequence or they fail the examination.
- Candidates must correctly identify the suspect.
- Upon completion of the test, candidates will be told their time and will be informed of their pass/fail status.

Test Components

All applicants will be given an orientation and walk through. No one will be allowed to take the test unless they fully understand what is expected of them.

1. **Patrol Car:** Wearing a police utility belt and the equipment listed above, the candidate will sit in the driver's seat of a patrol car with the doors closed and seat belt fastened and will await further instructions.
2. **Physical Description:** A test monitor will give the candidate verbal instructions to pursue a fleeing felony suspect (fictitious) by providing a description of what the suspect is wearing (for example, an orange shirt and black cap). Finally, the test monitor will tell the candidate to "GO." The applicant must then complete the following physical tasks.
3. **Run:** The candidate must get out of the car and run a distance of about 440 yards. Timing begins when the candidate's foot touches the ground.
4. **Incline Climb:** Shortly after beginning the run, the candidate must climb up and down an incline.

5. **Obstacle Run 1:** After coming down the incline, the candidate must run around obstacles in the manner specified by the test monitor. The candidate will then run under the training academy sign.

6. **Barrier Climb:** After the obstacle run, the candidate must jump over a 2-foot barrier and climb over a 4-foot barrier.

7. **Under Barrier:** The candidate must then run to and duck under a barrier.

8. **Fence Climb:** Approximately midway through the course, the candidate will encounter and climb over a wooden fence approximately 6 feet high. The candidate must climb over the fence and is not allowed to go around it.

9. **Stair Climb:** After climbing the fence, the candidate must climb up a staircase, and then climb down the other side of the staircase.

10. **Forced Door Entry:** The candidate will continue the course to a door with 55 pounds of weight on the other side of the door. The candidate must force the door open and proceed through the door.

11. **Obstacle Run 2:** After going through the doorway, the candidate must run under some monkey bars and around a pole.

12. **Window Climb:** Near the end of the run, the applicant must climb through a window opening, which approximates the type of windows commonly found in the City of Austin.

13. **Suspect Identification:** After climbing through the window, the candidate will run behind a wall and identify the suspect (silhouette) who matches the description provided at the beginning of the test. The candidate must identify the proper suspect by shouting out the number on the silhouette.

14. **Suspect Takedown:** After identifying the suspect, the candidate must take a punching bag, which simulates the suspect, down to the ground and past a line specified by the test monitor.

15. **Suspect Move:** The candidate will then move a dummy weighing approximately 165 pounds to a designated line 15 feet away. Timing of the events stops when the entire dummy passes over the line.

A candidate who is able to complete the entire series of events successfully, in proper sequence and in a certain amount of time passes the test.

Appendix C

COLUMBUS (GEORGIA) POLICE DEPARTMENT APPLICANT BACKGROUND BOOKLET

★

***** **IMPORTANT** *****

Failure to follow these instructions could cause your name to be removed from further consideration. Incomplete or incorrect information will delay or disqualify you from the hiring process.

- Applicants are encouraged to submit their applications IN PERSON. However, if the application must be submitted by mail, the applicant is responsible for contacting the Personnel

Office of the Columbus Police Department within 10 (ten) days to be scheduled for the required Physical Qualifications Test. Arrangements will also be made for fingerprinting, photographing, and completion of the Essay Exemplar.

- When submitting your application in person, you should also allow one (1) hour for the completion of the entire procedure. Applications should be submitted to the Police Personnel Office by 3:30 PM (Eastern Time) on normal business days.
- Print all responses in the booklet LEGIBLY and in BLACK INK. All supporting documents must be clear and legible.
- COMPLETE and ACCURATE addresses (numericals, streets, apartment #s., etc.) and phone numbers must be given in all requested areas. Incomplete or inaccurate information will delay your application process.
- All "yes/no" questions must be answered with a "yes" or "no" response. "N/A" stands for "Not Applicable." Do not use "N/A" when "No" or "None" is the correct response. Do not leave any blanks. Answer all questions accurately, truthfully, and in complete detail. Additional space is available in the last few pages of this application.
- All appropriate waivers and forms in this application must be completed. The Military Affirmation Form should be completed only if you have never served in the military.
- After submitting your application with the necessary background information, any changes in your address or phone number should be related to the Police Personnel Office. At any time during the application process, if you are issued a traffic citation, have criminal warrant or civil papers lodged against you or are the subject of a criminal investigation, you should contact the Police Personnel Office.
- If you have questions, contact the Police Personnel Office at (706) 653-3154.

It is necessary that all information be complete, truthful, and accurate. The Georgia Peace Officers Standards and Training Council manual (464-4.12) states: "The Council shall deny certification to any applicant supplying false information . . . or who uses fraud in securing employment."

Discovery of deliberate omissions, intentional misrepresentations, or any falsified information will be the basis for termination of the application process or employment. It could result in criminal prosecution as prescribed by Georgia Law (O.C.G.A. § 16-10-20).

It is imperative that any conviction be listed. This includes guilty pleas, guilty findings by a jury, or a plea of nolo contendre from any criminal proceedings, regardless of whether the judgment of guilt or the sentence is withheld or not entered. This also includes First Offenders under Georgia Law O.C.G.A. § 35-8-7.1. All information will be subject to verification through polygraph examinations and administrative investigations.

I understand the above instructions. I also understand that if I do not wish to answer a question in this booklet or application, I may choose to do so and the application process will be terminated.

Signature: _____

Date: _____

COLUMBUS POLICE DEPARTMENT
510 10th Street, Box 1866, Columbus, Georgia 31902

PERSONAL DATA

1. Name _____
    (First)   (Middle)   (Last)
    List any other names you have been known by and give reasons.

2. Date of Birth (mm/dd/yy) _____

3. Social Security Number _____

4. Race_____ Sex_____ Height_____ Weight_____
    Hair_____ Eyes_____

5. List any scars, marks or tattoos_____

6. Natural Born Citizen _____ or Naturalized _____
    Certificate Number_____

7. Location of Birth _____

8. Your Address _____

9. Your Home Phone _____

10. With Whom Do You Reside_____

11. List all organizations, clubs and associations which you are or have been a member of or associated with, including addresses.

_____

_____

_____

12. Your Work Phone _____

13. Marital status_____

If married, complete the following information concerning your spouse:

Name_____ Date of Birth _____

     (First) (Middle) (Maiden)   (mm/dd/yy)

Date Married _____ Occupation/Employer_____

Work Phone _____

If divorced, give names of former spouses:

_____

_____

14. What are your hobbies, special skills and abilities (including foreign languages)?

_____

_____

_____

_____

FAMILY HISTORY

15. List all of your dependants (exclude spouse if listed on previous page):

_____

_____

_____

_____

16. List all living members of your immediate family (include parents, siblings and in-laws). DO NOT list any names already shown.

_____

_____

_____

RESIDENCES

17. List all your addresses for the last ten (10) years. Start with your present address. Be sure to include college addresses and residences related to military service.

_____

_____

_____

_____

_____

_____

EDUCATION

18. If you obtained a G.E.D. certificate, list the name and address of the institution and the year obtained:

Institution	Address	City/State	Year

19. If you graduated from high school, list the name and address of the school and the year you graduated:

School	Address	City/State	Year

20. Please list each college or university you have attended. Please indicate quarter or semester hours.

Institution _____City/State_____

Date Graduated _____Degree/Hours Obtained _____

Major Course of Study _____

Overall Grade Point Average_____

Institution _____City/State_____

Date Graduated _____Degree/Hours Obtained _____

Major Course of Study _____

Overall Grade Point Average_____

Institution _____City/State_____

Date Graduated _____Degree/Hours Obtained _____

Major Course of Study _____

Overall Grade Point Average_____

21. Law Enforcement Academies (Georgia Only)

Name of Academy   City   Date Graduated

_____

Certification # Academic Score (Attach to Application) Position

_____

22. List any technical or other training/skills.

_____

_____

_____

23. Were you ever expelled or suspended from any school or disciplined by any school official?

If yes, explain.

_____

_____

_____

_____

EMPLOYMENT HISTORY

(Past and present employers should be listed in General Employment Application.)

24. Have you previously applied for employment with the Columbus Consolidated Government? _____

    If yes, list the approximate date, position sought and disposition.

    _____

    _____

    _____

    _____

25. Have you ever worked for the Columbus Consolidated Government? _____

    If yes, explain.

    _____

    _____

    _____

    _____

26. Do you object to wearing a uniform? _____ Shift work? _____

    If yes to either, explain. _____

    _____

    _____

    _____

    _____

27. Do you have any experience with shift work? ____

28. Have you ever engaged in any business as an owner, partner or corporate member? _____

If yes, explain.

_____

_____

_____

_____

29. Have you ever worked for any member of your family? _____
   If yes, explain.

_____

_____

_____

_____

30. Have you ever had any arguments concerning job duties or working conditions? _____
   If yes, explain

_____

_____

_____

_____

31. Has a supervisor ever reprimanded you for being late or absent
   from work? _____
   If yes, explain.

_____

_____

_____

_____

32. Has a supervisor ever reprimanded or suspended you for misconduct or for not doing your job correctly? _____
   If yes, explain.

_____

_____

_____

_____

33. Circle the number of times you have been asked to resign or have been fired from a job in the last 10 years.

    10 9 8 7 6 5 4 3 2 1 0

    If not zero, explain.

    _____

    _____

    _____

    _____

34. Circle the number of times in the last 10 years that you have resigned after being told your employer intended to fire you or take any form of disciplinary action.

    10 9 8 7 6 5 4 3 2 1 0

    If not zero, explain.

    _____

    _____

    _____

    _____

35. Circle the number of times in the last 10 years that you have left a job without giving notice.

    10 9 8 7 6 5 4 3 2 1 0

    If not zero, explain.

    _____

    _____

    _____

    _____

Financial

36. List information concerning all your current liabilities (including mortgages, auto loans, personal loans, credit cards, etc.).

Firm Name _____Balance _____

Firm Name _____Balance _____

Firm Name _____Balance _____

Firm Name _____Balance _____

Firm Name _____Balance _____

Firm Name _____Balance _____

Firm Name _____Balance _____

Firm Name _____Balance _____

37. Do you have any bills that are currently overdue? _____
    If yes, explain.

    _____

    _____

    _____

    _____

38. Have you ever had anything repossessed? _____
    If yes, explain.

    _____

    _____

    _____

    _____

39. Have you ever declared bankruptcy? _____
    If yes, explain.

    _____

    _____

    _____

    _____

40. Have you ever had any wage garnishments? _____

    If yes, explain.

    _____

    _____

    _____

    _____

41. Have you ever been involved in any kind of lawsuit, either as plaintiff or defendant (includes criminal, civil, traffic and divorce)? _____

    If yes, explain.

    _____

    _____

    _____

    _____

Military

42. Have you ever attempted to join any branch of the armed services and were refused? _____

    If yes, explain.

    _____

    _____

    _____

    _____

43. Have you ever served on active duty with any branch of the armed services? _____

    If yes, explain.

    _____

    _____

    _____

    _____

44. List dates of military service:

_____   _____

    Entrance (mm/yy)   Discharge (mm/yy)

45. List type of discharge (honorable, general, etc.)

_____

46. What was your highest rank and job title held?

_____

47. List all medals, commendations and decorations awarded to you as a member of the armed forces:

_____

_____

_____

48. Have you ever been an active or inactive member of any branch of the armed forces? _____

    If yes, what branch _____

    Rank _____Location _____

49. Have you ever been a member of the National Guard? _____

    If yes, what state? _____

    Rank _____Location _____

    Type of discharge, if applicable _____

50. Have you ever been court martialed, tried on charges or the subject of an Article 15, [received] Company level punishment, or any other disciplinary action while in the Armed Forces (including Reserves, National Guard, and active duty)? _____

    If yes, explain.

_____

_____

_____

_____

51. Have you ever been involved in any illicit activities while off duty during your military service? _____

    If yes, explain.

    _____

    _____

    _____

    _____

Illegal Drugs

52. In the space provided below, indicate when you first tried the drugs, when you last used them and the approximate number of times you used them. If you have never used a particular drug, write "Never" in the first column.

    A P P R O X I M A T E

	Date First Used	Date Last Used	Number of Times Used
Marijuana	_____	_____	_____
Hashish	_____	_____	_____
Angel Dust	_____	_____	_____
Cocaine	_____	_____	_____
Crack Cocaine	_____	_____	_____
Crank	_____	_____	_____
Crystal Meth	_____	_____	_____
Ecstasy	_____	_____	_____
Heroin	_____	_____	_____
Ice	_____	_____	_____
LSD	_____	_____	_____
Magic Mushrooms/PCP	_____	_____	_____
Mescaline/Cactus	_____	_____	_____

Morphine   _____ _____ _____

Opium   _____ _____ _____

Psilocybin   _____ _____ _____

Quaaludes   _____ _____ _____

Speed (Specify Type) _____ _____ _____

_____

Steroids   _____ _____ _____

STP   _____ _____ _____

THC   _____ _____ _____

Prescription Drug   _____ _____ _____
   Not Prescribed
   To You (Specify)

_____

Any Other Illegal Drug (Specify)

53. Have you ever used marijuana or any other illegal drug during working hours during the last 10 years? This includes lunch and coffee breaks as well as actually working. _____
If yes, give a brief explanation below to include the approximate number of times.

_____

_____

54. Have you ever sold marijuana or any other illegal drug to friends or anyone with or without profit to yourself? _____
If yes, give a brief explanation below (including when this occurred, the approximate number of times, the type of drugs involved, the approximate total dollar amount sold and how much profit was made.)

_____

_____

CRIMINAL ACTIVITY

It is important that you answer each of the following questions truthfully. You will be given an opportunity to explain or give an account of questionable situations, if needed.

Circle any of the following you have ever committed/done, whether it was undetected or you were caught or arrested:

Arson	Kidnapping
Assault	Murder
Breaking & Entering	Passing Bad Checks
Credit Card Fraud	Possession of Marijuana
Cruelty to Animals	Possession of Narcotics
Domestic Violence	Robbery/Armed Robbery
Drug Sales	Shoplifting
DUI/DWI	Steal Anything
Forgery	Vandalism
Auto Theft	Any Sex crimes (including rape, child molestation, incest, aggravated sodomy, peeping Tom, etc.)
Other	

Give a brief explanation in the space provided at the end of this application on any of the above you circled. Be sure to include your age at the time of the incident and the dates of occurrence.

55. Estimate the total dollar amount of cash and/or merchandise you have taken from all employers during the last 10 years. Write "None" if applicable. Do not leave blank. _____

56. Have you ever been fingerprinted? _____

If yes, give details.

Agency _____Date _____
Purpose _____

Agency _____Date _____
Purpose _____

Agency _____Date _____
Purpose _____

57. Are you being paid or urged by any person or organization to work for this Department? _____

If yes, explain.

_____

_____

_____

_____

58. Have you ever been a member of any foreign or domestic organization, association, movement, group, or combination of persons which is totalitarian, Fascist, racist, Communist, subversive, or which has adopted or shows a policy of advocating or approving the commission of acts of force or violence to deny other persons their rights under the Constitution of the United States by unconstitutional means? _____

If yes, explain.

_____

_____

_____

_____

59. Have you ever intentionally perjured yourself in a court of law?

_____

If yes, explain.

_____

_____

_____

_____

60. Have you ever been arrested, had to post bond or been detained by any police, sheriff, military police, or other municipal, county, state, or federal law enforcement agency? _____

If yes, give details below.

Crime Charged _____Date _____

Circle: Felony   Misdemeanor

Police Agency _____ City/State _____

Disposition _____

_____

_____

Crime Charged _____Date _____

Circle: Felony   Misdemeanor

Police Agency _____ City/State _____

Disposition _____

_____

_____

Crime Charged _____Date _____

Circle: Felony   Misdemeanor

Police Agency _____ City/State _____

Disposition _____

_____

_____

Crime Charged _____Date _____

Circle: Felony   Misdemeanor

Police Agency _____ City/State _____

Disposition _____

_____

_____

61. Have you ever been placed on probation or parole? _____
    If yes, give details (including date and length).

_____

_____

_____

_____

62. Are you presently under any subpoenas? _____
    If yes, explain.

_____

_____

_____

_____

IMPORTANT!
Please Read

It is the APPLICANT'S RESPONSIBILITY to assure all information given in this booklet and the employment application is accurate and complete. The instructions at the beginning of this document also apply to the employment application. Your ability to follow these instructions will be evaluated during the application process.

The following pages are waivers and various forms that you are required to complete in order to be processed for consideration for a position with the Columbus Police Department, Consolidated Government of Columbus, Georgia. When signing the waivers, please have them notarized by a Notary Public. If you are unable to have them notarized, complete the forms and we will notarize them later upon verification of your signature.

If you need additional space to complete any of the questions or information in this booklet or the employment application, please use the additional pages found near the back. Be sure to refer to page and question numbers when giving additional information. If additional information is from the employment application, please note that.

We request that you do not contact the Police Personnel Office just to find out the status of your application. Due to the volume of applicants we process and the amount of work involved, it will only slow down the background investigation process. Keep in mind that the application process is quite lengthy. It may take 6 to 8 weeks or longer to process the application AFTER the PQ test and the State Entrance Exam have been accomplished. You will be notified by the Police Personnel Office if any additional information is needed from you or from any references.

We ask that you call the Police Personnel Office at any time during the process if events require that additional or corrected information be added to the information already furnished. This includes address or phone number changes, traffic citations, arrests. etc.

Visit our Web site for more information:

www.columbusga.org/Police/

Columbus Police Department
P.O. Box 1866
510 10th St.
Columbus, GA 31902
Personnel Unit
(706) 653-3154

FOR APPLICANTS WHO HAVE NEVER
SERVED IN THE MILITARY

MILITARY AFFIRMATION

I, _____ , do hereby swear or affirm that I have never enlisted nor served in any of the military forces of the United States or in any foreign military service. I further swear or affirm that I have never served in any branch of the United States Reserve Forces or in any State National Guard.

Signature of Applicant_____

Notary Signature_____

My Commission Expires: _____

Notary Seal

TO WHOM IT MAY CONCERN

I, _____ , having submitted an application to the Columbus Police Department for the position of Police Officer, agree to participate in all phases of the applicant screening process to determine my suitability for employment.

I fully understand that a Physical Qualifications Test is required and that my participation in said test is a personal choice. In doing so, I hereby relieve the Columbus Police Department, The Columbus Consolidated Government and their representatives of any and all liability for personal harm or injury resulting from my participation.

Signed: _____ Date _____
Witness: _____ Date _____

Notary Signature_____

My Commission Expires: _____

Notary Seal

INDEX

★

ABOUT THE AUTHOR

━━━━━━━━━━━━━━━━━━━━━━━ ★ ━━━━━━━━━━━━━━━━━━━━━━━

Over his 25-year career as Special Agent with the FBI, John Douglas aided police departments and prosecutors from around the world. As founder and chief of the FBI's Investigative Support Unit—the team that tackles the most baffling and senseless of unsolved violent crimes—Douglas is the man who ushered in a new age in behavioral science and criminal profiling. He hunted some of the most notorious and sadistic criminals of our time: the Trailside Killer in San Francisco, the Atlanta child murderer, the Tylenol poisoner, the man who hunted prostitutes for sport in the woods of Alaska, and Seattle's Green River killer, the case that nearly ended his own life.

With several television series based on his exploits, he is one of the most dynamic personalities to emerge in modern law enforcement. In addition to providing pro bono assistance to police and victims of violent crimes, Douglas hosts a crime analysis radio show called "The Mindhunter" each week on the number one rated talk radio station in the country, KFI-640 AM. As a legendary figure in law enforcement, Douglas was the model for the Scott Glenn character in *The Silence of the Lambs*.

As a high-profile expert, Douglas provided consultation in the O.J. Simpson civil case and the JonBenet Ramsey murder investigation. He is the author of the national bestsellers *Obsession, Mind Hunter,* and *Unabomber: On the Trail of America's Most Wanted Serial Killer* (all coauthored with Mark Olshaker). He is also the author of *The Anatomy of Motive, The Cases That Haunt Us,* and *Anyone You Want Me to Be: A True Story of Sex and Death on the Internet* (coauthored with Stephen Singular). He is also the author of numerous articles and has done countless presentations on criminology. A veteran of the Air Force, Douglas holds a Doctor of Education degree. He lives in Virginia.

If you are interested in having Douglas speak at your group, please go to his Web site, www.johndouglasmindhunter.com.